Reunification Family Therapy

About the Author

Jan Faust, PhD, ABPP, is Professor at the College of Psychology at Nova Southeastern University (NSU), Fort Lauderdale, FL. While at NSU, Dr. Faust developed the Child and Adolescent Traumatic Stress Program, which is a clinical, training, and research facility serving children exposed to traumatic events, including child abuse, witnessing interpersonal violence, accidental injury, and medical traumas. Furthermore, she has developed a family forensic component to her trauma program wherein her doctoral students conduct forensic evaluations, post-dissolution therapy, reunification therapy, and individual therapy for children and their families experiencing family court issues.

Dr. Faust has conducted various research projects, and currently she is conducting treatment outcome research on treatment efficacy for families in reunification therapy, parent empathy training, and children with post traumatic stress disorder. She has published many articles in peer-reviewed journals and book chapters in the field of child, adolescent, and family psychology. Dr. Faust has served as Associate Editor for the APA trauma journal *Psychological Trauma: Theory, Research, Practice, and Policy* and was a founding editor of the *Journal of Trauma Practice*.

Finally, Dr. Faust also serves as an academic expert witness and conducts family reunification therapy, forensic evaluations, family mediation, and second opinion reviews in independent practice. She is a Florida Supreme Court Certified Family Mediator. She has also received Board Certification from the American Board of Professional Psychology in Behavioral and Cognitive Psychology.

Reunification Family Therapy

A Treatment Manual

Jan Faust, PhD, ABPP

Professor at the College of Psychology at Nova Southeastern University, Fort Lauderdale, FL

hogrefe

Library of Congress Cataloging in Publication information for the print version of this book is available via the Library of Congress Marc Database under the Library of Congress Control Number 2017952625

Library and Archives Canada Cataloguing in Publication

Faust, Jan, author

Reunification family therapy : a treatment manual / Jan Faust, PhD, ABPP, Professor at the College of Psychology at Nova Southeastern University, Fort Lauderdale, FL.

Includes bibliographical references.
Issued in print and electronic formats.
ISBN 978-0-88937-491-1 (hardcover).--ISBN 978-1-61676-491-3 (PDF).--
ISBN 978-1-61334-491-0 (EPUB)

1. Family psychotherapy--Handbooks, manuals, etc. 2. Family reunification--Handbooks, manuals, etc. 3. Parent and child--Handbooks, manuals, etc. I. Title.

RC488.5.F38 2017 616.89'156 C2017-905814-2
C2017-905815-0

The authors and publisher have made every effort to ensure that the information contained in this text is in accord with the current state of scientific knowledge, recommendations, and practice at the time of publication. In spite of this diligence, errors cannot be completely excluded. Also, due to changing regulations and continuing research, information may become outdated at any point. The authors and publisher disclaim any responsibility for any consequences which may follow from the use of information presented in this book.

http://www.hogrefe.com

PUBLISHING OFFICES

USA: Hogrefe Publishing Corporation, 7 Bulfinch Place, Suite 202, Boston, MA 02114
Phone (866) 823-4726, Fax (617) 354-6875; E-mail customerservice@hogrefe.com

EUROPE: Hogrefe Publishing GmbH, Merkelstr. 3, 37085 Göttingen, Germany
Phone +49 551 99950-0, Fax +49 551 99950-111; E-mail publishing@hogrefe.com

SALES & DISTRIBUTION

USA: Hogrefe Publishing, Customer Services Department, 30 Amberwood Parkway, Ashland, OH 44805
Phone (800) 228-3749, Fax (419) 281-6883; E-mail customerservice@hogrefe.com

UK: Hogrefe Publishing, c/o Marston Book Services Ltd., 160 Eastern Ave., Milton Park, Abingdon, OX14 4SB, UK
Phone +44 1235 465577, Fax +44 1235 465556; E-mail direct.orders@marston.co.uk

EUROPE: Hogrefe Publishing, Merkelstr. 3, 37085 Göttingen, Germany
Phone +49 551 99950-0, Fax +49 551 99950-111; E-mail publishing@hogrefe.com

OTHER OFFICES

CANADA: Hogrefe Publishing, 660 Eglinton Ave. East, Suite 119–514, Toronto, Ontario, M4G 2K2

SWITZERLAND: Hogrefe Publishing, Länggass-Strasse 76, CH-3000 Bern 9

Hogrefe Publishing
Incorporated and registered in the Commonwealth of Massachusetts, USA, and in Göttingen, Lower Saxony, Germany

Printed and bound in the USA

ISBN 978-0-88937-491-1 (print) • ISBN 978-1-61676-491-3 (PDF) • ISBN 978-1-61334-491-0 (EPUB)
http://doi.org/10.1027/00491-000

Dedication

For my family, and the families I have had the privilege of serving.

Contents

Preface

The inception of this book originated from observations gleaned and research conducted over the years, revealing that child problems do not occur in isolation and that many children are confronted with a variety of losses during childhood. Irrespective of a child's symptom presentation, its maintenance, exacerbation, and amelioration appears to be contingent on several environmental variables, including those exhibited in the family setting. For example, family conflict has been observed to drive children's adjustment to a myriad of life events, not just to a parent's divorce but also to chronic and life-threatening disease, exposure to various traumas (e.g., fire, terrorism, child sexual abuse, hurricane), and peer relational problems. In recent years, there has been a notable increase in the fracturing of the family system due to a host of factors such as military deployment, incarceration, and dissolution of the coparenting relationship (e.g., divorce and separation). The physical and/or emotional separation of a parent from a child can have deleterious emotional consequences for the child as well as the potential to permanently erode the parent–child relationship.

While lawmakers appreciate that children require opportunities to have healthy relationships with both parents, the vehicle employed to provide these affiliations is obscure in many cases. This is particularly true in high-conflict families, where parents are not only embroiled in overt conflict but also have multiple covert agendas from which they are operating, and which, at times, unexpectedly shift. These agendas often include the thwarting of one parent's time-sharing with the child in order to maximize the amount of child support payments, as an example. Frequently this leaves little recourse for officers of the court, who frequently call upon mental health professionals to assist in conflict resolution. For therapists who have been the recipients of these cases, they understand that conducting family therapy to repair intact families, while challenging, is nearly an impossible feat when attempting to repair those families comprising individuals who no longer desire to be together. Given societal mandates, scientific discovery, and the law, it is important for children to have healthy relationships with both parents irrespective of their parents' marital status, employment status (e.g., military), health status, and legal status (e.g., incarceration). It ultimately becomes incumbent upon the mental health professional to facilitate parent–child relationships, and while treatment outcome research is scant with respect to the best methods to assist these reunifying families, the incorporation of evidence-based treatments obtained from other realms of clinical psychology can be applied in the service of these cases. It is hoped that this treatment guide can serve as a manual to assist professionals in their work with reunifying parent–child relationships.

This book is divided into chapters that include the procedures of reunification therapy from the commencement of therapy to its completion. It incorporates instructional information as the therapist works initially with each member of the family and then when family members are subsequently joined together for family intervention. Additionally, ethical and legal considerations as well as the use of ancillary professionals in the reunification process are addressed. Alternative forms of reunification therapy, as well as special considerations when reunifying families, are also presented. Finally, a step-by-step treatment plan is provided as a reunification therapy template, and additional tools to effectuate change are included in the Appendices.

I would like to express my gratitude to Brandon and Nina for their unremitting unconditional support and faith in their mother. I would like to acknowledge Anita Alexander and Kelly Gibson for their invaluable assistance in preparing this volume and Colby Schepps for the use of her poignant maxims. I would also like to thank the Honorable Susan Greenhawt for her thoughtful feedback regarding this book and her valuable insights over the years from the bench. Finally, I would like to thank the Florida Family Court Bench and the family law attorneys who have entrusted me with serving the needs of their clients.

Jan Faust
Fort Lauderdale, FL
October 2017

CHAPTER 1

Introduction to Family Structure and Fragmentation of the Family

And love is love is love is love is love is love is love is love...
Lin-Manuel Miranda (2016, 70th Tony Awards, New York, NY)

The objective of publishing this book is to provide a blueprint for mental health professionals who are working with fragmented families of all constitutions and structures, to assist in reunifying parents and children. Family structures have changed considerably in the last 100 years, with the advancement of science and social revolution and reformation. The American landscape has been transformed with multigenerational family farming units collapsing into smaller entities and the scattering of family members across the country. Historically, farming parents bore a large number of children to assist with the servicing of the farm; however, with the invention of automated machinery, the need for multiple hands diminished. Scientific discovery, not only within the farming industry but also with respect to mass production of goods and expeditious transportation, has heightened human mobility. These changes have contributed to the dispersion of extended families such that there no longer remains a need for relatives to live in proximity to the nuclear family. Additionally, the women's movement has contributed to increased numbers of women in the work place, affording women greater self-sufficiency, which has had a cascading effect on divorce rates. No longer do women have to remain married for reasons of economic security; in fact, woman have chosen to marry less frequently in recent years and to have children out of wedlock in increasing numbers, such that since 1960, the number of live births to unmarried women has increased from 5.3 % to 40.3 % (Child Trends Data Bank, 2015). The impact of the women's movement coupled with the sexual revolution has assisted with the destigmatizing of divorce.

Economic changes have also episodically impacted the family structure, including adult children returning to their parents' home to reside, and adult children caring for their elderly parents in their own homes or those of their parents. Additionally, the notable increase in substance abuse and addiction in recent decades has contributed to children being raised by grandparents, other relatives, and non–biologically related caregivers. Similarly, there is an observed downward effect of substance abusing parents on child maltreatment; hence, in a cohort of abuse cases, substance use and abuse are factors detected in the family systems of abused children (Barth, Gibbons, & Guo, 2006). In fact, the United States Department of Health and Human Services (1996) identified parents with a substance use disorder were 3 times more likely to engage in child maltreatment than those without a substance use disorder.

Family composition has also been impacted by modern war such that between 2001 and 2013, 2 million children experienced a military deployment of a parent at least once (Clever & Segal, 2013). Other noted changes in the military family structure, in recent history, are observed in the fact that many more women are entering the military than previously, and concomitant with this change, many households are headed by two military parents. In 2014, the Department of Defense stated that 11.7 % of all active duty personnel included both married partners, with 19.3 % of all active duty Air Force personnel in dual military marriages (Office of the Deputy Assistant Secretary of the Department of Defense, 2014). Not only have military parents recognized the need to reconfigure family processes, structure, and operations given their impending absence from their children's lives, but courts have also recognized the need for adjudicating guardianships for children in these families when both parents are deployed simultaneously or when deployments overlap with each other. The federal government has sought to protect the child's interests in this regard (Burelli & Miller, 2013), and the majority of states have followed with similar laws as a result of the federal statutes. Currently, the Servicemembers Civil Relief Act (2014) is the only federal statute designed to protect single-parent service members. The parent's military deployment cannot be used as grounds for a change in custody, including time-sharing or modification of an existing parenting plan (e.g., Cal. Family Code § 3047, 2011, Division 8: Custody of Children, Chapter 2: Matters to Be Considered in Granting Custody; Temporary Time-Sharing Modification and Child Support Modification Due to Military Service, 2016; Modification of Order Based on Military Duty, 2009; Definitions, 2009). In fact, in some states, there are provisions for the deploying parent to appoint someone in their absence to stand-in for their time-sharing and parental decision making (e.g., Temporary Time-Sharing Modification and Child Support Modification Due to Military Service, 2016).

With respect to marital or partner dissolution and family court, the judicial climate has changed dramatically over the years regarding coparenting of children. For example, in 1996, researchers discovered that southeastern US judges' preferred time-sharing plan was for children to reside for the school year with one parent and the summer with the other parent, followed by the sole custody of one parent (Stamps, Kunen, & Lawyer, 1996). They also found that for visitation and time-sharing schedules, judges' preferred schedules were every other weekend as the most popular, followed in descending order of popularity by every weekend, more often than every weekend, one weekend per month, and less than one weekend per month. These 20-year-old findings contrast with the more recent statutory abolition of any demarcation of custodial or residential parent, and the current pending legislation in Florida of a presumption of 50/50 time-sharing (FLS SB 668, 2016). These statutory events highlight the dramatic changes in the views of the bench regarding time-sharing.

Despite a more restricted judicial perspective of time-sharing in the past, judges historically rated the parent–child relationship and the family unit as the most important factors in deciding time-sharing and access in divorce cases (Stamps et al., 1996). The focus on the parent–child relationship and the family as essential in considering a variety of parenting plans continues to be primary in judicial determination of parent–child time-sharing. In fact, most states employ "the child's best interests" standard when considering parent access to children. These best interests examine, in part, whether or not the parents can facilitate and encourage a close and continuing parent–child relationship. Some states expand upon this premise adding that the parents are required to honor the time-sharing schedule and to be reasonable when changes are required.

Finally, a more unusual need for reunification therapy can be discerned in the shifting age demographic as baby boomers age and are living longer than in previous decades. This, coupled with young-adult children returning home after college graduation or not leaving home as expeditiously as in earlier years, has created greater frequency of contact between adult children and their parents, as well as heightened reciprocal support-seeking relationships. Ultimately this change in family structure can create problematic interpersonal relationships leading to severed parent and adult-child relationships.

This treatment manual provides the therapist with a guide to assist the dissolving family unit which has been ruptured via several different mechanisms involving unified family law litigation, including marital or partner dissolution, paternity, dependency, domestic violence, and juvenile delinquency, as well as those families involved in military deployment and institutionalization (incarceration or hospitalization) and adult-child–parent relationship difficulties.

It should be emphasized that the content of this manual is based on the available scientific literature, including evidence-based practices and other empirical research, and well-established theories in the psychology literature, as well as observations gleaned in clinical practice. It also should be noted that the information imparted through this book and the example treatment template at the close of this book consider these scientifically derived sources of information, while noting that each individual and specific family is unique. The treatment utilized for each family is likely to vary to some degree from that which is imparted in this book. This treatment variance may be due to individual nuances of the problem areas leading to reunification therapy, individual differences in the family members and the family as an entity, and individual differences of the totality of the situation, including the specific legal issues in those reunification cases with court or other legal involvement.

CHAPTER 2
Bases and Elements of Reunification Therapy

Mechanisms Responsible for Breaches in the Parent–Child Relationship

Reunification therapy is a therapeutic process designed to repair relationships between parents and children in an attempt to restore not only physical contact but meaningful social, emotional, and interpersonal exchanges between parents and children. For families in need of reunification, the mechanisms responsible for the severed relationship include the following: First, the absence of the parent may be "intrapersonally" imposed for example, if the non-time-sharing parent has been hospitalized, incarcerated, or is unavailable due to substance use and abuse or major mental illness. In their 2015 article, Dallaire, Zeman, and Thrash (2015) cite statistics indicating significant increases in parental incarceration, with the most notable increases in recent years being in maternal incarceration. Approximately 1.7 million children in the US will have lost a parent to incarceration prior to their reaching 18 years of age, with many of the parents not released from prison until after the child has reached the age of majority (Hoffmann, Byrd, & Kightlinger, 2010). While in-person prison visits are a preferred method of contact to prevent the complete erosion of the child–parent relationship, two of the barriers to live prison visits are location and concomitant travel time and costs. On average, prisons are located 160 miles from incarcerated prisoners' children's homes (cited by Coughenour, 1995, in Hoffmann et al., 2010). There are some established programs that circumvent this potential barrier via the utilization of phone calls and video conferencing for parent–child contact (Hoffmann et al., 2010).

With respect to intrapersonal reasons for the severed parent–child relationship, the non-time-sharing parent may also have been absent due to the perpetration, or allegations of the perpetration, of domestic violence and/or child maltreatment. Statistics indicate a notable presence of child incest cases among fathers and mothers (Gover & Bosick, 2011). And while many permanently lose parental rights, there is a subset of these parents where reunification is the court's goal. Other noted intrapersonally imposed parent–child relationship breaches can be observed in the longevity and economic changes contributing to adult children residing with their parents and adult children having to care for their aging parents within their own home. A child's age when they depart their parents' home for the first time is increasing (Furstenberg, 2010), and more children than before are returning home to live. In fact, the term *Boomerang Age* was coined to demarcate these returning adult children (Mitchell, 2006), an event that appears to be a worldwide phenomenon. In a recent large-scale study, researchers observed different trajectories for a breach in the parent–adult-child relationship contingent on the family member's role. Parents reported relationship severing was the result of their adult children's unacceptable partner choice or sense of self-privilege, while adult children most frequently attributed the relationship breach to be a function of their parents' noxious behavior or their rejection or lack of support (Carr, Holman, Abetz, Kellas, & Vagnoni, 2015).

A second group of reunification cases that evolves from the parent's absence may be situationally imposed, for example, in those cases where the non-time-sharing parent has been relocated by the military or an occupation (job relocation). Approximately 1 million American children have experienced the military deployment of a parent (Clever & Segal, 2013; Park, 2011), and while there is literature to indicate the maladaptive effects of deployment on children, it is likely these negative effects and increased seeking of mental health services is the function of multiple factors. Researchers have indicated that increased mental health services for children, while possibly a direct function of the parent's deployment, may also be a function of the nondeployed parent, who may experience their own mental health issues and addresses those by seeking services for their child (Alfano, Lau, Balderas, Bunnell, & Beidel, 2016). Military children's problems evidenced at reunification with the returning deployed parent may also be multifaceted. These children may demonstrate a number of concerns such as worries about future parent deployments and the returning parents' impaired mental health status (Mmari, Roche, Sudhinaraset, & Blum, 2009). Researchers have shown that the returning parent who is afflicted by mental health concerns, particularly post-traumatic stress disorder (PTSD), may unwittingly negatively impact the child directly and the parent–child relationship (Brockman et al., 2016). With respect to reunification, Mmari et al. (2009) observed that adolescents cited reacquainting themselves with the returning parent postdeployment as the most challenging facet of the deployment process.

A rare environmental event contributing to a parent–child relationship breach is stranger abduction. Non-familial abduction has been cited in recent years as a traumatic event that requires the child to be reunited with all of their family members (e.g., Greif, 2009). In fact, researchers have developed a therapy model for transitioning families of children who have been abducted by a non-family member. The transitioning families therapeutic reunification model (TFTRM) for nonfamilial abductions of children includes a trauma-informed process incorporating the use of multidisciplinary teams who engage in a step-wise process with the incorporation of family systems and solution focus interventions to reintegrate the child within the family (e.g., Judge et al., 2016).

A third cluster of cases where a severed relationship exists between child and parent, originates from "failures in parenting" by the non-time-sharing parent, including failure to facilitate a bond or attachment to the child, inappropriate or severe parenting strategies, and the inability to negotiate cultural and value differences (see, for example, Darnall & Steinberg, 2008). Furthermore, maladaptive parenting practices by both parents can contribute to breaks in the relationship between the non-time-sharing parent and child, and these are typically observed in high-conflict families. For example, a parent who is angered by the child, perceives the precipitating adverse child behavior to be caused by the alternate parent and decides to abdicate their time-sharing for a night, week, few weeks, or months. Finally, active interference by the time-sharing parent may be the basis of the child's refusal to spend time with the other parent. There are a multitude of avenues for contributions to a disruption in time-sharing in high-conflict or divorcing families. Regardless of the factors which contribute to the estrangement between the non-time-sharing parent and the child, it is evident that reunification is typically the goal, as dictated by psychological science and the law. In fact, child outcomes are significantly enhanced when children have meaningful relationships with both parents (Amato & Sobolewski, 2001; Faust & Ko, 2016; Hetherington & Kelly, 2003).

While there are multiple mechanisms by which the parent–child relationship is ruptured, until recently, parent–child reunification therapy was a process typically reserved for the reconsolidation of the child–parent relationship through dependency court (Faust, 2010). In these dependency court actions, parents, confronted with the potential permanent removal of their children by the state generally due to parental neglect and/or abuse or the imminent potential of maltreatment, require a rehabilitative parenting plan. In fact, the scientific and legal literature is replete with papers that delineate the legal and social science approach to reunifying parents with their children who have been placed in foster care or relative care. Traditionally, it was not uncommon for substance-abusing mothers to lose custody of their children at birth or shortly thereafter (Famularo, Kinscherff, & Fenton, 1992; Wells & Marcenko, 2011). Many of these original attempts at reunification of parent and child involved group programs to repair the relationship between parent and child while the mother maintained recovery (Smith, 2003; Choi, Huang & Ryan, 2012). Haight, Black, Workman, and Tata (2001), who delineated in their foster care research that parents and children exhibit a broad variability of behaviors during mother–child visits, highlighted the need for appropriate reunification intervention. The mothers in their sample spontaneously reported the challenges of these interactions, with separating from the child at visit completion to be particularly problematic (Haight et al., 2001).

More recently, the legal system and mental health professionals have identified family law cases of marital or couple dissolution, wherein one biological parent holds the primary caretaking role and the other parent has not had contact with their child for varying periods of time. Often, the parent without contact wishes to develop or reestablish a relationship with their child. In rare hybrid family law cases, a breach in the parent–child relationship has occurred not only due to divorce or parental relationship dissolution but also due to parental abduction, with the child's time-sharing parent incarcerated for the kidnapping. Another uncommon phenomenon is the reunification of both parents with a child who has other adults as custodial agents. While there is a dearth of literature with respect to family law parent–child reunification, the need to remedy the separation between the parents and the children in these legal family matters is a reality in practice. Although many therapists actively try to avoid working with families involved in litigation cases, they often find themselves either wittingly or unwittingly having to address such parent–child separation issues in their practice.

Why Does the Need Exist for Reunification Therapy?

It is obvious that both divorce and death have varied negative consequences for children (Amato & Anthony, 2014). Irrespective of the mechanisms responsible for the breach in the parent–child relationship, there are a multitude of studies indicating that children are adversely affected by the loss of a parent and are better adjusted when able to maintain sound relationships with their parents. In fact, research demonstrates that children of divorce exhibit better overall adjustment when they enjoy adaptive and positive relationships with *both* parents (Hetherington & Kelly, 2003; Amato & Sobolewski, 2001). Furthermore, it appears the loss of the parent relationship has greater negative effects for children than exposure to family conflict, which has been cited as a primary variable of maladjustment for children in multiple domains and a variety of contexts. In a multimethod prospective study, Sturge-Apple, Davies, and Cummings (2006) observed that parental withdrawal had a direct negative effect on all areas of children's adaptation and functioning, whereas interparental hostility had an *indirect* impact on subsequent changes in child functioning. These researchers also discovered an intermediary role of parental emotional unavailability as related to interparental withdrawal and hostility and child adjustment. Hence it is evident that a parent's emotional and physical absence has a notable impact on child adjustment that is potentially greater than that observed when children experience interparental conflict only.

Interestingly, there are some longitudinal data to indicate that children are affected *prior* to the dissolution of the parenting relationship. Arkes (2015) observed that children experienced low reading scores and behavioral problems 2 years before the disruption of the parents' union. Amato and Anthony (2014) also detected that the estimated effects of divorce seemed to be the greatest for children with parents who have the maximum propensity to experience divorce, prior to the actual divorce. In this study, variables associated with a parent's greater proclivity toward divorce included issues of resources (Amato & Anthony, 2014). In a longitudinal study following a large child cohort from kindergarten through the fifth grade, Potter (2010) observed divorce to be associated with reduced psychosocial functioning in the youths, which was related to a decline in academic performance. In fact, the effects of divorce and loss on children have been globally and culturally observed. For example, Al Gharaibeh (2015) observed high rates of sleep disorders, stubbornness, and noncompliance in his sample of children from divorcing families of the United Arab Emirates.

Parent–child involvement is likely multidetermined. Pearson (2015) indicated a relationship between father involvement and the payment of child support, such that those fathers who paid child support were more likely to be involved with their children. This finding was bidirectional in that those fathers who were more involved in their children's lives were more likely to pay child support than those less involved. The benefits of both are paramount, since the literature supports the idea that children typically profit from the positive involvement of their nonresidential fathers, and that those who lack interaction are at risk for cognitive, social, and emotional deficits (Pearson, 2015). It is also evident that children benefit from financial integrity, which is often threatened or even adversely affected post marital dissolution (Amato, 2000). The financial resources of families are often considered as a potential risk or protective factor for children's emotional, academic, and cognitive state; physical integrity and health; and growth and social adjustment (Kelly & Emery, 2003).

Older research indicated that children benefit when they have contact with same-sex parents. However, in recent years, parent gender matching has been seen as not necessarily indicative of better outcomes for children who experience their parents' divorce (Faust, Ko, Alexander, & Greenhawt, 2017; Faust, Ko, Alexander, Tarver, & Gibson, 2016). More specifically, the literature indicates that children derive benefits from both parents postdivorce. The support for this includes research that identifies frequent and regular contact with fathers to be associated with more positive psychological adjustment in boys and young children than is the case with less contact. When children have close relationships with their father, and the father is actively involved in their lives, school-aged children have better psychological adjustment and academic achievement than children with a less-involved father (Amato & Fowler, 2002; Amato & Gilbreth, 1999). There is also evidence that daughters derive benefits from close and continuing relationships with their father. The better the quality of the relationship an adolescent daughter has with her father, the higher her self-esteem and healthier her romantic partner choice in early adulthood (Nielsen, 2011).

In a meta-analysis conducted by Bauserman (2002), it was observed that irrespective of who was rating the children (mothers, fathers, teachers, clinicians, or the children themselves) joint-custody children exhibited better psychological adjustment than sole maternal custody children. Viry (2014) observed that cohesive coparenting (the ability for separated parents to positively and supportively communicate and jointly problem solve child issues with the other parent) was linked more to frequent father–child contacts by phone and e-mail than to the proximity of the father's residence to that of the mother. Both cohesive coparenting and the father's residential proximity had positive and independent effects on children's adjustment. These researchers observed that children who had fathers living in proximity to the mother's residence exhibited fewer behavioral difficulties and showed more prosocial behavior than those whose father lived far away (Viry, 2014). These findings suggest that frequent contacts by phone or e-mail can substitute for distance in coparenting, but geographical proximity remains important for fathers' contributions to children's well-being. Furthermore, in one study, half of college students studied, who had experienced their parent's divorce on average 11 years earlier and who spent the majority of time with their mother, retrospectively desired additional time with their father (Fabricius, 2003). Additionally, Fabricius (2003) found that less than 10% of this sample in any time-sharing category (based on amount of time with each parent) desired less contact with their father than was previously realized.

For other populations, in a study conducted in 2015 by Dallaire and her colleagues, it was observed that children whose mothers were incarcerated manifested symptoms of both internalizing and externalizing disorders when they experienced the risks associated with their mother's incarceration, including loss. Zeman, Dallaire, and Borowski (2015) found that children with incarcerated mothers who engaged in emotion-focused responses to their children's sadness and who had high maternal incarnation risk experiences (e.g., mothers with three or more incarcerations and separation from siblings due to the incarceration) had poor psychological and social adjustment. Children separated from a parent due to military deployment also experience adverse effects with the separation. Researchers have found that youths report significantly more social and emotional difficulties with parental deployment than youths in a non-deployed-parent sample (Chandra et al., 2010). They also observed that length of parental deployment and nondeployed caregiver psychological functioning were significantly associated with adjustment difficulties for children both during deployment and after deployed-parent family reintegration. (Walsh et al., 2014; Laser, & Stephens, 2011).

The evidence in support of reunification intervention is demonstrated by research regarding the impact of parent–child relationship reparation. McWey and Mullis (2004) tested a model of the quality of attachment of 123 foster care children who received monitored time-sharing with their biological parents. The results indicated that for children reunifying with their biological parents, the children who had more regular and recurrent contact with their biological parents had stronger attachments than children who had less contact. In turn, the children with greater levels of attachment had better behavioral and emotional adjustment, were less frequently prescribed psychiatric medication, and were less likely to be diagnosed with developmental delays than were children with less adaptive attachment (McWey & Mullis, 2004).

In family court, the need for reunification therapy is evident, as highlighted in cases where the time-sharing parent is intentionally withholding the child from the non-time-sharing parent. While judges have had the means to shift custody from the time-sharing parent to the non-time-sharing parent; they are hesitant to do so, as there is a lack of data that support (or invalidate) such a shift, and this remedy is often viewed as extreme by the judiciary. Furthermore, there is both implicit and explicit pressure on judges not to shift custody from the time-sharing parent to the non-time-sharing parent (Warshak, 2015a). Hence, in these cases, if a parent–child relationship is to be established or reestablished between the non-time-sharing parent and the child, the only recourse is to effectuate some form of intervention.

Why Not Let the Child Decide? Application of Developmental Psychology

Overall, having a child contribute to decision making in areas of parenting and child behavior has been shown to have positive results with respect to overall child adjustment. Parenting-style research indicates that parents who partially include children in rule development and consequences for infractions of the rules, combined with a parent's explanation for the rule, have children who exhibit the best outcomes versus those parents who are authoritarian, laissez-faire, and uninvolved (Givertz, 2016). However, while it is important for children to express themselves and be involved in family decision-making processes, there are some life areas for which children should not finalize the decision. Health and education are two of the most obvious examples where the decisions in these domains should remain with the parents or guardians. Parents generally do not allow children to decide whether they should or should not take medicine for an acute or chronic medical condition, as the health risks are potentially great. This is true even if religion dictates the refusal of medical treatment, as the parent is the one declining medical treatment, which often involves other adults such as members of the judiciary in this decision-making process. Similarly, there are laws that enforce education for children in the US, and the mores and cultural values of the US society place a premium on education for children. In fact, when the time-sharing parent informs the therapist that they cannot obtain compliance from the child to share time with the non-time-sharing parent, it is useful to ask the parent what they would do in the event the child refused to go to school. These parents often appear mortified at the thought that the child would be allowed to decline school attendance. This question is often a useful launching point for a discussion of the importance of forging a relationship with the alternate parent.

There are excellent developmental data that indicate that children's developmental processes at different stages of their lives prohibit their decision making with full contextual adult understanding. Most obvious are babies and very young children who are unable to understand let alone communicate time-sharing beliefs and feelings. Furthermore, given the importance of attachment and the critical evolution of adaptive attachment from birth, it is extremely important that the adults ensure positive attachments occur to all primary caretakers, irrespective of a young child's beliefs or statements. Furthermore, as indicated previously, there are a multitude of reasons proffered as to why children have a severed relationship with a parent. Many of these causes or beliefs are complex in nature, requiring advanced cognitive development and socioemotional maturity for the child to enter a well-reasoned decision regarding time-sharing with a parent. In fact, while there is an extensive literature that indicates that children derive significant benefits from forging a relationship with both of their parents, children are not consumers of the scientific literature and hence are unable to make well-reasoned decisions that are in their best interests regarding time-sharing with their parents.

There is a wealth of data that indicate that children are not able to achieve formal operational thought until early adolescence, and in many cases, children do not ever attain this level of cognitive functioning. The development of formal operational thought is a perquisite to considering many different options and hypotheticals; hence such a level of cognition is often necessary for understanding complex relationships and the child's role in these relationships. Furthermore, children lack experiences from which to build their cognitive base, including their problem-solving skill set; consequently, they are often unable to make correctly reasoned decisions for themselves. Likewise, the brain's frontal lobe is generally not sufficiently developed in children and adolescents, rendering them susceptible to impulsivity and hasty decision-making processes (Silveri et al., 2013).

Additionally, children and adolescents are egocentric; consequently, they are likely to be self-absorbed with their own lives as well as to take the path of least resistance if it provides immediate gratification of needs and minimizes hassles and discomfort. Therefore, the decisions they make may be derived from immediate gratification of self-perceived needs and reduction of hassles in their lives, without regard to the consequences of these decision-making processes. For example, in a child whose social life is primarily centered in the neighborhood of one parent, that focus may be a barrier to the child's motivation to spend time with the alternate parent. Similarly, children with split time-sharing plans often find it frustrating and troublesome to relocate their belongings between homes on a fairly regular basis. By being self-focused, the youth's ability for cognitive flexibility and to have the perspective to consider the impact of environmental events on their lives is restricted.

With respect to making informed decisions, children and adolescents are not objective masters of their lives. If given a choice, there are many variables that potentially influence children and adolescents regarding with whom they choose to live and spend time. Some of these may be biased, such as loyalty issues. For example, the child who observes the mother's devastation after the father leaves her for another romantic relationship may feel protective of mother, wishing not to contribute to any additional psychological pain for her. Ultimately, the child may desire to forgo a relationship with father, based primarily on the mother's reaction to the divorce. Furthermore, the loyalty issue may be fear-based, such that the child may observe the non-time-sharing parent to be impaired in some manner, or they may have been told by others that the parent is impaired, and since the child cannot not yet live independently, they need to align themselves with the time-sharing parent for self-perceived survival purposes (e.g., food and shelter).

In family law cases, judges are often compelled to consider the opinions of preteens and adolescents with respect to sharing time with a parent. Laws in many states provide for child testimony regarding time-sharing and custody, with specific provisions in family law cases. In fact, child testimony in parents' dependency litigation (i.e., for retainment or removal of parental rights) is expected in these types of cases (Section 4085 of Fla. Statute 39, 2016). Unfortunately, empirical data which elucidate the psychological impacts that testifying in these actions have on children are lacking. In dependency court, the potential impact is more obvious, such as in cases where a child, desirous of reuniting with a parent, testifies, and the judge decides, based on other evidence, that their best interests are better served by terminating parental rights. The child is left to contemplate the role this testimony had on the adverse outcome, placing them at risk for self-blame, guilt, and potentially depressive symptoms, as the cognitive behavior literature empirically supports a relationship between guilt and self-blame, on the one hand, and depression, on the other (Kim, Thibodeau, & Jorgensen, 2011; Green, Ralph, Moll, Deakin, & Zahn, 2012). In family court (non-dependency actions), children's testimony has the potential to adversely impact the child in a number of different ways. First, should the child feel compelled to testify due to the pressure of one parent while simultaneously desiring a relationship with both parents, that places the child in an untenable situation. Second, providing hurtful testimony against a parent also places a child in a difficult position when subsequently they are required to spend time with that parent. Third, the message of power disseminated to the testifying child is evident, as the child may easily believe that the determination of parental access and time-sharing rests squarely on their testimony. While children often desire to have this power, it also comes with a cost, such as heightened anxiety and disruptive behavioral issues in other areas of their lives. Testifying children may believe that since they can make important decisions about whether or not they have a relationship with one of their parents, that they can make other power-based adult decisions. For example, this transfer of power is evident in other areas of their lives, such as academic (whether or not they go to school on any given day) and social (e.g., who they see and when they see their peers, ignoring any curfew). Finally, as previously discussed, due to a child's developmental status, they may be unable to accurately determine what is in their own best interest with respect to maintaining or developing a relationship with their parent(s).

Spontaneous Reunification

Darnall and Steinberg (2008) define *spontaneous reunification* as the child's request to reestablish a relationship with the non-time-sharing parent without court order, direct incitement, or being the result of required therapy. This request may be made directly by the child, or alternately, through some conduit of the child's request: a family member, a court-related professional, or other nonforensic professional. Darnall and Steinberg (2008) identified four motivational models for spontaneous reunification, based on international crisis and negotiation models. These models include that of the *hurting stalemate,* which is derived from both parents' knowledge that they, together, with the child are in a no-win situation, which if not addressed will lend to further problems for all three family members (Darnall & Steinberg, 2008). The crisis in the family serves to disrupt the stalemate. An example of this is a child who has been caught cheating in high school and is faced with suspension or expulsion during the time they are applying to college. Once the non-time-sharing parent is called upon to assist the child and alternate parent, the stalemate resulting from the child not seeing that parent and from the time-sharing parent supporting the child's position to not spend time with that parent is broken.

The second model of spontaneous reunification includes a *recent catastrophe*, which is based on the premise that catastrophes often bring people together to work toward the common good as they put aside their differences (Darnall & Steinberg, 2008). An example includes the non-time-sharing military parent being transferred to a war zone in the Middle East or a parent dying of a terminal illness.

Darnall and Steinberg (2008) describe the third model of spontaneous reunification as based on the *impending catastrophe* or *deteriorating position.* In this model, the parents unite to prevent an impending catastrophe such as substance abuse or suicide attempts by the child.

Their fourth model of spontaneous reunification is the *enticing opportunity,* which requires both parents to work together to meet some important specific need of the child, such as assisting the child with financial aid applications for college (Darnall & Steinberg, 2008).

For this category, the parents must set aside their own differences and needs in order to place the child's desires first.

It is not unusual for the non-time-sharing parent to feel emotionally devastated and hopeless when there have been breaches in the parent–child relationship. This is particularly evident in highly litigated and contested family law cases; although these feelings may be present in other forms of severed parent–child relationships. The devastation and futility are often communicated by the non-time-sharing parent via their statements of resistance to the intervention process. These parents state that maybe they should abandon reunification, and they express the hope that as the child ages they will wish to be reunified with the parent – in effect, a wish for spontaneous reunification. Unfortunately, there are no data to support the "coming around" of the child without intervention or without the aforementioned four motivators for spontaneous reunification. In fact, Warshak (2015a) reported that while some cases spontaneously reunify, many families do not reconsolidate without intervention. Many other professionals state that to allow a campaign of alienation and denigration against the non-time-sharing parent to continue in the presence of the child has deleterious consequences for the child even into adulthood (Rowen & Emery, 2014). Without the proverbial crystal ball to predict which cases will spontaneously reunify, the costs are too great to leave reunification to chance in the hopes of eventual, spontaneous reunification.

Treatment Selection Guided by Empirical Evidence and Specific Characteristics of Family

Selection of treatment is based upon the specific characteristics and needs of the family as well as the available empirical literature to support its efficacy. Irrespective of the reason for the breach in the parent–child relationship, the core issues that have emerged in reunifying families include the anxiety of the child, dysfunctional communication among family members, poor behavioral exchanges (e.g., low on positives and high on negatives) between family members especially between the reunifying parent and the child, maladaptive parenting and problem solving, developmental issues, and any psychopathology of a parent or parents. Additionally, the absence of the non-time-sharing parent (the one in need of reunification) at critical periods in the child's development and for particular lengths of time can impact the quality of the parent–child relationship. In fact, it is apparent that the longer the separation from the non-time-sharing parent, the more resistant the child often is to reunification (Warshak, 2015b).

Observed child resistance to time-sharing can be due to a number of different factors including interference by the sheltering parent; however, it is evident that the child's anxiety can play a significant role in their resistance toward a relationship with the other parent, irrespective of the reasons for the child not having seen their parent. The old maxim of it being "difficult to get back up on a horse once one has fallen off" is operative in these cases, because of principles of operant conditioning, in addition to other factors including the residential family's script. With respect to operant conditioning, avoidance, a core component of anxiety disorders or symptom clusters, is negatively reinforcing because anxiety decreases when the anxiety-provoking stimulus is not present (Wenzel, 2013). One way not to be in the presence of the anxiety-provoking stimulus is to avoid it; consequently, the non-time-sharing parent or the time-sharing situation is avoided by the anxious child. It is evident that the child's contextual anxiety must be treated as part of the reunification process. Cognitive behavior therapies for a variety of childhood anxiety-based disorders and symptoms have empirically supported efficacy (e.g. Brown et al., 2017; Warner et al., 2016; van Starrenburg, Kuijpers, Kleinjan, Hutschemaekers, & Engels, 2017).

In addition to anxiety as a factor in the breach in the parent–child relationship, poor communication between the parents can lead to high interparental conflict and poor communication with the child, contributing to the severing of the parent–child relationship. Poor communication can increase conflict between parents. Marital or couples' therapy research indicates a positive relationship between dysfunctional communication patterns and couples' conflict (Shapiro, Gottman, & Fink, 2015). This is likely exacerbated when couples have dissolved their relationship because the motivation to repair it has abated. Furthermore, conflict exacerbation can be the result of contentious and acrimonious litigation and the adversarial factors leading to the divorce (e.g., extramarital relationships, financial problems). Ultimately, this conflict contributes to diminished positive exchanges between the couple. Divorcing parents in high-conflict cases often have frequent negative and adverse behavioral and verbal transactions. It is evident that these maladaptive communicative exchanges are longstanding for the conflicted couple relationship. In a longitudinal study, Lavner and Bradbury (2012) discovered that newlyweds who eventually divorced evidenced more negative communication than those who remained married after 10 years. Related to adverse communicative exchanges because they also impact the parent–child relationship are poor problem solving and ineffective parenting strategies (Bastaits & Mortelmans, 2016; Hetherington, 2006). In fact, *diminished capacity to parent* has been an enduring concept proffered by professionals when referring to the deterioration of parenting skills and behaviors upon marital dissolution (Wallerstein, 1985; Wallerstein, Lewis, & Packer Rosenthal, 2013).

Further family system theories have evolved via communication research and include intergenerational communication transmissions and metacommunication among family members. Accordingly, the term *family scripts* refers to the mores and belief systems transmitted by parents to children, which can be further sustained as a child integrates this knowledge into their own belief systems and ultimately behaves according to this script themselves (Byng-Hall, 1998). For example, for some cultures, fathers are considered the more powerful and knowledgeable parent, and mothers are passive and ineffective. This message can render the mother as powerless in her parenting role, which can thwart an adaptive and functional relationship between mother and children. This cultural message of powerlessness can be transmitted directly (e.g., in phrases such as "You are a useless mother") or indirectly, such as when the father does not include the mother in important child decisions.

Furthermore, there is evidence that such scripts and family beliefs are intergenerational, as they serve to maintain equilibrium within a family and keep the family connected across generations. In fact, Amato and Cheadle (2005) conducted a study that examined the links between divorce across three generations and observed that divorce in the first generation (grandparents) was associated with lower educational attainment, more marital discord, and weaker ties with mothers and fathers in the third generation (grandchildren), despite the majority of these grandchildren not being born at the time of their grandparents' divorce (less than 10%). These researchers discovered that these effects were mediated by second-generation characteristics of low education, marital discord, divorce, and tension in the early parent–child relationships (Amato & Cheadle, 2005).

Developmental problems have also been shown empirically to impact the parent–child relationship such that parents who may not understand and appreciate their child's developmental challenges have unrealized expectations of the child which leads to maladaptive parenting behavior. Additionally, the quality of the marital or parent relationship has been identified as an important predictor of the parent's acceptance of a child's disability (Sae & Yoko, 2004). Others have identified that the quality of the parent–child relationship is negatively impacted by the severity of a child's autism spectrum disorder (ASD) and can be improved with intervention (Hobson, Tarver, Beurkens, & Hobson, 2016).

Finally, a parent's psychopathology has been observed to mediate the parent–child relationship, which can ultimately disrupt a child's relationship with their parent. For example, research demonstrates that parental antisocial behaviors are related to maladaptive parenting practices, family conflict and poor quality of parent–child relationship (Bornovalova, Blazei, Malone, McGue, & Iacono, 2013). Parental depression has also been observed to impact the parent–child relationship. Researchers have noted that the quality of parenting is adversely impacted by parent depression (Dempsey, McQuillin, Butler, & Axelrad, 2016). Furthermore, Wade, Llewellyn, and Matthews (2015) observed that parent mental health impacted parenting practices to which children with intellectual disabilities were subjected. With respect to child maltreatment, Cohen et al. (2014) observed distinct personality disorder symptoms to be related to different forms of child maltreatment.

Reunification Therapy: Terms and Related Concepts

Prior to delineating the treatment approach for the reunification of families, it is important to clarify the terms used for reunification therapy as well as related concepts.

Therapy Terms

The two most frequently used terms for the reparation of a child–parent relationship via family therapy are *reunification therapy* and *reconciliation therapy*. With respect to the former, reunification is defined as "to come together again" (Reunite, n.d.) or "to unify again after being divided" (Reunification, n.d.). Reconciliation, alternately, is defined as "to put people back on friendly terms, to end conflict" (Reconciliation, n.d.) and "to make friendly again; to settle; bring into harmony" (Reconciliation, n.d.), according to *Webster's New World Dictionary* (Guralnik, 1986). While the goal of reunification therapy is to reduce conflict, and heighten positive exchanges between parent and child, thereby facilitating the reconciliation of the dyad, in many cases the breach in the relationship that is in need of mending is not conflict driven but rather a result of logistics such as military deployment. Consequently, the purpose of this book is to serve as a treatment manual for unifying divided families irrespective of whether the division is due to conflict or other issues, and the term *reunification therapy* is best used to denote this process.

Terms Referring to Parents

When conducting reunification therapy for individuals from intact homes with the breach in the relationship due to time and place (e.g., lengthy hospitalization or military deployment), the use of parent terms is clear: *mother, father,* or derivatives thereof. With respect to reunification therapy for families undergoing high-conflict parent relationship dissolution proceedings or dependency court proceedings, the demarcation of the legal status of each parent includes a multitude of terms such as *divorcing parents, time-sharing parent* and *non-time-sharing parent, custodial parent* and *noncustodial parent, residential parent* and *nonresidential parent, preferred parent* and *nonpreferred parent, aligned parent, estranged parent, alienated parent, target parent, reunifying parent,* and *reconciling parent.* Regarding the terms for divorcing parents, there are many cases where reunification occurs in homes with married parents, such as is the case with institutionalized parents or those in the military. Furthermore, there are emerging trends for biological parents who cohabite but do not marry, and therefore do not divorce if they dissolve their relationship. The number of cohabiting parents with children under the age of 18 years has practically tripled from the late 1990s until 2014, from 1.2 million cohabiting parents to 3.3 million (Child Trends Data Bank, 2015).

Given that there are different laws in different states regarding dissolution proceedings and children's best interests, these terms carry different valences and hold varying meanings for individuals in different states. In some states, the concepts of *custody* and *residential parent* have been abolished by statute, with the intent that children have a right to equal access to their parents and that no one parent has greater rights than the other to have contact with and to make decisions for that child. The term *preferred parent* may not truly reflect the child's preferences, as in many cases a child may have equal preference for both parents; however, they may not be in a position to express this preference. The term *preferred* also carries with it some implied or assumed stature of the parent who is exclusively spending time with the child. For the purposes of this book, the terms *time-sharing parent* and *non-time-sharing parent* will be used to demarcate the true relationship parents have with their children in the face of the time-limited nature of the relationship all children have with their parents concurrently and over the course of a child's development. Also, such a demarcation prevents one parent having greater power or preferred status over the other parent and does not indicate any preferential stature of a particular parent.

Interparental Conflict Terms

In family law litigation, children are often perceived as chattel, and parents frequently battle over the children as a possession to be won rather than as a young life, on loan, in need of nurturance and caretaking. Given specific sets of circumstances, parents often have a separate agenda apart from their assigned parent role and time-sharing schedule. These agendas are often multifaceted, and the individual may have direct awareness of their own agendas or these agendas may lie outside of the parent's awareness. For example, for many divorcing parents, one manner in which the marital relationship continues is through the interparental conflict. Conflict requires various forms and degrees of contact and is emotionally charged, thereby eliciting a response. As conflict continues, so does the relationship, as it requires at least two individuals' interchanges; hence the parents, despite being legally divorced, remain "married" through the conflict which can be discharged via time-sharing schedule disputes, for example.

Alienation, Estrangement, and Interference

Wallerstein and Kelly (1980) were the first to initiate a discussion of child refusal or resistance to time-sharing with a parent following parental marital dissolution. Subsequently, Richard Gardner developed the concept of *parental alienation syndrome* (PAS) to encompass a cluster of symptoms and behaviors frequently detected in child custody evaluations in which a child is unwilling to have contact with one parent (Gardner, 1999, 2003). Gardner delineated PAS parameters of a child's investment in unwarranted denigration of a parent resulting from the amalgamation of both the programming of the child against the non-time-sharing parent and the child's own vilification of the target parent (Gardner, 1999, 2003).

With respect to alienated parents and PAS, there has been much controversy regarding the concept of alienation and the judiciary's discrediting of the notion that a syndrome exists, in the face of a lack of clear and convincing evidence regarding the existence of alienation as a "syndrome" (Gardner, 1999; Gardner, 2003). This is because empirical research with a priori hypotheses and appropriate statistical analyses, including those of a factorial nature, has not been conducted, and therefore, data do not exist which support such a construct. To encapsulate the premise that episodically parents interfere with the other parent's attempts to have a healthy and meaningful relationship with their children, professionals have clarified this parental interference as alienating *behaviors*. Unfortunately, the legal system is extremely resistant to such efforts at clarification, since a derivative of *alienation syndrome* is included within the phrase *alienating behaviors*, thereby foreclosing the consideration of alienating behaviors as operative in family systems. This does not mean that the term *alienation* has been completely eradicated in professional communications – as one can discern from the use of the term in a multitude of recent publications on the topic; however, mental health professionals may wish to use behaviorally based synonyms of *alienation,* such as *parental interference* or those phrases which have not been subject to prejudice in court.

Interestingly, other professionals have offered different interpretations regarding alienation, with different emphasis as to the impetus for the breach in the relationship. For example, Reay (2015) stated that within the literature, *alienation* is a term used for a child who has rejected a parent without a realistic or legitimate reason. Furthermore, research indicates that alienation is distinguished from the term *estrangement*, such that with estrangement, a child has a legitimate reason for the refusal to spend time with the other parent. However, others have used the term *estrangement* to denote any breach in the parent–child relationship irrespective of the legitimacy of the reason (Carr, Holman, Abetz, Kellas, & Vagnoni, 2015).

To address some of the problems inherent in PAS, Kelly and Johnston (2001) focused on the end product: the child. This removes the focus on the malevolent conditioning maneuvers of the alienating parent as the only etiological agent for the child's unwarranted rejection of the non-time-sharing parent. Furthermore, in their divorce model, they considered a continuum of different parent–child relationships, with children having positive relationships with their parents as one continuum anchor, and children expressing complete parent rejection at the other end of the continuum. The focus on the child forces the clinician to assess the origins of the child's refusal or resistance to spending time with the time-sharing parent. By focusing on the child's refusal, the model by Kelly and Johnston (2001) considers multiple sources (e.g., both parents and the child) as influential in the child rejecting time-sharing with a parent. Well-trained clinicians examine problems from numerous perspectives, including listening to the child's disclosures, observing child behaviors, and considering the child's systemic relationships including parental, sibling, and extended-family relationships.

Operationalizing a term to describe a time-sharing parent's role in a child's refusal to spend time with the non-time-sharing parent reduces the observed behavior to discrete units and increases the likelihood of effective intervention. This empirical reductionist approach reduces the potential for adult inflammation of the process. For example, the term *interference* may be used to describe overt behavior without identifying the motivation or intent of this behavior (e.g., intentional or accidental). Irrespective of the terminology used when referring to a child's hesitancy or refusal to spend time with the alternate parent, the focus of reunification therapy is on establishing meaningful relationships between parent and child.

Factitious Disorder Imposed by Another

Regarding parental divisiveness, recent attention has been focused on factitious disorder imposed on another (FDIA), previously known as *factitious disorder by proxy,* as a possible contributing factor for estrangement between the non-FDIA parent and the child. FDIA is also known as *Munchausen syndrome by proxy.* FDIA is defined in the *Diagnostic and Statistical Manual of Mental Disorders,* 5th edition (DSM-5) as

> A. Falsification of physical or psychological signs or symptoms, or induction of injury or disease, in another, associated with identified deception. B. The individual presents another individual (victim) to others as ill, impaired, or injured. C. The deceptive behavior is evident even in the absence of obvious external rewards. (American Psychiatric Association, 2013, p. 325)

The concept of FDIA serves a purpose in drawing attention to the parent sabotaging the child – in some cases rendering the child incapacitated – thereby fusing the relationship between the afflicted parent and the child victim. Adshead and Bluglass (2001) identified attachment problems between the perpetrator and the child in these cases.

With respect to fabricated illness behaviors, Sanders (1995) originally proposed a multiple family process, which includes not only considering the behavior of the afflicted parent but also child behaviors and the behavior of other family members who engage in creating the illness symptoms. Sanders (1995) further proposed that physicians often unwittingly become coauthors of these individuals' fictitious medical stories in an effort to assist in resolving the often mysterious illness. Typically, a parent manufactures a child's medical history and symptom presentation, and as children age, they may collude with the parent in this invented symptom presentation (Sanders, 1995; Barber & Davis, 2002). Sanders (1995) also proposed that this level of collusion ranges from complete child awareness, to the child's unconscious collusion, with varying levels of awareness in between these ends of the continuum. This observation is not surprising given children's susceptibility to memory alteration (Loftus, 2005).

In some extreme cases of parental alienation, the time-sharing parent can be observed to manufacture events to justify withholding the child from the non-time-sharing parent. An example of this process includes allegations of child sexual abuse levied by the time-sharing parent against the non-time-sharing parent in an attempt to impede time-sharing, where, upon investigation, the probability of the abuse occurring is nonexistent. As the child ages, however, for those FDIA cases where intervention has not been adequate, the abuse stories reemerge in an altered form and/or are relayed as continuing to occur despite the unfeasibility of abuse, given supervision of the non-time-sharing parent and videotaping of the public access areas leading to private areas within the home. As a result, the time-sharing parent has effectuated a memory for the child of a manufactured event. Not only does the child believe they are justified in not time-sharing with the parent and hence loses that relationship, but they also believe they have been abused, which can contribute to trauma symptoms (vicarious traumatization) and potentially other psychological sequelae. This manifestation of FDIA is psychological in nature, whereas historically FDIA has been based in the generation of physical symptoms and contrived medical illness by the perpetrator of these events. While for traditional FDIA cases, the medical practitioner is inadvertently drawn into the "story," for family law cases, attorneys, guardians ad litem, and even judges can unwittingly be "coauthors" of the story. Alternately in these family law cases, there have been occasions where a parent has attempted to withhold a child from another parent by making that child sick, which reflects more directly traditional FDIA than psychological FDIA.

In extreme cases, time-sharing parents not only contribute to making the child ill but also levy complaints that the non-time-sharing parent was either causing the illness or neglecting the child resulting in the child's symptoms. Examples included a time-sharing father, overfeeding a toddler and then supplying that child with laxatives, immediately prior to time-sharing with the non-time-sharing parent (mother). This caused the child to have explosive diarrhea for 24 hours, and subsequently to have a diminished appetite during the mother's limited time-sharing (two weekends a month). Upon the child's return to father, he would immediately have the child weighed by a medical practitioner to demonstrate weightloss. In fact, this practice evolved into the father having the child weighed before and after the mother's visit; thus, a record of weight loss after visiting with the mother was maintained. Immediately prior to the mother resuming her full 50 % time-sharing schedule, the father asserted to the pediatrician that mother was starving and neglecting the child; the physician promptly called child protective services, and the mother was prevented from exercising any time-sharing with the child.

Another case example involved a mother communicating to her 4-year-old son not to eat, drink, or speak in the presence of the father during his time-sharing. The father was greatly concerned about the child's potential for dehydration and other systemic problems inherent with lack of food and liquids. In both case examples, the parents were observed to have co-slept with the child since birth, and they voiced opinions that they were the only parent who could adequately parent and protect the child. Neither parent had successfully separated from their own parents. The child sabotage was an effort to maintain the fusion between the parent and the child, preventing healthy separation and individuation.

Typically, by the time the reunification therapist receives the referral in cases of medical FDIA, physicians (sometimes in conjunction with child protective services) have identified the disorder or have expressed concerns that the physical sabotage of the child by the time-sharing parent is present. For cases of psychological sabotage of the child, these are often more difficult to identify but may be elucidated through custody evaluations or social investigations or by the reunification therapist during initial child reunification sessions.

Gatekeeping

The term *gatekeeping* has evolved to denote one parent's management of the other parent with respect to their parenting, and as such can vary in extremes, ranging from the hypervigilant overprotective parent who has no intention to estrange the child from the time-sharing parent, to the intentionally estranging parent. Gatekeeping has been described as both attitudes and actions that impede cooperation between parents by reducing opportunities for the non-time-sharing parent's engagement in child caretaking (Allen & Hawkins, 1999). Children in these cases often feel stuck between the opposing wishes of both parents when exposed to interparental conflict, contributing to the child's feeling that they are responsible for causing or even resolving these disagreements (Healy, Stewart, & Copeland, 1993). Specifically, researchers have proposed gatekeeping as a prominent issue frequently noted in cases with high levels of conflict post couple dissolution that may result in decreased involvement by the non-time-sharing parent, increased conflict between the non-time-sharing and time-sharing parents, and a poorer parent–child relationship between the child and their non-time-sharing parent (Kelly, 2000; Doherty, 1998). Although children who have gatekeeping parents may directly reject the non-time-sharing parent, in many cases, gatekeeping may not necessarily involve the child's rejection of the non-time-sharing parent, as occurs in parental alienation, interference, or estrangement, but in fact it is the parent who prevents the non-time-sharing parent from actively parenting the child.

CHAPTER 3
Reunification Therapy as a Specific Form of Empirically Based Family Therapy

Reunification therapy is a form of family therapy that differs from traditional family therapy with respect to the type of family problem and the focus of problem resolution. Most family therapies are oriented toward problem resolution within a family, where family members have frequent and continuing contact with one another. Reunification therapy is employed in situations where there has been a physical and emotional breach in the parent–child relationship, and generally, continuing and frequent contact is absent in the relationship. Furthermore, it is expected that there is a notable disruption in the coparents' relationship as well, particularly since the child typically does not live or interact with the one non-time-sharing parent, while spending exclusive time with the other. While the primary situations in which the severing of the relationship between child and parent is observed include military parent deployment, institutionalized parents (e.g., prison or hospitalization), and parents in family law cases (e.g., parents in dependency court or divorced or separated parents), the last of these clusters, family law reunification cases, are most frequently the target of intervention. Furthermore, when working with parents who have engaged in family court, these situations are further complicated by the addition of a number of individuals (e.g., guardians ad litem, extended-family members, and attorneys) and other factors such as legal barriers.

What Reunification Therapy Is NOT

With respect to family court cases, interventions by psychologists and other mental health counselors in family law matters are wide-ranging and varied, including, but not necessarily limited to, social investigations and custody evaluations, forensic psychological evaluations, individual or multiclient therapy, mediation, parenting coordination, and reunification therapy. While some of these roles are specifically and deliberately adopted by a psychologist based on their family forensic psychology area of practice, other mental health professionals are often placed unwittingly in the center of a family law action. Such instances include when a therapist is treating a child for a psychological issue and over the course of treatment, the parents dissolve their marriage and petition the therapist to testify in court.

Traditionally, family forensic psychologists have been primarily characterized by their work in conducting custody evaluations or social investigations and forensic assessment of the individual. For some states, *social investigations* have replaced custody evaluations; however, the outcome remains the same, with the professional ultimately making recommendations to the court regarding time-sharing and access for parents and children. While the court is tempted to use the reunification therapy process as a method of discovery for adjudicating custody issues, reunification therapy is not an assessment. The role of a reunification therapist is not to delineate which parent is better fit to take care of the child and how much time each parent should spend with the child for a formal parenting plan, and in fact, a therapist making these recommendations is at risk of violating their ethical code and practice laws. If the reunification therapist is asked to make a determination of the suitability of time-sharing or custody, the attorneys and the court will need to be apprised of the unsuitability of such a referral.

The inappropriateness of the family reunification therapist *custody-determination referral* is based on the nature of custody evaluations versus treatment. While assessment is not inherently incompatible with treatment – and in fact, it can guide treatment in many non-family forensic settings – it has the potential to derail the family therapy process and compromise the therapist–client relationship during reunification therapy, as the "fight" subsequently shifts from a constructive approach to a dismantling or deconstructive approach in order to determine which parent is best suited to spend the majority of the time with the children (which is often viewed as which parent is the winner). In contrast, the family reunification therapist's approach is designed to construct and mend family relationships, building upon a synthesis of interactions. Finally, many of the reasons attorneys and judges wish for the reunification therapist to assess whether or not the child should have access to a particular parent stem from concerns over child maltreatment. If in fact the child has been maltreated by a parent and neither the child nor the parent have engaged in their own therapy, the potential for further damage exists in placing the child and parent together in a family reunification therapy situation. Furthermore, if a parent demonstrates potentially harmful behavior during sessions or during one of the out-of-session homework assignments, not only does this potentially place the child in harm's way and derail the therapy process, but it also has the potential to harm the child's receptivity to the therapeutic process and the trust the child holds in the therapist and theoretically in future therapists. In summary, reunification therapy is not assessment.

Similarly, officers of the court have attempted to bypass forensic psychological evaluation of one family member, by utilizing reunification family therapy as a manner to assess the "psychological fitness" of one person, or to determine if one particular parent is responsible for the breach in the parent–child relationship (i.e., alienation). This is ordered with good intentions, as judges and lawyers may believe that reunification therapy is the ultimate goal of the case, regardless of the individual's mental health. Alternately, reunification therapy may be ordered under these circumstances to save the clients money, as a "two for the price of one," desiring the therapist's clinical impressions of the clients, while they simultaneously provide reunification services.

Professionals also intervene from an individual therapy perspective in cases where people need assistance in adjusting to the dissolution of the family unit as it was originally formed. Since inherent in the psychotherapy process is the creation of a supportive relationship, there is an element of advocacy built into the relationship. Furthermore, through this trusting relationship, the client renders themselves vulnerable and shares the most personal of information to their therapist. The therapist's goal in these cases is to serve as an advocate for the individual client; hence the client–therapist relationship is often one-sided, whereas the interests of more than one family member must be considered in reunification therapy. While all family members' needs must be balanced – unlike in traditional family therapy with cohabiting family members – reunification therapy may skew this balance of individual family members' needs. For example, a time-sharing father who has the need to be the most important parent in the children's lives may have to relinquish this need to the non-time-sharing parent and to the children themselves in their quest for healthy autonomy and independence, and to establish a healthy relationship with the non-time-sharing parent.

Mental health professionals may also be hired as consultants by parents who request information on child development and the impact of divorce on children. These parents may seek knowledge as to the best method to inform the child about the impending dissolution of the marriage. Also parents may seek information supporting the best methods by which to structure time-sharing plans revolving around the child's best interests. Consultations in this vein may continue throughout the life of the divorce or dissolution, and thereafter; for example, regarding postdissolution dating and introducing new partners into the child's life.

Additionally, subject to the laws of their state, mental health professionals after meeting the requirements of their state can serve as mediators or parenting coordinators. Mediation is an alternative form of conflict resolution to litigation, often empowering parents to creatively craft their own parenting plans which are subject to ratification by the court. This form of dispute resolution has better outcomes with greater satisfaction with time-sharing agreements by both parents and noticeable reductions in postdivorce litigation and interparental conflict compared with adjudicated parenting plans (Emery, Laumann-Billings, Waldron, Sbarra, & Dillon, 2001; Shaw, 2010).

While not typically statutorily determined, *therapeutic mediation* has evolved from statutory mediation and is occasionally ordered by judges for a mental health expert who is a certified mediator to assist parties in their readiness and ability to reach decisions regarding parenting and time-sharing, further assisting with parenting plan composition which also ultimately becomes the parents' legal contract. Therapeutic mediation, given its basic premises of assisting the parents in evolving a mindset conducive to entering into an agreement regarding a parenting plan may occur over time with episodic meetings, unlike traditional mediation, which occurs during a large block of time (consecutive hours). The goal of mediation is typically twofold: equitable distribution of the parents' financial resources, and determination of a specific time-sharing and parental decision-making document. Neither of these outcomes is the explicit goal of reunification therapy. Rather reunification therapy is not mediation or a tool for developing specific time-sharing plans, but rather it is a tool to assist in rebuilding families and strengthening familial relationships. It may be that a byproduct of the outcome of reunification therapy is that parents jointly agree separately and apart from the reunification therapist on the structure and content of their time-sharing plan.

Parenting coordination is typically effected to assist the parents with their coparenting, with an emphasis on the reduction of interparental conflict and the enhancement of communication between the parents. At times, parenting coordination is court ordered, is a component of the parents' marital settlement agreement and parenting plan ratified by a judge, or is entered into voluntarily by both parents. Parenting coordination is most typically requested or ordered after filing for marital dissolution, prior to the final divorce judgment and/or after the divorce (postdissolution) as interparental conflict continues or reemerges. In most states, parenting coordination is not a confidential process, and there is a possibility if not an expectation, that the parenting coordinator will report to the court. Within some models of parenting coordination, if the parents cannot agree on specific parenting decisions, then the parent coordinator will make the recommendation to the parties and to the court if necessary, regarding resolution of the disagreements. In some states, there has been a movement among some attorneys and mental health experts toward allowing the parenting coordinator to have binding authority, such that parents are bound by the parenting coordinator's recommendations in the event that parents cannot agree to a resolution of the problem area. Despite the aspiration for some that the parenting coordinator be bestowed with binding authority, the law does not support this practice because only the trier of fact (e.g., the judge) can exert such authority.

Other models of parenting coordination in a few states demarcate parenting coordination as a confidential process, with limited exceptions such as when a parenting coordinator is privy to child maltreatment or domestic violence exposure, or if one or both parties is noncompliant with the process (Parks, Tindall, & Yingling, 2011; Kelly, 2008). The confidentiality of the process and the inclusion of both parents as well as the children, at times places parenting coordination in a category akin to family forensic therapy. However, in some states, attorneys who are mediators and undergo parenting coordination training can become certified in this procedure; it is likely then that contingent on one's originating profession, the tenor of parenting coordination will differ, with psychotherapists focusing on skills-based and communication-training approaches, and attorneys focusing on problem solving and potential legal issues. Although no data exist with respect to determining any differences in parenting coordination outcomes based on the profession of the practitioner, future research should elucidate whether or not disparities exist and the impact of extant differences on conflict resolution and parenting outcomes. Similarly, there are no data available that delineate the impact confidentiality has on the parenting coordination process and outcomes. Some professionals have suggested that by protecting the process via confidentiality, parents are able to stay stuck in their conflict. This is particularly important for couples who continue in their "marriage" with their coparent via the conflict and despite being divorced. Attorneys attempt to bypass the confidentiality of parenting coordination by utilizing family therapy as an alternative. Despite family therapy being subject to the laws of confidentiality, privileged communication, and Health Insurance Portability and Accountability Act (HIPAA, 1996), it is at times easier to obtain a waiver of confidentiality in therapy than in parenting coordination.

Finally, there are many jurisdictions that do not have parenting coordination laws, and in fact in the Ohio Supreme Court mandates that counties decide whether or not to adopt parenting coordination as a process (Rules of Superintendence for the Courts of Ohio, 2014); consequently, family therapy is the default intervention for these families in crisis, if there is no provision for parenting coordination.

Reunification therapy is neither traditional family therapy nor is it parent coordination that is shrouded with a promise of confidentiality. In many reunification therapy cases, confidentiality is removed by the order of the judge, and in fact, the abatement of confidentiality via court order is recommended, if not required, by many professionals. While it includes elements of parenting coordination, reunification therapy goals and timing of interventions are different. For example, for a child who has never met the non-time-sharing parent, parent coordination may not be introduced until reunification is proceeding. Additionally, sessions spent with the time-sharing parent initially are often to assist that parent in preparing the child for meeting and spending time with the non-time-sharing parent, as opposed to addressing issues that the parents have with each other regarding the parenting of the child – a central feature of parenting coordination. As reunification therapy evolves, however, it is often mandatory that the reunification therapist conduct dyadic sessions with the parents to assist in their conflict resolution and coparenting issues related to reunification, since left untreated, these coparenting problems can derail any parent–child relationship.

Reunification Therapy: A Composite Treatment

Change is hard at first, messy in the middle and gorgeous at the end

Robin Sharma (April 8, 2016, via Twitter)

Empirical Bases of Reunification Therapy

Prior to addressing the reparation of the parent and child relationship, it is important to discern the etiology of the maintenance of the fragmented relationship. Garber (2015) postulated that the mechanisms responsible for a child's avoidance of a parent in reunification cases follows the same learning paradigms as other stimuli that are avoided with anxiety. The non-time-sharing parent has become the feared stimulus for the child and is the result of a true pairing of previously neutral stimuli with an unconditioned stimulus such that the non-time-sharing parent (conditioned stimulus) has physically hurt the child by administering corporeal punishment (unconditioned stimulus), as an example. These are the core components of classical conditioning. The fear or anxiety regarding contact with the non-time-sharing parent is further reinforced by avoidance, because when anxious, the child avoids that parent and anxiety diminishes; hence, avoidance is reinforcing (e.g. Murray, Creswell, & Cooper, 2009). Ultimately, avoidance is maintained or increased through the principles of operant conditioning. In addition to conditioning, anxiety theories contain a cognitive component such as the information processing component in PTSD paradigms (Foa & Rothbaum, 2001; Foa, Steketee, & Rothbaum, 1989). Alternately, in cases where fear is not acquired or learned via conditioning, such as in cases of a parent's undue influence, avoidance may be learned via modeling and operant conditioning (reinforcement including rewards) as well as an altered cognitive map in response to the time-sharing parent's negative-valanced scripts about the non-time-sharing parent and associated stimuli (e.g., events).

While replication is the cornerstone of science (Simons, 2014), empiricism is an important tenet of hypothesis testing, such that empiricism is based on observation in an attempt to objectify and realize conjecture, opinion, inquisition, and invalidated theory. In recent years, the field of psychology has adopted a framework, which is steeped in empiricism forming the basis of evidence-based practices. Not only do psychologists and other mental health professionals adhere to the importance of evidence-based practices, the legal profession has also adopted this orientation to legitimize psychology as a science.

In fact, the acceptable legal standard for expert opinions is based on the Frye standard that allows witnesses who have special experience or knowledge, and who are skilled "in that particular science, art, or trade" (as this is phrased in the standard) render opinions as admissible evidence (Frye v. United States, 1923). Frye is considered the "general acceptance test" (Bernstein, 2001) to determine if opinions offered can be admitted into evidence. In more recent years, some states have replaced the Frye standard with the Daubert standard, which considers expert opinions based on the tenets of science (Black, Ayala, & Saffran-Brinks, 1993). To meet the Daubert standard, opinions must be formulated based on scientific inquiry, including hypothesis development, and testing with known error rates, subject to peer review and publication, with methods, procedures, and outcomes according to accepted standards in the professional community. Consequently, for the purposes of reunification therapy, interventions are anchored in empirically based science. Even if the Frye Standard is operative in the state where the therapist is practicing, it is useful to consider Daubert principles in all cases, because of the attention that is placed on the tenets of science that should guide practice regardless.

The literature is rife with papers which advocate for reunifying children with their parents, from a myriad of theoretical orientations including cognitive behavior, family systems, Adlerian theory, play therapy, attachment theory therapy, and ecosystemic models (Chaffin, & Friedrich, 2004; Goldsmith, Oppenheim, & Wanlass, 2004; Guardia & Banner, 2012; Nelson, Mitrani, & Szapocznik, 2000; Timmer et al., 2006). Reunification in family law cases typically involves reestablishing a relationship between child (children) and one parent. Rarely, it involves the reunification of both parents with a child who has other adults as time-sharing agents, and this phenomenon is mostly observed in dependency cases. Similarly, in cases where both military parents are deployed or adult children are estranged from both their parents, both parents may be the ones reunifying with the child.

Selection of treatment is based on the specific needs of the family, including symptomology and the available empirical literature to support the treatment's efficacy. Irrespective of the reason for the breach in the parent–child relationship, the core issues that tend to emerge in reunifying families' cases include (a) the anxiety of the child; (b) dysfunctional communication among family members; (c) poor behavioral exchanges (e.g., low on positives and high on negatives) between family members, especially between the reunifying parent and the child; (d) maladaptive parenting and problem solving; and/or (e) developmental problems (e.g., Greenberg, Doi Fick, & Schnider, 2012). Additionally, the absence of the non-time-sharing parent (the one in need of reunification) at critical periods in the child's development and for particular lengths of time can impact the quality of the parent–child relationship.

As stated previously, anxiety can play a significant role in the resistance of the child toward a relationship with the other parent, irrespective of the reasons the child has not seen their parent. Operant and classical conditioning, in addition to other factors including the residential family script, contribute to anxiety's development and maintenance. With respect to operant conditioning, avoidance, a core component of anxiety disorders or symptom clusters, is reinforcing because anxiety decreases when the anxiety-provoking stimulus is not present. One way not to be in the presence of the anxiety-provoking stimulus is to avoid it (Foa & Kozak, 1986). Children estranged from their parents often actively avoid parent contact. It is evident that the child's contextual anxiety must be treated as part of the reunification process.

In addition to anxiety as a factor in the breach in the parent-child relationship, poor communication between the parents can lead to high interparental conflict and poor communication with the child, contributing to the severing of the parent–child relationship. Further family systemic theories have evolved via communication research and include intergenerational communication transmissions and metacommunication among family members. As discussed previously *family scripts* are the mores and belief systems transmitted by parents to children. These belief systems are ultimately adopted by the children who behave in accordance with the script. These scripts are communicated generationally and serve to maintain family stability and link the family across generations (Byng-Hall, 1998).

Poor communication can contribute to significant conflict between parents. Marital and couples' therapy research indicates a positive relationship between dysfunctional communication patterns and couple conflict. This is likely exacerbated when couples have dissolved their relationship, as the motivation to repair the couple relationship is greatly diminished, because the couple has parted ways. Likewise, adult children estranged from their parents also have problems with communication. Agllias (2016) reported that researchers have observed adult-child–parent estrangement occurs in response to feelings of betrayal by a parent and/or problematic dispute negotiation patterns and a maladaptive communication style. In fact, adult children have reported psychological maltreatment at the hands of their parents, including forceful and spiteful communications (Scharp, Thomas, & Paxman, 2015). Conflict evolves in part from diminished positive exchanges between the dyad. Divorcing couples in high-conflict cases often have frequent negative and adverse behavioral and verbal transactions (Ayoub, Deutsch, & Maraganore, 1999; Maclean, 2007). In fact, Gottman and Driver (2005) in an empirical study of newlywed couples found that intercouple conflict was likely the result of unspoken interactions. Gottman and Levenson (2000) observed in their 14-year longitudinal study, that couples' lack of positive emotions and perpetuation of conflict-laden discourse significantly predicted delayed divorce. Early divorce was significantly determined by negative feelings during conflictual couple exchanges. Dorrance, Hall, and McNallie (2016) reported that those families who emphasized the value of open conversation within the family had greater positive relationship outcomes both inside the home as well as external to the family unit. Furthermore, in a meta-analysis of 52 studies, Schrodt, Witt, and Messersmith (2008) discovered that familial conversational style was associated with relationship satisfaction, interpersonal connectedness, relational commitment, physical and psychological well-being, and self-regard.

When applying the concept of diminished positive exchanges to the parent–child relationship, research regarding parent ineffectiveness is illustrative of adverse child impact. In these studies, parents attend to the negative or maladaptive behavior via attempts at correction, which at the very least are negative (e.g., explanation as to the inappropriateness of the child's behavior) and at the other extreme are coercive (e.g., physical methods of discipline). A feedback loop is created such that the child acts out to obtain attention from the parent, and the parent's primary attention toward the child is negative or adverse, thereby reinforcing and increasing the unwanted behavior (Goldstein, Arnold, Rosenberg, Stowe, & Ortiz, 2001).

With regard to poor problem solving and ineffective parenting strategies, it has been well established that coercive parenting practices, including physical discipline, contribute to the manifestation of child disruptive behavior (Latham, Mark, & Oliver, 2016; Patterson, 1982). These maladaptive parenting tactics can be observed in all realms of reunifying parents, including in parents of adult children (e.g., Agllias, 2015, 2016). While Carr et al. (2015) found that parents of adult children perceive their children to have a sense of unjustified entitlement, it was likely that that sense of unwarranted entitlement was derived from the parent reinforcing the privileged behavior by overindulging the adult children; thereby enabling the adult children to maintain their expected dependency on the parent(s).

Developmental problems have also been noted to impact the parent–child relationship, such that special needs children require greater resources, including time, energy, and financial support than those children with typical abilities. Resource demand often stresses both the parenting skills of the parents and their coparenting relationship. Keenan, Newman, Gray, and Rinehart (2016) observed parents of children with ASD to display significantly greater levels of parenting stress and attachment-related anxiety than typically developing children's parents. Additionally, children experiencing potentially life-threatening illnesses have reported significant levels of family conflict and family dysfunction (Leeman et al., 2016).

While reunification family therapy is not traditional family therapy, it is family therapy none-the-less, and the confluence of different family members and their impact on one another are evident whenever addressing problems within a family. Traditional systemic family therapies, from which both structural systemic family therapy and strategic systemic family therapy originate, frequently commence with an identified patient who is exhibiting some problematic behavior. From systemic family therapy perspectives, the therapist uses the symptom as the key to understanding a larger comprehensive problem manifestation that reverberates throughout the family system, with the structural systemic family therapist emphasizing the family hierarchy, power, and role of each member, and the establishment of a family hierarchy through interpersonal boundaries. Alternatively, the strategic systemic family therapist focuses on the symptoms as communicated metaphors of problems inherent in the family system. While the reunification therapist often assists in the reparation of family boundaries via alterations in intrafamilial communication, the focus is not on specific symptom resolution but rather on reparation of relationships within the family system. Similarly, behaviorally oriented family therapists include family members to address problems observed in an identified client via parent effectiveness training to address a child's oppositional defiant symptoms, or via behavioral couple's therapy to address problems within the marital or couple relationship. Likewise, while components of these behavioral family therapies are used within reunification therapy, reunification therapy encompasses a broader range of struggles and contexts than specific symptom resolution. Reunification therapy often involves multiple layers of problems across family members that co-occur or occur sequentially, including poor problem-solving ability of parents, poor parenting skills, a lack of adaptive communication skills, anxiety observed within children, and lack of motivation or resistance by the custodial parent, as examples.

While there are some treatment outcome data to support the reunification process and treatment, overall the literature is sparse. Nonetheless, available outcome research indicates that children who have been separated via interference from a parent and who are required to have contact with that parent have greater likelihood of having relationships with both parents than those children who are not obligated to have contact (Rand & Rand, 2005). While individual therapy was observed to be counterproductive in the Rand and Rand 2005 study, the argument for therapy that is family focused, with the goal to heighten contact between both parents and child, is tenable.

In a longitudinal study, spanning 6 years, of children and divorced mothers, a social learning and cognitive behavior intervention program was designed, which included different therapy components for the children and the mothers (Vélez, Wolchik, Tein, & Sandler, 2011). Program elements for the mothers included addressing the mother–child relationship quality, effective discipline, the father's access to the child, and interparental conflict (Vélez et al., 2011). In this study, the children's interventions included increasing effective coping, reducing negative thoughts about divorce-related stressors, and improving mother–child relationship quality (Vélez et al., 2011). Results indicated improvements in the mother and child relationship, which had a cascading effect, with increased levels of child coping efficacy over time (Vélez et al., 2011).

With respect to other reunification therapy observations that do not include the estrangement or alienation custodial parent component, Digiorgio-Miller (2002) presented a comprehensive approach to family reunification following incest which included each family member having individual therapy to maintain a protected environment for unrestricted communicative exchanges. She discussed different goals for each family member's individual therapy, contingent on the role each member had in the family, such as that of offending parent, nonoffending parent, child survivor of abuse, and non-abused child survivor. Eventually family therapy was integrated into the process, with the goal of reunification; however, in these cases, the therapy was child survivor–driven and primarily guided by the child's comfort level (Digiorgio-Miller, 2002). Furthermore, including the perpetrator in the family sessions was not realized until the individuals had made significant gains in their own individual therapy.

To address the core issues noted in reunifying families as delineated above (child anxiety, dysfunctional communication among family members, poor behavioral exchanges between family members, maladaptive parenting and problem solving, and developmental problems), reunification therapy involves seven primary components within the cognitive behavioral domains and two secondary theoretical operational components within the humanistic and client-centered and systemic family therapy domains.

Cognitive and Behavioral Domains

Behavioral Parent and Behavioral Coparent Training: Interventions Based in Operant Conditioning

With respect to family therapy for parents who have dissolved their relationship, there is also empirical literature that supports the utility of heightening parents' ability to parent and coparent together to the betterment of the child. Lamela, Figueiredo, Bastos, and Feinberg (2016) observed in their sample that parents who were in the high-conflict coparenting group exhibited significantly greater levels of divorce-related negative affect and inconsistent parenting behaviors than parents in the cooperative coparenting cluster. Additionally, they discerned that those in the cooperative coparenting group reported higher levels of positive family functioning and lower externalizing and internalizing problems in their children than parents in the high-conflict coparenting group. Consequently, interventions designed to heighten parenting and coparenting skills have been observed to be effective in assisting families and their children. In fact, Stallman and Sanders (2014) conducted a treatment outcome study with divorced families focusing on increasing the parents' ability to coparent. They discovered that those receiving the intervention engaged in fewer coercive parenting practices, had better communication with the coparent, had better psychologically adjusted children, and evidenced less acrimony toward the alternate parent than those not receiving the intervention.

In addition to the ability to coparent, parents in reunification cases are often lacking in parenting knowledge and skills. This includes deficiencies in child development knowledge, attunement, and discipline. Research focusing on parent training or parent effectiveness training demonstrated empirical support for the use of protocols that are based in operant conditioning. Accordingly, behaviorally based parenting interventions have enjoyed a lengthy history of scientific validation and are recognized as first-line therapies for children with disruptive behavior problems (Forehand, Jones, & Parent, 2013). Additionally, parent–child interaction therapy (PCIT) has been effectively used for children who have diverse diagnoses and who exhibit externalizing behavior problems (Ginn, Clionsky, Eyberg, Warner-Metzger, & Abner, 2017). In addition, the dissemination of information regarding children's cognitive, emotional, moral, physical, and social development is important to enhance parenting skills. There is evidence that maladaptive parenting practices and lack of child development knowledge can contribute to the maintenance of the breach in a parent–child relationship. For example, a parent who bit a 2-year-old to discipline her for biting a peer in day care, temporarily lost parenting contact with her daughter. The parent, in this example, generally believed that by biting the child, she would learn not to do the same to others.

Communication Skills Training for Parents and for Parents and Children

Related to adaptive parenting and coparenting in reducing conflict and enhancing parent–child relationships is the development of adaptive communication skills. Afifi, Huber, and Ohs (2006) observed that children's communications with their parents were positively associated with their own ability to cope adaptively with their parents' divorce. Others have detected that conversation orientation was associated with positive child adjustment and child prosocial behaviors during the returning military parent's family reintegration (Wilson, Chernichky, Wilkum, & Owlett, 2014). Furthermore, communication and relationship interventions disseminated through family therapy have been linked to decreases in drug and alcohol use in substance-abusing mothers, contributing to greater family harmony (Slesnick & Zhang, 2016). There is a large body of data that indicate couples' enhanced communication skills contribute to greater relationship congruence. This finding has been noted in a large variety of populations. For example, Backhaus et al. (2016) discovered that relationship skills training, including communication intervention, significantly improved couple functioning in those couples who had one partner with a brain injury. Reunifying parents and children often have difficulties in adaptive communication; in fact, they often use withdrawal from contact in these situations, or alternately they use coercive and negative communicative exchanges that contribute to loss of interpersonal contact. Likewise, disruptions and poor communication are evident in the exchanges of both parents, which also instigate parent–child divisiveness.

Behavioral Activation Therapy

Behavioral activation therapy was developed from principles of operant conditioning for depressed individuals, with its primary premise that environmental context is responsible for mood and behavior change. These individuals experience low levels of positive reinforcement and high levels of negative reinforcement from their environments. With respect to the latter, depressed individuals typically withdraw as a coping strategy. Behavioral activation targets avoidance as an ineffective coping strategy. During the early stages of treatment, the client identifies the association between affect and behavior, in an attempt to determine and engage in adaptive behaviors that are reinforcing thereby diminishing maladaptive symptoms and nonreinforcing behaviors (Hawley et al., 2017). It also assists the client in identifying goals and affords an opportunity for mastery (McCauley et al., 2016). In their treatment outcome study, Hawley et al. (2017), observed behavioral activation to decrease mood symptoms in their participants with mild to moderate levels of depression. Others have also detected a decrease in depressive symptoms in their samples, including in youths. In a recent study, McCauley et al (2016), observed the efficaciousness of behavioral activation for their depressed adolescent sample. Behavioral activation in reunification therapy is used similarly to address the lack of motivation and the coping strategy of avoidance in reunifying children. It also serves to provide the reunifying child with opportunities for mastery through engagement with the reunifying parent. As the reunifying child has incremental successes by engaging in pleasurable activities with their reunifying parent, their avoidance decreases, and their confidence in both their own behavior and their interactions with that parent are likely to increase.

Systematic Desensitization and Exposure-Based Therapy: Interventions Based in Classical Conditioning

The use of therapies that have their roots in classical conditioning have demonstrated efficacy for individuals with anxiety. While flooding techniques have ethical and moral constraints when used in child treatment, those that combine the instruction of counter-conditioning elements such as relaxation techniques to replace a feared response with graded exposure to feared stimuli have been used for a number of disorders in childhood including PTSD (Faust et al., 2014).

For many of these feared stimuli, systematic desensitization is conducted both imaginally initially and subsequently in vivo, with the feared stimulus. This methodology has been used within a wide range of anxiety based disorders, ranging from specific phobia to generalized anxiety disorder (Clementi & Alfano, 2014). Desensitization procedures have been used for children with special abilities as well such as those with ASD (Flood & Luiselli, 2016). For other cases, in vivo desensitization is not possible, such as in the case of a sexual abuse perpetrator as the feared stimulus. With respect to the latter, reducing a child's PTSD symptoms may be particularly important, as the youth may be obliged to confront the perpetrator in court. In these cases, the use of *quasi in vivo* methods such as still photographs as well as video and audio recordings that approximate live exposure are utilized (e.g., Faust, 1996, 2000). The use of these stimuli not only approximates more directly the feared stimulus but also prevents avoidance of the stimuli that may occur with imaginal desensitization. In fact, anxiety sensitivity has predicted children's avoidance of sensations of anxiety, and those who are high in anxiety sensitivity are motivated to avoid any feared stimulus (Lebowitz, Shic, Campbell, Basile, & Silverman, 2015).

Likewise, systematic desensitization can be used in addressing children's anxiety regarding interacting with an estranged parent or a parent they have never met. In fact, Garber (2015) also promoted the use of systematic desensitization procedures for children of high-conflict divorce who are undergoing reunification interventions. After the instruction in coping procedures, including progressive muscle relaxation (PMR), and development of a fear hierarchy, exposure mechanisms are selected contingent upon the child's level of anxiety. First, either imaginal desensitization is conducted or quasi in vivo methods are employed through exposure to photographs, audio, and audiovisual recordings. Subsequently, live telephone contact, visual screen (electronic) contact, voice contact through the therapy door or walls, and eventually direct in-session contact with the non-time-sharing parent are employed. Treatment focuses on assisting the child with altering these maladaptive cognitions which concomitantly reduces anxiety.

Information Processing Theory and Cognitive Restructuring

Information processing theory emerged from research on anxiety and fear responses in adults. While both operant and classical conditioning have been identified as central in the development of the fear response, they are not exclusive anxiety determinants. Researchers have identified a cognitive component to the development and maintenance of fear. In a seminal paper regarding the manifestation of PTSD, Foa, Steketee, and Rothbaum (1989) identified an information processing factor regarding stimuli associated with rape trauma that explains some PTSD symptoms. The manner by which an individual interprets stimuli and its context determines, in part, the fear response. Likewise, other cognitive processes can contribute to negative affects and maladaptive behavior. Children with trauma or anxiety responses may make erroneous attributions and assumptions regarding their safety (Cohen, Mannarino, Berliner, & Deblinger, 2000). Relatedly children are prone to catastrophizing, such as cognitively rehearsing the worst and typically extremely rare possible outcomes, contributing to the development and maintenance of anxiety symptoms (Cohen et al., 2000).

With respect to reunification therapy, often a child's refusal to develop a relationship with the non-time-sharing parent is embedded in fear that emerges through maladaptive self-statements such as "If I spend time with my estranged parent then I will never see my time-sharing parent again"; "If I see my non-time-sharing parent then they may kidnap me"; "If I spend time with this parent, then something bad may happen to my time-sharing parent if I am not around"; or "If I time-share with this absent parent then what if they leave again?"

Motivational Interviewing for Children and Parents

Motivational interviewing is an integrated therapy that contains components of cognitive behavior therapy (CBT) delivered through humanistic applications such that motivation is elicited rather than levied, and empathy is a vehicle in this regard. The goal is to increase the intrinsic motivation via the client's autonomous commitment to change in order to facilitate adaptive problem solving (e.g., Catley et al., 2006). Historically, motivational interviewing was developed by William Miller and subsequently was highlighted in the work of Miller and Rollnick (Miller & Rollnick, 1991, 2002) for those with substance abuse issues.

Ultimately, the focus of motivational interviewing is to assist the individual in identifying and successfully negotiating ambivalence that prevents adaptive change. Furthermore, motivational interviewing has been used for a wide variety of problems where resistance to change prevents healthy growth and development, and some models have included its use with adolescents (e.g., Naar-King & Suarez, 2011). Motivational interviewing assists the client with identifying the discrepancy between current behavior and important goals and values, utilizing or rolling with resistance (not fighting against it), and validating the client's self-efficacy for change. These are addressed through the therapeutic relationship via person-centered facilitating skills, with a focus on change talk and self-affirming commitment. The core motivational techniques and skills disseminated via this process include affirmations, offering feedback or advice, soliciting permission of the client, normalizing struggles with change, use of open-ended questions, reflective listening, use of summaries, utilizing change talk, and addressing the pros and cons of change (Sobell & Sobell, 2013).

In the course of natural development, adolescents demonstrate resistance to adults in an attempt to become independent and to learn about themselves. This "knowing about knowing" or metacognition is also evident in adolescent communications. Motivational interviewing treatment outcome data have indicated motivational interviewing to yield significant positive outcomes for a variety of youth problem behaviors including substance abuse, weight loss, and anxiety (Westra, Constantino, & Antony, 2016; VanBuskirk & Wetherell, 2014).

Children and teenagers who are being reunified with a parent are often stuck in their view of the family problem. This is observed in both resistance and hopelessness of the child. With respect to the latter, children's comments such as "It is no use; they won't change; I have already given them many chances" are indicators of being bound by cognitive inflexibility. The resistance to change, while internal, may also be influenced by external factors such as the time-sharing parent's direct pressure or indirect anti-reunification pressures. By assisting the youth to identify for themselves the incongruity between their present behavior and their core values, change is likely to occur. For example, an adolescent who is extremely benevolent in their volunteer work identify their core values and goals of helping others, and yet is unwilling to help their repenting, remorseful parent. The therapist assists the adolescent in identifying the incongruency and reconciling the behavior with the core value of helping others. Validation of the concordance that is aligned with the adolescent's self-perception of helping others is applied in the relationship with the non-time-sharing parent.

Acceptance and Commitment Therapy

Acceptance and commitment therapy (ACT) has guided, mindful action as its primary value (Harris, 2009). ACT includes acceptance and awareness of, and adherence to, one's valued objectives. While considered a CBT, it departs from traditional CBT, as its focus is on personal growth as opposed to symptom resolution (Simon & Verboon, 2016). One of the core features of ACT is the development of flexibility, which allows a person to seek central ideals and objectives by selecting behavior in accordance with these tenets, while tolerating all experiences including unpleasant ones (Hayes & Strosahl, 2004). This includes the acceptance of negative thoughts as opposed to the refutation of unpleasant cognitions, which is a hallmark of traditional CBT. Although initially developed for work with adults, more recent research has demonstrated ACT and its components to have notable utility for children (Coyne, McHugh, & Martinez, 2011; Simon & Verboon, 2016). Giving reunifying children permission to have unpleasant thoughts about reunification, while assisting them in identifying their own valued objectives in the outcome of reunification can assist in parent–child relationship reparation.

Humanistic (Client-Centered) Domain

Humanism or client-centered therapy offers to the child self-understanding through empathic reflection, and as a result, the child's identity is formulated. From the work of Virginia Axline (2013), theoretically, children do not develop an identity apart from their parents' when the parents' own expectations and desires are levied onto the child. The child incorporates these parental emotionalized attitudes originating from the parent, by subsuming them into their identity as if they are their own (Axline, 2013). Alternately, the child learns who they are by receiving empathic reflections of all realms of human functioning including feelings, cognitions, and behavior.

It is not unusual to observe parents' lack of empathy toward their children in cases where a child does not have a relationship with one or both of their parents. This is most obvious in cases where parents are embroiled in acrimonious dissolution of their partnership; their fight becomes the primary focus, and the children are collateral damage, since the focus is on the couple's anger. Also in dependency cases where parents' custodial rights are in dispute due to child maltreatment and/or substance abuse, parents' inability to place the child's needs above their own and concomitant lack of empathic attunement are prevalent.

Dillman Taylor, Purswell, Lindo, Jayne and Fernando (2011) conducted a treatment outcome study examining the impact of filial therapy on children and families undergoing divorce. The core tenant of this approach includes humanistic principles that capitalize on the current parent–child relationship and employ client-centered techniques taught to the parent, to use with children. These techniques are designed to assist a parent in greater understanding of their child as well as to assist in positive relationship building between parent and child. The results of the treatment outcome study by Dillman Taylor et al. (2011) indicated a reduction in parenting stress and child behavior problems in those families receiving their manualized filial therapy treatment (Dillman et al., 2011).

The transmission of empathy not only assists in identity formation for children and adaptive relationship building for parents and children, but is a core component of establishing a therapeutic alliance of client and therapist irrespective of theoretical orientation. The nonspecifics of positive treatment outcome, including the empathic relationship between the client and the therapist, have a lengthy history in psychotherapy research (Martin, Garske, & Davis, 2000). Given the often painful nature of reunification therapy, therapist empathic responding and attunement are essential in establishing meaningful relationships with children and parents, as well as in creating a safe environment for children. If a child deems that the therapist understands them (empathic attunement), they will trust the therapist to act in their best interests even if these run counter to the child's expressed desires. For example, if a child is anxious about meeting their non-time-sharing parent, their willingness regarding the interaction may increase if they trust the therapist – a trust gleaned through the therapist's propagation of empathy.

Systemic Family Therapy Domain

While reunification therapy includes elements of cognitive behavior and person-centered (humanistic) therapy, it is also a process closely linked to strategic family therapy, which has, as its foundation, communication theory, such that families operate and interact through a series of communicative and metacommunicative exchanges, and the goal in treatment is to alter these transactional exchanges (e.g., Haley, 1960). Strategic family theorists believe that psychological symptoms evolve from both direct and nonovert metacommunication exchanges. For example, an adolescent who informs the therapist that they would like to have a relationship with the estranged mother and readily agrees to the pre-set activity with the mother, but is absent when the mother attempts to retrieve them from school to engage in the activity, is demonstrating communication incongruence. The verbal message is incongruent with the behavioral message. Overt communication indicates not only willingness but also desire to spend time with the mother; however, the covert message, as can be discerned by the adolescent's no-show, is one of rejection or disinclination to forge a relationship with the mother.

Another form of systemic family therapy that is operative in reunification therapy is structural family therapy, which hinges on hierarchical roles and the power assigned to these roles (e.g., Minuchin, 1974). Parents are heads of household and hold the majority of power; however, in reunification cases, this parenting power is often abdicated to the children. The non-time-sharing parent's parenting leverage is absent in many cases, and frequently that parent is relegated to the child position with respect to status and power. This power disparity is reinforced by the time-sharing parent's communications to the child indicating the estranged parent's powerlessness and incompetence. The *non-time-sharing* parent's own fear intercedes to reduce their parenting assertiveness. Furthermore, the time-sharing parent often elevates the child to a parenting role by allowing them to make the decision about spending time with the other parent and may bestow special privileges on the child if they assume their own parenting role in this regard. The goal of strategic and structural family therapies is to alter transactional exchanges and family structures and roles via communication and metacomunicatin.

CHAPTER 4
Pretreatment Decisions and Process

Appropriateness for Reunification Therapy in Military Deployment and Institutionalization Cases

Most individuals pursuing reunification in response to separation via military deployment or institutionalization seek services independently or on the recommendation of another, such as a health care professional. Occasionally these cases, particularly institutionalization cases such as those involving incarceration or psychiatric hospitalization, are attorney referred.

For institutionalization cases, it is important to ascertain the mental status of the parents wishing to be reunified. For military families in particular, the practitioner should refer those reunifying parents who have debilitating PTSD or other potentially interfering mental illness to the appropriate mental health expert before commencing treatment. In fact, children exposed to military parents' PTSD have been noted to experience psychological and behavioral problems themselves (Brockman et al., 2016). Similarly, for those incarcerated or psychiatrically hospitalized, it would be prudent to ensure that any psychological issues are well-managed and controlled, lest the children be placed in an untenable situation. Consultation with these parents' mental health providers will assist the reunification therapist in elucidating the feasibility of reunification therapy.

With respect to incarceration, therapists are often consulted prior to the parent's incarceration as to the manner in which to best prepare the child for the separation. This preparation may include a prison visitation plan. If a prison visitation plan is anticipated in these cases, it is prudent to work with the custodial parent regarding the prison's visitation structure and the logistics of the custodial parent facilitating these visits. Many prisons have family visitation days and structure the visits in a warm and supportive environment (Sam Houston State University, 2015). A prison visitation arrangement can be developed via a live in-person format or through electronic means in order to heighten predictability for the child. There are, of course, some occasions when the incarceration is not anticipated; this sudden separation can have debilitating effects and should be addressed in treatment quickly.

In considering the appropriateness of reunification of incarcerated parents when parent incarceration was due to child maltreatment or domestic violence, it is necessary for both the child and parent to have addressed this problem in individual therapy prior to commencing family treatment. Furthermore, this type of reunification therapy generally requires a court order, as many incarcerated abusive parents are not only prevented from therapeutically reunifying with their children, but their parental legal rights including child access may be permanently terminated.

Appropriateness for Reunification Therapy in Family Law and Guardianship Cases

The appropriateness of a referral for reunification therapy in family law matters is dependent on a number of factors. First, cases of allegations of abuse that have not been investigated are not appropriate for reunification therapy. In family law matters, it is not unusual for parents to accuse the alternate parent of child maltreatment. If these allegations have not been investigated, evaluated, or assessed, then reunification therapy should not be attempted until the accused is cleared of these allegations. There have been occasions when attorneys and/or judges have referred cases for reunification therapy with a hopeful anticipation that the therapist can discern if the parent has engaged in child maltreatment. This may not only have a chilling effect on the therapy process, but also have the potential for creating more adverse reactions in the alleged maltreated child – if in fact, the parent has been abusive. The practitioner should be aware, however, that *child abuse* and *child maltreatment* are terms that may be levied by the time-sharing parent against the non-time-sharing parent in a generic manner, such that one parent whose discipline barometer is relatively low may accuse the other parent of abuse when in fact the parent has administered appropriate discipline. Similarly, there is an assumption that the parents and caretakers are "good to go" when engaging in reunification therapy. It is possible that despite adequate evaluation and assessment, some reunifying children have been abused by the non-time-sharing parent. The therapist does not discount this possibility throughout treatment and is always alert to any indication of child maltreatment.

On occasion, judges and attorneys will refer parents for reunification therapy in anticipation that the therapist will evaluate parental mental health. It is incumbent on the therapist to delineate the boundaries of the therapy and the therapist's role, and as a result, communication with the referral agents is of paramount importance in these cases, since a reunification family therapist cannot serve as a parent's psychological evaluator.

Secondly, with respect to the appropriateness of the referral, and as stated previously, reunification therapy is not mediation or a tool for developing a specific time-sharing plan. Referrals that are proffered with the primary goal of developing a time-sharing and access plan are not appropriate. While reunification therapy is a tool by which eventually parents come to some resolution regarding a time-sharing plan for their child, the end goal for the therapist is not to hammer out their legal parenting document, but rather to assist the parent in establishing or reestablishing a healthy relationship with the child. The distinction between having a parent and child spend time outside of a session as part of the reunification therapy process, on the one hand, and the development of a specific time-sharing plan, on the other, needs to be underscored not only with the parents but with their attorneys. It is often useful to discuss with these individuals that various outings are recommended as treatment homework assignments. Just like academic homework, this form of extra session work is intended to give an opportunity to practice and reinforce skills learned in session, as well as to provide exposure to foreign or new subject matter for both parent and child. Information gleaned as a result of these homework assignments serves to guide treatment and the reunification process, whereas a parenting plan that is eventually ratified by a judge is a binding contract for the duration of childhood.

A third pretreatment decision is the necessity for both caretakers to have some commitment to the process. This level of commitment, not surprisingly, can vary among parents and caretakers who have guardianship. For those primary caretakers who are completely resistant to the process, external motivation can be provided at the outset, with the sharing of therapy costs between the parties, so that the estranged or non-time-sharing caretaker is not the only one to pay the retainer. The retainer serves as a form of response-cost paradigm such that the sooner reunification occurs, the less financial burden is placed on the individuals. In fact, the caretakers may obtain reimbursement of any unused funds should reunification occur prior to the depletion of the retainer. Furthermore, it is not unusual for the one seeking "time-sharing" (the non-time-sharing parent) to be responsible for fees associated with reunification therapy; this often evolves through the non-time-sharing parent's desperation to swiftly reunite with the child. Frequently this is realized through a so-called agreed court order between the parties; alternately the judge may order the non-time-sharing parent to pay 100% of the fees without prejudice for determination at final hearing, at which time, the time-sharing parent may be ordered to pay a portion or all of the fees. Many judges astutely realize, at the outset, that commitment to the process requires "skin in the game" by the time-sharing parent and will order the parties to share costs.

Fourth, major mental illness of either parent must be considered prior to the referral of these cases for intervention. Not only can a parent's active psychotic symptoms expressed in a parenting capacity derail reunification and reunification therapy, these symptoms may also have a deleterious impact on the child apart from the parenting role. Additionally, it is not unusual in high-conflict families for parents to have symptom clusters other than psychosis that need to be addressed prior to, or simultaneously with, reunification therapy. In these cases, symptom control must be obtained prior to and during attempts to reunify the parent with the child.

Ethical and Legal Considerations

While there are laws that govern the mechanisms by which children and families are reunified in dependency actions where a parent or both parents have temporarily lost parental rights (such as in the use of case plans), as of yet there is no specific statute that delineates or regulates *the practice* of reunification family therapy – other than the statutes, administrative laws, and ethics that delineate the practice of psychology and mental health interventions. Ethical principles of the profession are often adopted into law as well, such as the American Psychological Association's ethical principles (APA 2002, 2010) concerning confidentiality, multiple relationships, informed consent, and custody recommendations, which are not only demarcated in the ethical code but have also been integrated into many state practice statutes.

With respect to confidentiality, reunification therapy is subject to the laws that govern the practice of psychotherapy and the practitioner is bound to maintain information gleaned in treatment as confidential. However, cases with family court involvement, which is often true for reunification therapy, include a forensic component. Accordingly, there is typically a necessity of having to report to the court, a guardian ad litem, and attorneys, regarding these cases, and for some, there is a mandate to report information concerning the reunification process; hence confidentiality must be waived in these cases. The waiver of confidentiality should be accomplished via a signed court order and should be included in the practitioner's initial contract for services, also known as a *statement of understanding*. It is extremely important to re-review the limits of confidentiality, as well as other components of the statement of understanding, in-person with each family member at the initial interviews. The statement of understanding serves as a vehicle by which to obtain informed consent; however, in many cases, the court order dictates the process, and parents are left with little choice but to participate. The statement of understanding delineates the process, scope, and role of the reunification therapist, which heightens the probability of parents' or caretakers' commitment to the process, as well as prevents misperceptions and misunderstandings while engaged in therapy. Furthermore, if the statement of understanding is sent to the attorneys prior to the writing of the agreed order, the attorneys will know in advance the parameters of reunification therapy and be able to assess the appropriateness of reunification therapy for their clients and their case, ultimately counseling their clients accordingly.

In cases where litigation is typically not contemplated, such as in working with parents returning from long absences due to the military or those hospitalized for lengthy periods of time, confidentiality of disclosures by the child to a third party may not be at issue, and privacy is maintained. However, confidentiality issues relevant to within–reunification therapy sessions may remain. For example, the child or adolescent may be worried about disclosing information individually to the reunification therapist lest it be divulged to one or both parents. Furthermore, the nature of reunification therapy is a family process, and confidentiality may not be in the best interests of repairing the family. This should be discussed with the children or adolescents during individual sessions, and a request should made to the youth to inform the therapist regarding any information they do not wish for the therapist to disclose during the family sessions, which can be held in confidence, subject to state laws (e.g., regarding release of information due to child maltreatment, court proceedings, or self-harm or harm to others). Interestingly, clinical observation has shown that, while initially youths may wish for some communications to be held in confidence, more often than not, the child or teen discloses the information of their own accord, or ultimately, they give the therapist permission to disclose this information during family sessions. It is likely, through the reunification therapy process, that the youth has gained insight into the value of disclosing this information.

Informed Consent: Statement of Understanding

For non-court-involved cases, the statement of understanding includes all components of a therapy contract's *consent to treatment*. Confidentiality and the management of information gleaned in sessions via HIPAA (1996) and other governing bodies apply for these cases. All family members involved in the process, including both parents, sign the consent for treatment form as well as the HIPAA disclosure forms, and within these forms, it is delineated who has access to this information and under what circumstances. It is common practice for case initiation to target one identified patient, typically the child, with family therapy being the modality of treatment; consequently, a child-friendly version of the statement of understanding should be available for the child to sign. In these cases, where one person is demarcated as the identified patient, consent to release information among family members should be obtained, as an additional method of communicating the fact that information gleaned from family members may be disclosed to other family members to effectuate the reunification process. In the rare event that these initially non-litigated cases become contested and the reunification therapist is subpoenaed to testify or release information in other formats, the therapist will require a court order allowing for the release of the information – a subpoena to facilitate disclosures will not suffice. Similarly, in many states, signed consent forms even by both parents will not suffice when disclosure of therapy information which involves minors is to be made in court or other legal proceedings. In fact, a judge is mandated to appoint an attorney ad litem or guardian ad litem to evaluate whether or not the release of protected information is in the child's best interest. Once the judge receives the guardian ad litem's case-specific recommendation regarding release of information, the judge renders a ruling on the matter (e.g., Attorney ad Litem for D.K. v. Parents of D.K., 2001). Reunification cases that have current court involvement are forensic in nature and require both the time-sharing parent as well as the non-time-sharing parent to sign a statement of understanding contract. In these forensic cases, confidentiality is waived as it is often incumbent on the professional to report to attorneys, a guardian ad litem, and the court. In fact the reunification family therapist is often operating via a court order for these family law cases.

Given the unique nature of family reunification therapy, it is important to have all family members sign the statement of understanding even if there is one identified client. The statement of understanding is a comprehensive mechanism by which to obtain informed consent from all family members.

The Contract, Court Order, or Agreed Order

There are different trajectories by which the reunification process is initiated. For reunification cases that do not involve the courts, such as military or medically ill parents, a therapeutic contract that includes the elements of consent to treatment and family therapy will suffice. For those cases where active litigation or legal action is imminently *contemplated* (e.g., with married but physically separated parents), it is necessary to have both a contract and a court order. The *agreed court order* is an order agreed on by the parties and drafted by their attorneys, submitted for ratification by the judge. A nonagreed court order may initially originate from one party's motion of the court; after the judge listens to arguments regarding an appointment of a reunification therapist, the judge rules on the motion, and thus the reunification therapist may be appointed by the judge without agreement of the parties.

Reunification therapists are often contacted by the attorneys prior to court appointment, requesting their preferences for the components to be included in a court order, particularly the agreed order, but even those attorneys petitioning the court for an order may contact the therapist. Two essential elements that should be included in the order include the waiver of confidentiality and a specification of the division of the therapist fees. With respect to the former, the lifting of confidentiality pertains to speaking to the necessary adjunctive professionals such as the guardian ad litem and individual therapist. It also enables the therapist to communicate with the attorneys, which is often necessary for status conferences, access and homework, time-sharing planning, and parent noncompliance. Furthermore, by waiving confidentiality, this allows the therapist to testify in court should the need arise. The parents' accountability to the process and to each family member is heightened with the waiver of confidentiality, particularly when they understand that the therapist may be called upon to discuss, in court, treatment adherence.

Do No Harm

It is important to consider children's psychological composition and needs when conducting reunification therapy. In fact, Dallam and Silberg (2016) maintain that the process has the propensity to be unethical if abuse allegations are present. Reunification is predictably an uncomfortable process, because if it were not, then therapeutic services would not be required. As with any children's anxiety and worry, these symptoms must be addressed first to decrease anxiety and increase adaptive coping. Furthermore, the ethics of allowing a parent to be eliminated from a child's life must also be considered, especially in cases of alienation or estrangement, in cases where the non-time-sharing parent may have many benefits to supply the child, and in cases where the child may have had a previous attachment to the non-time-sharing parent. Furthermore, in an attempt to balance the discomfort of the process with reunification, the focus may shift toward an emphasis on the child's preferences regarding reunification. As stated previously, children often do not have the cognitive ability, maturity, and life history to make a truly informed decision about repairing their relationship with a parent. Furthermore, these weighty decisions have the propensity to place significant pressure on a child. This child decision-making ability also communicates to the child that they hold their own parenting power, which can translate into other areas of their lives. Finally, it is inevitable that legislators and judges will continue to compel reunification of a parent and child, and without well-trained and knowledgeable therapists to assist these families, children may be at significant risk for an adverse response.

Avoiding Multiple Relationships

Engaging in multiple relationships in any service offered by a mental health professional is prohibited both by American Psychological Association ethics (American Psychological Association, 2002; Knapp & VandeCreek, 2006; Bersoff, 2003) and by the mental health practice laws of most states. Adherence to these becomes exceedingly important in legal matters where the neutrality of the court-ordered professional is paramount in the collection and evaluation of evidence. The trier of fact must have the ability to rely on professional opinion and scientific data to adjudicate family court petitions and motions in the best interests of the child.

Role shifts from individual or marital therapist to reunification therapist, even with the informed consent of all family members, may give rise to accusations of bias when one parent who is not happy with either the process or outcome of reunification therapy raises potential prejudice issues in court proceedings, motions, hearings, or trials. While such bias may not be present, once the allegation has been asserted, doubt regarding a lack of therapist neutrality may linger obtrusively.

Furthermore, the goals of reunification therapy may contradict the goals of individual therapy, thereby having the potential to cause the individual client confusion, at the very least, and emotional pain or distress, including the enhancement of distrust, as a harmful outcome. Irrespective of court involvement, by the very nature of the therapeutic relationship of individual therapists, these exchanges are supportive and project advocacy of the individual client. Individual therapy is much more client-centered and client-led than family therapy. With respect to family therapy, not only does the therapist shift unilateral alliance away from the individual client, but also the therapist has to forge and balance alliances with all other family members. An example of a worst-case scenario would include a child's individual therapist who has been supporting the child's feelings about not wishing to engage in a relationship with the mother, is subsequently retained to conduct reunification therapy for the family. The individual therapist is then placed in the untenable position of violating their former client's wishes, due to the role shift, which now explicitly demands the reunification of child with parent.

Avoiding Making Custodial and Time-Sharing Recommendations

As discussed previously, reunification therapy does not have as one of its goals to memorialize the parents' time-sharing plan nor determine which parent should have decision-making authority with respect to the children. The American Psychological Association's Guidelines for Child Custody Evaluations in Family Law Proceedings have been adopted into law in a number of states (American Psychological Association, 2010). These guidelines not only emphasize informed consent, avoidance of multiple relationships, and minimization of the possibility of conflicting relationships, but also underscore using comprehensive culturally fair evaluation methods for the family and each of its members, with multiple methods of data gathering when making custodial and child access recommendations. Given that the goals and methods of family reunification therapy depart widely from those associated with family law evaluations, family reunification therapists are not in a position to make time-sharing recommendations and other custodial determinations as part of the reunification therapy, nor can they switch roles to effectuate these recommendations. Reunification family therapists should make themselves familiar with these Guidelines for Child Custody Evaluations in Family Law Proceedings (APA, 2010) as well as its recommended Specialty Guidelines for Forensic Psychology (APA, 2013) when engaging in reunification therapy. In addition, the reunification therapist should not only familiarize themselves with these guidelines as well as the primary American Psychological Association ethical principles (American Psychological Association, 2010; Carter & Sanders, 2001; Robinson, Tharinger, Urbina, & Witt, 1994), practice laws, and statutory administrative rules of their state, but should also familiarize themselves with their state's family law and administrative rules regarding the practice of family law. While at times, family law and mental health practice laws conflict, it is important for the practitioner to inform parties when such conflicts exist and to reconcile these conflicts as expeditiously as possible.

Practicing Within the Scope

While reunification therapy involves specific intervention tools, all are based on empirical research, including CBT and its theoretical underpinnings, client-centered approaches, and systemic family therapies, applied in a multifactorial context. In addition to the specific interventions, a broad knowledge base is necessary, including adult and child psychopathology, family composition functioning, multiculturalism, child development, forensics, and conflict resolution, at a minimum. While psychotherapists working within the forensic arena become well-versed in applicable family law, they are not legal experts, and as tempting as it may be to offer legal advice, the need to resist making these recommendations is of paramount importance. For example, a child's individual psychotherapist in family court began testifying about the parent–child relationship and completed her testimony by recommending a time-sharing plan as well as the distribution of assets, including which parent should keep the marital home. The judge was incensed by her testimony and reprimanded the therapist during the court proceeding.

Communicating With Attorneys and Allied Professionals Prior to Treatment

It is not unusual for attorneys to contact the reunification therapist prior to treatment initiation. Typically, lawyers desire to know the reunification therapist's availability, procedures, and fee structure. As stated previously, some may request the reunification therapist's requirements or preferences for court order content and structure. Usually these attorneys will give some background of the case so that the reunification therapist can better elucidate both the parameters of the court order as well as other areas of practice, such as if there are active restraining orders in place between the parents, how many children are in the family so the retainer may be calculated, and any other issue that is relevant to the treatment and therapy process or its impediment. It is in this initial telephone contact that it is helpful to suggest e-mailing a copy of the statement of understanding to the attorney to familiarize them with the process.

Occasionally an attorney will not consult with the reunification professional before drafting and submitting an agreed order for the judge's signature. Similarly, in cases where the judge directly orders the parties to undergo reunification therapy, the reunification therapist will not be consulted regarding the language delineated in the order. It is extremely prudent of the reunification professional to review the order prior to commencing reunification therapy in order to determine the scope and limits of the therapist's role in the process. If there are items in the order that conflict with the practice ethics and laws and/or could interfere with therapeutic process, the therapist will need to address these at the outset with the attorneys, parties, and on occasion, the judge. Often reunification is the last resort to resolve a family case, and these families have had a long legal history with multiple professionals involved with little resolution; hence court orders for reunification therapy may contain everything including the kitchen sink such that officers of the court may wish for the therapist to serve as a pseudo guardian ad litem, monitor of the parents (e.g., reunification therapist may call in drug testing), and evaluator. The therapist will need to instruct the attorneys, parents, and on occasion the court regarding the limits of their role in the case. If the therapist has concerns of parent substance abuse, then the therapist will inform the guardian ad litem (if there is one on the case) and/or state protective services about these concerns. Similarly, if issues of child maltreatment including physical abuse, sexual abuse, psychological abuse, neglect, and/or domestic violence emerge, state protective services as well as the guardian ad litem will be notified, but it is not the role of the therapist to assess these potential deleterious events directly, unless suspicions of maltreatment imminently emerge during treatment.

Once the reunification therapist agrees that they can perform reunification therapy as set forth in the court order, it is crucial that the therapist follows the parameters identified in the court order as written. For example, if the order instructs that the parents must include reports to the court prior to the non-time-sharing parent spending time with the children outside of session, the therapist must comply with this mandate.

Once a signed court order has been obtained, the signed statement of understanding and retainer have been received, during the initial phase of treatment, it is important to consult with other nonattorney professionals, who by the nature of their role in the case have the propensity to either negatively or positively impact reunification therapy. Case-active guardians ad litem typically have a wealth of case information to share and, in fact, may have been the impetus to obtaining reunification therapy for the case. Additionally, developing a positive working relationship with the guardian ad litem early on in treatment may also expedite the reunification process. Finally, it is important for the reunification process, for the family therapist to forge a collegial working relationship with children's and parents' individual psychotherapists.

When Reunification Therapy Is Inappropriate

Implementation of reunification therapy is inappropriate when there are allegations of child maltreatment including child sexual abuse, physical abuse, and witnessing of domestic violence in the home that have not been investigated. In addition, in cases where allegations of child maltreatment have been confirmed, and the child and parent have not received treatment for the abuse, reunification therapy should not be initiated. Similarly, if there are active orders of protection (e.g., restraining orders) between non-time-sharing parent and the child, reunification therapy should not be attempted, unless the dyad is cleared to participate by both having had therapeutically addressed the issues which contributed to the order of protection, and a judge has lifted the order for the purposes of reunification therapy. As stated previously, reunification therapy is not for the purposes of assessment to determine the psychological and parenting health of a parent, nor is it a method by which to develop a parenting plan and time-sharing or custodial document.

Necessary Therapist Characteristics

With any psychological service, the ability to engage in meaningful therapeutic working relationships with clients is the vehicle for effective service delivery. Family therapy introduces an additional process-related variable of the inclusion of multiple individuals in treatment and balancing the needs and preferences of each family member to assist in effectuating change; in fact, family members' preferences may be diametrically opposed to one another in these reunification family therapy cases. This may be particularly relevant in those reunification cases where there is high interparental conflict (Gritzer & Okun, 1983; Olson, 2000; Minuchin, 1985).

Particularly for high-conflict cases where there is resistance from the time-sharing parent to assist in facilitating a relationship between children and the non-time-sharing parent, thereby interfering with the process, it is exceedingly important for therapists to understand the feelings of the estranging parent even if these do not align with their own beliefs or feelings about the reunification process. The validation of time-sharing parents' feelings via empathic reflection is important not only in facilitating a therapeutic relationship with this parent, but also this validating empathy may illuminate possible methods by which to intervene as treatment focus becomes person-centered as opposed to directive and therapist driven. Therapist directiveness may increase the time-sharing parent's defensiveness and resistance, adversely altering the reunification course; whereas empathic client-centered validation is a vehicle to reduce defensiveness and heighten client–therapist alignment and collaboration.

It is not unusual for parents to initially approach reunification therapy with consternation, in anticipation of being judged by the therapist. This orientation often emanates from lengthy histories of being judged by the time-sharing parent (irrespective of whether or not in litigation) and by adult children in cases of adult-child–parent reunification, court personnel, and other institutional employees. Also with respect to a nonjudgmental orientation, Garber (2015), citing Dejong and Davies (2013), stressed the importance of maintaining neutrality as a family reunification therapist and avoiding taking sides, with the goal of repairing parent–child relationships so that the child can develop healthy relationships with both parents.

Therapist's Thick Skin

Typically, in reunification cases, the parent who holds the primary parenting position and the majority if not all of the time-sharing with the child has some hesitancy, at the very least, about the reunification of the non-time-sharing parent with the child, irrespective of the reason for the breach in the parent–child relationship. In these circumstances, the "momma or papa bear" orientation toward the child emerges regarding the reunifying therapist, and disparaging remarks and degradation of the therapist's skill may be cast. This hostile stance is often intensified in family and dependency court cases where a parent may feel empowered to be antagonistic merely by being represented by counsel, and/or parental hostility toward a reunification therapist may be fueled, on occasion, directly by the attorney. Furthermore, given the adversarial nature of these cases, some attorneys who do not want reunification to occur, typically because their client does not desire reunification of child with the other parent, will attack the reunification therapist to strengthen their case. With respect to attorney aggressiveness, it is important for the reunification therapist to understand that attorney demeanor is not personal, against the therapist, but rather a matter of "business," as attorneys attempt to win their case, justify billing, and market their reputation for future cases. This winning orientation is merely in the nature of the profession; however, such an orientation while neither good nor bad is often diametrically opposed to the orientation of the training of psychologists. Furthermore, the legal profession focuses on facts and events, often reducing situations to discrete units, whereas the psychologist, while also concerned with facts and events, is additionally focused on internal events and process, with the goal of reconstruction as opposed to reduction. Hence an attorney in their approach to a case is as a reductionist, whereas a mental health practitioner's approach is holistic. Attorneys and judges often require discrete finite answers that often cannot be provided in the field of psychology. This disconnect of the professions requires the therapist to have the requisite communication skills and finesse to bridge the chasm.

Activating the Expectancy Set

During initial contact with all family members, two events must co-occur: explanation of the process of reunification therapy and highlighting the goals of reunification therapy to both the caregivers and the children. Not only is it the clinician's ethical responsibility to fully disclose the process of treatment to participating family members, but it also primes their expectancy set, enabling therapy to proceed much more smoothly than in cases where the participants are not prepared. Even in cases where the therapy is court ordered, it is important to engage in as much of a collaborative relationship as possible with all family members; the need to develop exceptional working relationships is of paramount importance for the most unreceptive family members to reunification. In family law cases, the most unwilling family members to engage in the process are generally the time-sharing parents who, irrespective of their reasons, are likely the ones who have the most to lose. The losses include turning the child over to someone who they perceive as harmful to the child, the loss of time and contact with the child, and the potential loss of revenue through child support, since child support is calculated by the amount of time each parent spends with the child. Research supports better therapeutic outcomes when therapist and client form a collaborative working relationship (Lambert & Barley, 2001; Horvath & Symonds, 1991), and while this may be counterintuitive to those under the looming specter of an order of the court, there are techniques which can enhance the collaborative relationship between residential caretaker and the therapist. These will be discussed in chapters devoted to the different individual family members, below (see Chapter 5: Working With the Child; Chapter 6: Working With the Non-Time-Sharing Parent; and Chapter 7: Working With the Time-Sharing Parent). Additionally, at the initial session with each family member individually, the therapist not only explains the process and begins to establish effective therapeutic relationships with each family member, but the clinician is also attentive to each individual's communication style, coping ability, interpersonal style, personal agendas, culture and subculture, and resistance to the process, as well as the parents' parenting skills and effectiveness.

In addition to disseminating information regarding the process and goals of reunification therapy as well as verbally explaining the statement of understanding, initial session time focuses on establishing effective working relationships with all targeted family members. The approach used when establishing meaningful working relationships with each family member differs to some degree contingent upon the role of each member within the family and is explained within each chapter devoted to a different family member.

CHAPTER 5
Working With the Child

Kids do things at times not on purpose but they have a purpose.

Colby Schepps, Doctoral Student

At the commencement of treatment it is important to cover the limits of confidentiality with the child or adolescent, including those limits that are statutorily mandated (e.g., child maltreatment). In most marital dissolution cases, paternity actions, or dependency motions, children have knowledge that there are multiple people involved in their family's issues, and many are not surprised to learn that the family reunification therapist cannot necessarily maintain confidentiality. As stated previously, in cases where litigation is generally not anticipated, such as with absent parents due to military deployment, parents working abroad, or parents' lengthy hospitalizations, confidentiality of disclosures by the child to a third party may not be at issue, and privacy is maintained. However, absent public arenas for the dissemination of private information, confidentiality concerns of youths may remain. These concerns include those relevant to within treatment, such that the child and adolescent may be worried about disclosing information to the therapist lest it be divulged to one or both parents. It is often useful for the therapist to indicate that they will attempt to protect the child's privacy as much as possible, but that at times, it may be important to have this information disclosed in session. The therapist may include the youths in how and when this information is disclosed in family sessions, thereby empowering them in situations where they may feel that they have little power or in situations where they have too much inappropriate power. It is important to take notice when the time-sharing parent and/or the child complain to the therapist that the "previous therapist" disclosed private information to the non-time-sharing parent, even when this information was the primary complaint leading to the breach in the relationship. For example, a time-sharing parent was concerned when the 15-year-old daughter, a competitive swimmer, complained to the therapist that the non-time-sharing parent, the mother, was remiss in not taking her to swim practice. This issue of attending swim practice was central to the child's refusal to spend time with mother. However, when the therapist attempted to address the issue with mother and child together, the father removed the daughter from therapy, stating that the therapist had breached the child's trust by disclosing the swim practice issue to the parent. A double bind was created such that should the crux of the problem be addressed in treatment, the therapist would have allegedly contravened the trust of the child who no longer wished to remain in therapy. Ironically, in these cases, everyone is privy to the problem that contributed to the disruption in the parent–child relationship because that was the impetus for seeking therapy at the outset.

Explanation of the Reunification Process to the Child or Adolescent

The Use of Metaphors

Metaphors have been proffered as an important foundation of communication theory within family systems theoretical orientations as well as within child psychotherapy domains. With respect to the former, the early research conducted by communication theorists including Gregory Bateson, Jay Haley, and the Palo Alto group identified communication patterns within families who have children with schizophrenia and that such communication patterns have unique characteristics that are delivered on a number of levels of consciousness (Bateson, Jackson, Haley, & Weakland, 1956). These patterns indicated that both parents and adult patients with schizophrenia engaged in specific communication exchanges that demarcated problems within their interpersonal relationships (Bateson et al., 1956). Jay Haley and Milton Erickson who developed, in part, the foundations for strategic family therapy, based their work on different levels of communication, including metacommunication. Metacommunication is a form of communication that is indirect and yet can appeal to different levels of consciousness (Haley, 1960). The use of metaphors can transcend direct verbalizations, allowing the individual to communicate in such a manner that more than one message can be transmitted via different levels and forms of communication (Haley, 1960).

Additionally, the use of metaphors has proliferated in the child psychotherapy treatment literature (e.g., Mills & Crowley, 2014), and there is empirical support for metaphor use with children in psychotherapy (Heffner, Greco, & Eifert, 2003). Metaphors provide children with a unique anchor by which to ascribe meaning to incoming messages. For example, a metaphor can link previously learned information with either new information or similar information originating in a new context. Ultimately the metaphor can assist in retrieval of previously stored information (De Grauwe, Swain, Holcomb, Ditman, & Kuperberg, 2010).

In the context of a parent–child relationship breach and the attempts to reestablish a relationship between the child and one parent, one approach to explaining the purpose of reunification therapy is via a pizza metaphor. Children hailing from wide age ranges can identify with pizza, and many families have made or attempted to create their own pizzas. The pizza is an explanation for children, through metaphor, for a renewed parent–child relationship. When utilizing this metaphor, the therapist asks the child if they have ever made a homemade pizza or have observed someone make a homemade pizza. Typically, these pizzas are irregular in shape, unlike their commercially made counterparts, which appear to be more nearly perfectly round. The therapist states that while most people would like their pizza to turn out perfectly round, it generally is not the case for homemade pizzas, and yet the homemade variety is often tastier than the commercially produced pie. This is true of everyone's wish for a parent, such that "We all wish for the perfect parent like the perfectly round pizza." However, typically children's individual parents, who are homemade, are not perfect; they are like misshapen pizzas: Some are more oblong, curvy, or merely misshapen than the manufactured professional variety, without negatively impacting the taste of the pizza. The therapist explains to the child that while the goal of reunification therapy may be to develop the parent into a more round, perfect parent, this may be extremely difficult as there really is no such thing as perfection. This concept may divert the conversation to some degree to a discussion about the subjectivity of perfectionism. At this juncture, the therapist will need to explain that the meaning of perfectionism for one person may not be the definition of perfectionism for another person. The use of examples regarding child and parents or child and teacher discrepancies in the meaning of perfectionism may be helpful in this regard. The therapist can state,

> Haven't you ever cleaned your room to your idea of perfection; however, your parent's idea of perfection was different? Perhaps you neatly stacked your books as opposed to lining them up on the shelves because you find that the stacking method is more pleasing to your eye than the shelf-lining method.

With respect to the pizza metaphor, the therapist can explain that the reunifying parent may never be able to obtain the perfectly round state of a pizza; but perhaps the child will have a newly defined relationship with that reunifying parent, and although not perfectly round, that parent, like a homemade pizza, may have some unusual characteristics. Some of those the child will enjoy, or some they may not enjoy, like those pizzas with edgy air pockets or areas that are completely missing cheese and toping. The therapist may also explain that they can establish a relationship with that parent who represents only a slice of pizza. In other words, the child may take a relationship that is merely a slice or a portion and focus on that segment, as opposed to the complete relationship; they may choose the slice (or that part of the relationship) that has the most desirable construction, not unlike the most desirable toppings, such as the playful, supportive parent component. Or they may recreate a pizza with that parent with some new and creative design and toppings, as an opportunity for growth and exploration in the relationship. Adolescents appear to be particularly receptive to the slice of pizza metaphor and to recreating a different type of pizza, as they redefine their relationship with the reunifying parent and emerge into young adulthood.

In addition to clarifying the reunification process, children are often confused as to their parents' behavior in these fractured families. Young children may be at a particular loss to explain their parent's absence, and both younger as well as older children may not understand the motivations behind their parents' behavior. Data indicate that children may not be able to attribute accurate explanations of adults' behavior and their motivations driving it, until they are in the concrete operational or formal operation stage of development (Harter, 1978, 1988). In fact, the literature indicates that children are not as adroit in explaining motivations of others as older individuals are (Cheung, Siu, & Chen, 2015; Filippova & Astington, 2010).

Furthermore, children are egocentric at different developmental stages from early childhood through adolescence (Piaget, 2000). This developmental phenomenon explains why many children blame themselves for their parents' divorce or disappearance from their lives. Children often believe they could have directly prevented the divorce or the relocation of the parent, and it is not unusual for the child to say that they should have tried harder to prevent the marital dissolution or to have prevented a parent from leaving despite the circumstances. It is also typical to hear the children discuss more indirect methods by which they should have kept their parents together or present in their lives. These communications include references to their own behavior as being operative in maintaining the family.

Basically, the underlining theme to these communications includes statements regarding the child's needing to have been good enough or special enough or to not have been a problem for the parents or departing parent, or otherwise the family would have remained intact. These feelings and perceptions regarding self-blame are further reinforced when the parents have open disagreements about parenting, including discipline of the children. Somewhat subtler than discipline, couples' primary arguments regarding children often include finances (Beckerman & Shepherd, 2002), and it is not unusual for parents to argue over money spent on the children. Even though finances are an adult issue, it is easy for children to translate the blame to themselves, since in many cases parents argue over child items and responsibilities that are expensive. Furthermore, children have learned from their parents that their requests from the parents are too expensive, thereby reinforcing the belief that they have contributed to the interparental conflict, which leads to the dissolution.

One method to explain to children the seemingly inexplicable behavior of adults and parents, including their absence from their lives, is via a puzzle metaphor. Most children hailing from an extensive variety of cultures throughout the world have been exposed to puzzles albeit differing in content and form. The therapist asks the child, "Have you ever had a puzzle that you have nearly finished but you couldn't because you were missing a puzzle piece?" The therapist continues, "The picture of the puzzle cannot be completed without the final piece or two." Discussion ensues with the child about puzzles being problems for a child to figure out by putting together all the pieces until the complete picture emerges, and the problem is solved. The therapist discusses the fact that grown-ups have big puzzles, and problems they need to solve, and that they are missing a piece or two of their puzzle before they can solve the problem. These adult puzzles may not be observable or tangible, explaining to younger children that they may not be able to see these puzzles with their eyes or touch them with their hands, because adult puzzles are somewhat different from children's puzzles. The therapist may say, "The reason your mother or your father has not seen you is because they are attempting to find their missing puzzle piece of their grown-up puzzle." The therapist may also add that the adults are working on finding their puzzle piece, and that is why they have not been able to see them and their siblings. The grown-ups need to find the missing pieces and figure out the puzzle so that the family can mend.

An example of the use of this metaphor emerged when a psychologist was treating a 4-year-old girl when she, her 8-year-old brother, and 6-year-old sister had been held hostage by their military officer father, who threatened to kill the children while on the phone to their mother. Local law enforcement intervened, and everyone, while physically intact, experienced psychological repercussions. The 4-year-old was referred for treatment for trauma symptoms, including separation anxiety from the mother. The father was diagnosed with a major mental illness for which he had never received treatment, an order of protection was secured, and an extensive individualized treatment plan, as well as a family plan, were structured. In effect, the father had to undergo intensive psychological and psychiatric treatment prior to having contact with the children. As he met specific treatment and behavioral goals, a hierarchical plan with fading in of contact between the father and the children was initiated. Initial contact included supervised phone contact and family reunification therapy with a therapist present. Despite the trauma the father had inflicted on his children, they had previously bonded to him and experienced the loss that was a by-product of the separation. The 4-year-old asked the therapist the reason she could not see her father, and in response, the therapist relayed the adult puzzle metaphor, which was repeated at various points in the process, when the father would make parenting errors, such as promising the children specific Christmas presents to be delivered on a specific date, and failing to follow through. Eventually, the father abandoned the individualized and family therapy treatment plan, which resulted in the reunification process remaining in the preliminary stages, consisting of only supervised telephone contact. At this point, 2 years had passed, and the now 6-year-old little girl was questioning the father's lack of contact, adding her own perception of the problem and stating, "I wish he would find those missing puzzle pieces already." It was evident that the puzzle metaphor had been meaningful to her and elicited an emotional understanding of her father having problems, without parental denigration.

Establishing Effective Working Relationships: The Buy In, The Child

In addition to explaining confidentiality and the need for and goals of reunification therapy, initial sessions should also include individual therapy time with the child to establish an effective working relationship, including the development of rapport, as well as to lay the groundwork for the reunification family therapy sessions. This groundwork includes acquiring from the child positive memories, associations, and events that they have regarding their non-time-sharing parent. These previous positive experiences are used as a launching point to reintegrate the non-time-sharing parent into the child's life through a reestablishment or realignment of the child's cognitive schemas that have been derailed due to the elapse of time and/or the undue influence of outside sources. These positive experiences establish points for behavioral activation that allow the child to experience incremental successes through engaging in enjoyable activities with their reunifying parent. The pleasurable events serve to reinforce behavior allowing for heightened probability of increased positive behavioral exchanges between child and parent.

Capitalizing on Children's Natural Curiosity

Over a half of century ago, researchers postulated that curiosity is innately determined. Alvarez and Booth (2016) in an article showed that Jean Piaget had delineated a connection between curiosity and learning. More recently, developmental psychologists conducting empirical studies, such as Alvarez and Booth (2016), have observed a link between even very young children's desire for causal explanation and information-seeking behaviors. Children have been observed to be driven directly to pursue causal information and use explicit communication strategies to obtain this causal information (Frazier, Gelman, & Wellman, 2009). Interestingly some developmental psychologists, in an attempt to generate an operational definition of curiosity, have concluded from their research, that curiosity is a "cognitive conflict or a gap in knowledge" that contributes to the child's investigative behavior (Jirout & Klahr, 2012, p. 157). The implications of this knowledge in working with children who are being reunified with an absent parent is readily apparent. Clearly, in many reunification cases, the absence of a parent irrespective of the reason for the absence generates gaps in knowledge for the child even if the time-sharing parent and others attempt to fill the gaps with information, either to honestly ameliorate distress for the child, in the case of a non-time-sharing parent who is incarcerated or who elopes from parenthood, or in the case where a time-sharing parent is intentionally providing erroneous information to push an agenda. With respect to the latter, cognitive conflict can occur. In either case, if the child does not have sufficient knowledge to close the gap or ameliorate conflict, then the child is driven to seek out additional information.

Some examples of parents attempting to fill the gap for their child to protect their feelings and perhaps to preserve the relationship between non-time-sharing parent and the child include statements such as "your father is away working" or "your mother is away visiting her mother (who lives out of state)." Children, given their drive to satisfy their curiosity, begin to seek out information that may diverge with a conflicting, unusual, or vague premise. As a result, as time passes, these gap fillers may not hold. One little girl in session tearfully lamented, "Where is my mother? She has been working for 100,000 nights." Furthermore, children may overhear information from adults that conflicts with their gap filler and hence contributes to the child's even greater drive to seek out additional information.

"Are You My Mother?"; "Are You My Father?"

On occasion, children may not realize that the parent exists with whom reunification is being sought; furthermore, it is not uncommon for the time-sharing parent to have not prepared the child for this fact prior to commencing treatment. The therapist will need to ascertain from the time-sharing parent what information has been relayed to the child (and excluded in discussion with the child) in preparation for reunification therapy. Generally, parents may have told the child that they are meeting a friend or a special friend of the time-sharing parent's. It is often most beneficial for the therapist to work with the parents or other caretakers on preparing the child together, regarding the relationship status of the reunifying parent.

If the interparental conflict between the caretaker and reunifying parent is too great to facilitate a joint meeting with both parents at the commencement of treatment, then the therapist should first meet individually with the time-sharing parent to address the disclosure of the non-time-sharing parent's true relationship with the child. The therapist can subsequently have a joint session with the child and the time-sharing parent to explain the true relationship of the reunifying parent to the child. The therapist can assist the parent(s) in facilitating this discussion. If the time-sharing parent is reluctant to address this issue with the child, it is critical to explain to the resistant parent that children are often aware of the "secret," as they will undoubtedly have overheard pertinent discussions and are either too anxious or protective of the time-sharing parent to broach the topic with them. Time-sharing parents should be informed that maintenance of this secret can generate anxiety for the child as they attempt to elucidate the meaning of the information they have overheard and/or as they attempt to harbor the secret in order to protect the caretaker. Furthermore, in some cases disclosing the parent status to the child is a legal issue; some court orders dictate that the child be told the nature of the relationship in therapy. Alternately in cases with active litigation and if the time-sharing parent refuses to discuss the non-time-sharing parent's role in the child's life, consultation with both parties' attorneys and the guardian ad litem is necessary to effectuate the disclosure.

The child's developmental level should dictate the language and constructs used in information dissemination. Regarding the true relationship of the non-time-sharing parent to the child during discussion with the child about the existence of the non-time-sharing parent, current and future plans with this parent are discussed, as well as their characteristics, attributes, and proclivities (e.g., career and hobbies). The reasons for the separation between parent and child should be delicately addressed, lest either parent perpetuate hostility regarding the relationship division that they attempt to externalize in discussion with the child. Likewise, if the reason for the breach is imbued with adult themes such as an affair, the focus of the discussion should instead be on the ultimate separating event, such as "Mommy and Daddy love the part of each other that loves you, but they could not get along together."

Assessing and Addressing Resistance: The Child

While there may be a primary origin to child resistance such as anxiety, resistance may have secondary roots. It is important to assess the origins of resistance as a component of anxiety, oppositionality, or the effects of interference by the time-sharing parent or other interpersonal factors such as nonalienating loyalty. Clearly when the resistance is a function of anxiety, once the anxiety is addressed and abates, the child will be able to engage with the non-time-sharing parent.

Resistance Due to Anxiety and Fear: "Getting Back Up on the Horse"

Anxiety begets avoidance, which is reinforcing, because avoidance decreases the adverse feeling state thereby increasing the propensity to engage in further avoidance of the target stimulus (Borkovec, Alcaine, & Behar, 2004; Paulus & Stein, 2006; Maner et al., 2007). While this anxiety is generally targeted toward spending time with the non-time-sharing parent and evident in the child's behavior, it is also apparent in worry and concern that the non-time-sharing parent may disappear again. The antecedents to this constellation of fears may include the child's attempts at cognitively reconciling events and behaviors they have observed, as well as reconciling conflicting accounts of information obtained, including information they have gleaned from others regarding the loss of the parent. For example, a mother who abdicated parenting in response to dissatisfaction with a court case involving her estranged husband impulsively gave up her custodial rights to the child; ultimately, she regretted the decision. For approximately 10 months, the girl did not see her mother and worried she had died. The father did not know what to tell her about the mother's disappearance because it was unclear whether the mother would ever return. Consequently, he did not discuss the mother's disappearance with the child at all.

The loss of a parent can contribute to grief and traumatic reactions; consequently, when children reunite with the "lost parent" they experience a myriad of feelings. In addition to joy and happiness, children reuniting with the absent parent likely experience feelings of emotional pain, sadness, and anger. Furthermore, it is not unusual for children to be hypervigilant to future losses. The feeling of hypervigilance is ego dystonic and children may wish to reduce these feelings by avoiding situations and the persons who activate these feelings; consequently, despite a child loving and desiring closeness with the non-time-sharing parent, they actually avoid this parent lest they experience abandonment and concomitant negative feelings should the parent desert them once again. Similarly, it is not unusual for children who have not shared time with their non-time-sharing parent to express concern that this parent may be angry with them due to the separation. The presence of this concern is particularly surprising in cases where children have not overtly expressed preferences to not have contact with the non-time-sharing parent.

The reunification therapist must determine the source or antecedents of avoidance of contact with the non-time-sharing parent as well as the anticipated response to this parent. If the anticipated response is fear based, but *not* due to PTSD and legitimized previous trauma perpetrated by the non-time-sharing parent, then the therapist assists the child with enhancing effective coping and desensitization to the feared stimulus – that is, the non-time-sharing parent. If the child has PTSD due to the non-time-sharing parent's maltreatment, this needs to be addressed by an individual therapist prior to commencing reunification therapy.

When addressing non-PTSD reunification fears, the first step is to instruct the child in empirically supported coping strategies including therapeutic breathing (diaphragmatic breathing), PMR with guided imagery of a relaxing scene, and adaptive cognitive rehearsal or restructuring. With respect to PMR with relaxing imagery, at the completion of the PMR protocol, the therapist has the child imagine themselves in the most relaxing place they can conceive of, which can be fictional, such as a candy land, or a real place such as the beach. The therapist audio records the relaxation protocol of diaphragmatic breathing and PMR with the relaxing scene. The time-sharing parent is then meant to assist the child in practicing these strategies between sessions, including listening to the pre-recorded relaxation protocol, and is instructed in incentive-based methods to enhance adherence to the practice plan of these strategies (see the section "Resistance Due to Oppositionality," below).

The next step is to develop, with the child, a fear hierarchy regarding contact with the non-time-sharing parent, from the least feared to the most feared stimuli. The time-sharing parent's input may be required for hierarchy development as well, given that due to the nature of anxiety, children may avoid discussion of specific feared stimuli. The following is an example of a reunification fear hierarchy from least to most anxiety-provoking stimuli: 3 days prior to the first phone call with the non-time-sharing father, 2 days prior to the phone call, 1 day prior to the phone call, calling father and only listening to father on the phone, calling father and asking him specific questions, calling father and answering his questions, 1 day prior to seeing the father in the therapist's office for first time, sitting in the waiting room of the first live session, walking down the hall to the therapy room where father is waiting, walking into the therapy room where father greets child, sitting in session with father, going to the movies with father, and having a meal with father.

Subsequently, the therapist conducts imaginal systematic desensitization and quasi in vivo desensitization to the items on the fear hierarchy. With respect to the latter, photographs and audio or video recordings of the non-time-sharing parent are used. Conceptually the use of nonimaginal images is a closer approximation to live experience and hence is likely to provide more effective stimuli for anxiety reduction, since research supports in vivo desensitization to be more efficacious than imaginal desensitization (Ultee, Griffioen, & Schellekens, 1982). As anxiety abates and the child becomes skilled at utilizing the anxiety reduction techniques, cognitive self-statements related to self-efficacy are incorporated into treatment. Examples of these statements include "I can do this. I am in control of my anxiety. I can do my deep breathing. I can think about my special place. I am safe."

With respect to systematic desensitization, many professionals believe it is actually the exposure to the feared stimuli that reduces the anxiety response through extinction, as opposed to reciprocal inhibition, which indicates the replacing of the feared stimuli with an incompatible response (i.e., relaxation). Additionally, by giving children additional cognitive coping strategies, they are self-empowered, thereby heightening self-efficacy and reducing anxiety. It is also likely, as shown by information processing theory, that children are able to reinterpret their situation with the bolstered coping skill base. As children's anxiety abates in individual sessions, the therapist exposes the child to the non-time-sharing parent in increasing increments via family therapy sessions and outside-of-session homework (see Chapter 8: Conjoint Sessions and Effecting Change), which further reduces the child's anxiety and increases the likelihood of child and non-time-sharing parent contact.

Finally, the time-sharing parent can transmit anxiety to the child via modeling, or in cases of parental interference, direct disclosures of fear regarding the non-time-sharing parent. The therapist addresses this directly in sessions with the time-sharing parent and may subsequently include the child in these sessions. This work is addressed in the time-sharing parents section below (see Chapter 7: Working with the Time-sharing Parent).

Resistance Due to Oppositionality

Periodically children will refuse to time-share with a parent due to oppositionality unrelated to interference by the time-sharing parent. In these cases, children are often noncompliant with other adult requests and this noncompliance is often best addressed through parent effectiveness training, a form of behavioral therapy, where the emphasis is on extinction of maladaptive behavior and replacement of the noncompliant behavior with new adaptive behaviors (e.g., Forehand et al., 2013; Ginn et al., 2017). While initially, the time-sharing parent is instructed in these parenting skills, the non-time-sharing parent should be versed in these methods as well, since an ultimate goal is coordination of parenting at both households. Although a formal parent training protocol can be used for reunifying families, especially with families who have children who meet diagnostic criteria or exhibit symptoms of externalizing disruptive behavior problems, time and concomitant problems with the passage of time in these cases (e.g., heightened anxiety of the child, increased child exposure to the custodial parent's interfering or alienating behaviors) may prohibit the implementation of a formal parent training regime. Consequently, a modified version of parent training protocols can be incorporated into family reunification therapy to enhance the reunification process.

With respect to parent training, the first step in reunification cases is to instruct the parent to identify the child's approach behaviors and compliance with respect to time-sharing with the non-time-sharing parent. This is often the most difficult step, as it is typically the child's noncompliant behavior that gives a loud signal, through statements of refusal and complaints, escalating to yelling, screaming, and crying, which draws the parent's attention to the "noise." This attention then reinforces the noncompliance and maladaptive behaviors toward time-sharing. Subsequently, the parent is instructed in assisting the parent to "turn down the volume," by not attending to it and ignoring it until the channel is changed or the noise dissipates. At this point, the parent "locks in the channel" by attending to and praising the child for the change in tune (adaptive behavior) with statements such as "Now that you have lowered your voice and are packing your bag for a visit with your mother, I can talk to you about having your friends over next weekend." Hence during this initial parent training phase, parents are instructed to follow and attend to the child's adaptive behavior and are informed that these methods increase adaptive behavior. This, coupled with ignoring the maladaptive behavior (the child's "fall-out" when they do not wish to comply with parent directives), has the benefit of extinguishing maladaptive behavior and enhancing the desirable behavior of the child. It is important that the therapist prepares the parent for an extinction burst, that is as the parent changes the channel, the child's static will get louder or the volume will be raised in an attempt to redirect the parent to their channel.

In this early phase in the process, the parent with the therapist should create in session a list of the child's complaints and resistant behaviors that the parent will need to ignore and, more importantly, make a list of those adaptive behaviors and communications the parent should attend to and reinforce. It will be difficult to predict what exactly those communications and behaviors will be, so some exploration will be necessary, and the general themes of what the parent should scrutinize will need to be addressed.

Subsequent to teaching parents to attend to adaptive behavior and ignore maladaptive behavior, the therapist instructs the parent in the use of praise when the child is exhibiting the appropriate adaptive behavior and appropriate communications (Forehand & McMahon, 1981). There are two forms of verbal rewards: labeled and unlabeled rewards. Unlabeled rewards are, for example, "Great," "Terrific, and "Fabulous"; labeled rewards are "Great job speaking to your mother on the phone for 5 minutes," for example. The latter identifies for the child behaviors that are positively attended to by the parent and increases the probability of child repeating them, due to the principles of reinforcement (Forehand & McMahon, 1981).

In addition to verbal rewards, small rewards may be used to enhance compliance. A quick and effective method to heighten the probability of the child engaging in adaptive and positive approach behaviors toward the non-time-sharing parent is the use of a grab bag. Grab bags include small toys or prizes that hold enough valence to be reinforcing for the child. Wrapping the small prize in tissue or wrapping paper and placing it in a container from which the child retrieves the reward heightens the appealing nature of the reward. In fact, this serves as a double reward via the wrapped nature of the prize and the prize itself. An additional purpose of wrapping the reward is that it prevents the child from excavating the reward container and taking the most rewarding toys and prizes, while leaving the less-valued toys, which may have been rewarding had they been received as a wrapped surprise, but are less so when the child can make a visual comparative analysis.

In addition, an alternate version of a grab bag that more directly addresses time-sharing is a treasure hunt at the non-time-sharing parent's residence. The advantage of a treasure hunt is that this approach can be modified for children of all ages. An additional advantage of the treasure hunt for the non-time-sharing parent is that it can be useful in encouraging a hesitant child or teen to visit the non-time-sharing parent's residence at the commencement of residential time-sharing. Not only is it a behavioral motivator and reinforcer, but also it changes the cognitive valence for the youth regarding the visit, especially when adolescents complain that the non-time-sharing parent's home is boring or gloomy, for example.

An example of this process involved a mother with four daughters (aged 11, 13, 14, and 15 years). While the three youngest were willing to visit their mother at her residence, despite not having been there for 2 years, the eldest child was the most resistant. Unfortunately, the resistant daughter also held the most power in the time-sharing family and was directly aligned with the father. Her anger was formidable, which bled into her relationship not only with her non-time-sharing parent but also with the time-sharing parent, her father, despite the alignment. It was evident that all family members were either intimidated by or afraid of the eldest daughter; consequently, the siblings who would have typically attempted a home visit with their mother were too frightened to do so, given their fear of retribution or retaliation by their eldest sister. This was particularly worrisome for them given they were living full-time with their sister. It was evident that these girls had a natural curiosity and were competitive with each other, as well as with others, as evident by their need to excel and be at the top of their class academically. Capitalizing on their natural curiosity and competitive nature, and using the principles of cognitive behavior therapies, the therapist and mother devised a treasure hunt for the girls, such that each clue rendered a new clue to a subsequent location. Attached to each clue were smaller prizes such as chocolate coins and nail polish, all enough for four girls. Ultimately, it was also stipulated that if more than one daughter arrived at the final treasure spot, then those girls would receive a larger treasure. The ultimate prize was a $25 gift card to a popular girl teen clothing store. All of these items were reinforcers that were appealing to these girls.

Another version of this treasure hunt includes the hiding of a prize in the parent's house without clues but with some physical boundaries regarding where it was contained, such as the main living areas, the first floor, and the patio. Some parents have also used verbal cues for such treasure hunts, such as "you are getting warmer or colder" for children struggling with locating the treasure.

For older children and adolescents, reinforcers or incentives to engage in the adaptive behavior may also be offered in a structured behavioral contract. For example, the adolescent who refuses to spend time with a parent because they prefer to spend time with their friends, will work for social time with friends by spending time with the non-time-sharing parent in increasing increments. The terms of the contract can include the demeanor of the child as well, so that the child is required to spend time with the non-time-sharing parent without hesitation or negative vocalization while exhibiting an agreeable attitude (which is behaviorally defined). These behaviors are tracked during the opportunity for time-sharing (e.g., Monday, Wednesdays, and every other weekend), and if the youth has exhibited a predetermined amount of these behaviors over time, then they earn a specific social event with their friends. To reduce adverse behaviors during time-sharing with the non-time-sharing parent, the contract tracks, via check marks every hour or predetermined time block, prosocial behavior during time-sharing. The peer socialization reward may be contingent on earning enough checks at the initiation of time-sharing as well as during the time-sharing with the targeted parent. It is evident that parents and child will all need to be involved in varying degrees with respect to the development and implementation of a formal behavioral contract to increase compliance.

Resistance Due to Alignment With the Time-Sharing Parent

A child who has anxiety regarding a previously conflictual relationship with a parent may have worked through the anxiety but be resistant about seeing their non-time-sharing parent because they are worried about the time-sharing parent's feelings. This may not only be the result of fear of either angering or disappointing the time-sharing parent if the child willingly spends time with the non-time-sharing parent, but rather may also be the consequence of protective feelings as the child empathizes with the pain observed in the time-sharing parent. Generally, in these circumstances, the therapist will need to work with both the time-sharing parent and the child individually initially, and subsequently, jointly. The goal is for the child to reconcile these feelings of loyalty for the time-sharing parent in order to progress with a relationship with the non-time-sharing parent, whereas the goal for the time-sharing parent is to model adaptive coping for the child and relay messages that they are strong and not in need of protection from the child, as well as to proffer explicit and implicit messages of the importance of, and support for, the child's rebuilding a relationship with the non-time-sharing parent.

With respect to the child's treatment goals, a cognitive behavior paradigm examining the child's self-statements as they impact both emotions and behaviors, and intervening to alter these, is used. The gentle use of challenges to maladaptive cognitions via motivational interviewing can assist in identifying and altering unfounded cognitions. Primary themes include beliefs that the child either caused or could not prevent the time-sharing parent's emotional pain related to the dissolution of the parent relationship. Other maladaptive self-statements include beliefs that the time-sharing parent is weak or injured due to the breach in the interparental relationship and hence is impaired in their ability to take care of themselves or another child.

Addressing Anger

Children being reunified with their parents are often angry, which may emerge from different sources. This anger can have roots in the non-time-sharing parent's behavior via poor or ineffective parenting choices or other inappropriate behavior, the time-sharing parent's maladaptive behavior or inappropriate parenting behavior, and/or behavior that is unrelated to either parent, such as in a child who is meeting a parent for the first time. The child may also be angry about not having a relationship or having a disruptive relationship with a parent despite the reasons for this relationship breach. It is not unusual for the time-sharing parent to indicate that a child is anxious and fearful of seeing the non-time-sharing parent, when, in fact, the child is angry and not anxious. The therapist should listen to and closely observe the child to elucidate the actual situation. The most overt indicator of anger is when a child replaces terms like *mother* or *father* with the parent's given name or surname. Prior to establishing a therapeutic relationship with the child, the therapist *should not* reinforce this by using the same language as the child – that is, referring to the parent by their given name (e.g., John) or surname (e.g., Mr. Smith) – nor should the therapist correct the language choice. Rather, in the beginning of treatment, the therapist should merely ignore the reference and refer to the parent as "your mother" or "your father" to the child. Once a working relationship is established, the therapist can model the acceptability and desirability of referring to parents as "mother" or "father," by using these terms without having to directly correct the child.

It is not unusual to receive a literal mixed message from a child contributing to concerns about a child's anxiety. However, when taken in totality, the communication likely reflects anger and not fear. Frequently, children will communicate that they "do not want anything" to do with the non-time-sharing parent but are in fact angry that the parent left. For example: "I have no interest in having a relationship with my mother. She abandoned my brother and me. Who leaves their children? I cried so many nights after she left." It is evident in this example, that the child had an attachment to the parent who "abandoned" her; hence it is exceedingly unlikely that the child does not desire a relationship with her mother. In fact, this level of distress indicates the contrary position.

Similarly, the adolescent who robotically tells the therapist that they have no desire to have a relationship with their non-time-sharing parent, as tears stream down their face, is another example of a contradictory message – one that indicates a strong desire to reunite with their parent. Youths will complain that they have no feelings for the non-time-sharing parent and yet will divulge nearly every hurt that the non-time-sharing parent has inflicted on them which includes hurts, related to the lack of emotional support and absence of the parent from the teen's life. For example, Joanie said, "I have no interest or desire to have a relationship with my father. He never attended any of my dance recitals, school award assemblies, and soccer league games. Furthermore, he missed my fifth-grade graduation ceremony." The mixed message in this communication includes apathy toward the relationship and yet also hurt about not having a connected relationship with the non-time-sharing parent.

Finally the child may display anger via a mixed-message that also serves as a double bind. For example, children often exhibit their anger and resistance by telling the time-sharing parent, "if you really loved me, you wouldn't make me see you or spend time with you." It will be important to dismantle these double binds that are based in anger through motivational interviewing, cognitive restructuring, and skills that eliminate face-saving maneuvers.

Face-Saving Maneuvers

Many adolescents as well as pre-adolescents become entrenched in their position of refusing to see the non-time-sharing parent even if they are desirous of re-establishing the relationship. This is an example of cognitive dissonance, which was originally demarcated by Festinger (1957) "as a state in which two or more cognitions (including attitudes, beliefs, behaviors, etc.) conflict such that one follows from the inverse of another" and of a student of Festinger's, Elliott Aronson (2000), who defined it as "a state of tension that occurs whenever an individual simultaneously holds two cognitions (ideas, attitudes, beliefs, opinions) that are psychologically inconsistent with each other."

Therapeutic challenges in this regard occur when during the reunification process, the therapist actively intervenes so the child abandons the position of not wishing to visit with the non-time-sharing parent and adopts the opposite time-sharing view, despite having an underlying desire to engage in a relationship with the non-time-sharing parent. For adolescents and sometimes children, having to adopt this opposite view engenders feelings of powerlessness, of losing, of surrendering something, or even of shame that somehow they were wrong to have the feelings they had or to engage in the resistant behaviors toward the non-time-sharing parent. Researchers have identified power, autonomy, and situational factors such as familiarity of individuals, to be related to the engagement of face-saving maneuvers (Leichty & Applegate, 1991).

Furthermore, these feelings can be heightened when a child engages in dishonesty or lying to maintain their position of not wishing to spend time with the parent and when such dishonesty is revealed during the reunification process. In these circumstances, the therapist, to enhance compliance and a smooth transition toward reunification, will need to deploy goal-directed reunification methods without the child perceiving that they have lost, or that in some way they are admitting to being wrong or dishonest in their prior position of not wishing to spend time with the other parent. One method is to shift ownership of the reunification to the therapist, to other adults (except the non-time-sharing parent), and to events beyond the control of the youth, avoiding discussions of adult issues such as courts and judges, unless the child is previously well-versed in these adult issues by those around them. At times the therapist may "throw themselves under the bus" and invite the teen to blame them for the reunification process while simultaneously presenting a team approach. In these instances, the therapist conveys the message that while the therapist's role is to assist in reunifying the family, they do not make the ultimate decisions regarding reunification; hence the therapist, who is overtly wielding the power toward reunification, is modeling helplessness and the idea that they too do not have power in the decision-making process about reunification. Having a solid working relationship with the child can enhance this process, as the child is often more forgiving of the therapist than of others in their life for "making them" go see the other parent. Therapist and child often unite over this lack of power in the ultimate decisions regarding time-sharing.

Another face-saving maneuver that can be deployed when a child's staunch refusal to engage in contact with the non-time-sharing parent emerges during discrete interventions is giving that child permission to wait to make a decision regarding adherence to a specified plan. This affords the child some power and control and the ability to change their mind and engage in the process, as opposed to having to maintain their professed refusal of contact. For example, a child who tells the therapist that they are not willing to speak to a non-time-sharing parent during an initial phone call is told that they do not have to decide at that moment whether or not to speak to that parent, and that they can wait for a future scheduled phone call to speak with the non-time-sharing parent. Alternately, they may be told that they do not have to speak at all, while listening to the parent on the telephone.

Other face-saving maneuvers are to explore the child's cognitive processes and attribute any reversal regarding the position of wishing to spend time with the non-time-sharing parent, to the child's volition, thereby reassigning the power to time-share to the youth themselves. This may be accomplished partly through motivational interviewing such that the child uncovers the positive or adaptive reasons for time-sharing. Once this is accomplished, the therapist can rely on those child-identified reasons, rendering them the child's idea for the time-sharing. For example, a child says, "One of the good things about seeing my dad is that he is Italian, and I could learn about his parents who live in Italy and maybe even visit them. That would be really cool." The therapist responds at one point in the reunification process, because the child is perhaps feeling ambivalent, with:

> You know you had a great idea about having a relationship with your dad so that you could learn more about yourself by visiting your grandparents

in Italy. That is such a mature and well-thought out idea. You are really making healthy choices for yourself. (Therapist)

Appropriately Empowering the Child

In addition to some of the face-saving maneuvers that can appropriately empower children, the child's development of a list of questions for the non-time-sharing parent can also give some situational power to the child. This list will likely include two sections: one list that is relatively benign, and the other list that may be more affectively charged and engender some anxiety in the child. The child and therapist make a determination as to the manner in which these lists are to be discussed in session. By allowing the child to determine the content of the questions as well as the timing of the dissemination of the questions, this heightens their sense of power in a process that seemingly has stripped them of a power they once held or perceived themselves to have. Many children wish to begin with the benign list such as "Daddy what have you been doing?" or "Mommy do you still have that plate that we made at the ceramics store?" The child and therapist should also develop a list of items the child would like the time-sharing parent to know about them, as well.

Appropriate power can also be disseminated to the child as they assist in planning the activities and outings for out-of-session homework assignments as well as activities for in-session work. Furthermore, allowing the child to make in-session choices of where they will sit, where others should sit, and additional in-session protocol activities are effective methods by which to empower children in seemingly hopeless situations where they perceive themselves to be powerless. In fact research indicates that giving children with life-threatening illnesses that involve concomitant, complex and often painful medical regimens, developmentally appropriate choices such as which arm the venipuncture goes in and the design of bandaging, will often help the child feel empowered and reduce their distress (Slifer, 2013; Manne et al., 1992).

Similarly, choices over situations where children perceive someone is making them do something they do not wish to do even if they are attempting to reconcile cognitive dissonance can appropriately empower a child. For example, a hug, while often extremely important to the non-time-sharing parent, for the child may feel like a breach of interpersonal boundaries and space or like a defeat in cases where the child is attempting to save face. Hence, giving the child a choice of not being hugged or touched by the time-sharing parent during the initial phase of treatment can empower the child and assist them in saving face, particularly, for these children who would desire affection from the non-time-sharing parent, but have maintained a stance of non-contact from the parent.

Another method to appropriately empower the reunifying child is to give the child permission to be a child; this is particularly important for children who have been given too much information about the parents' dissolution and related matters. Ironically as much as children believe they want to know everything about their parents' legal matters, relationship dissolution, and other adult concerns, they also wish to be removed from the conflict and enjoy all of the freedom of living and playing that childhood affords. Furthermore, they feel trapped in an untenable situation which renders them powerless; the goal is to remove them from the middle of their parents' conflict, which will appropriately empower them by freeing them to assume their authentic role – that of a child – and not to assume an adult role or other parent role. The therapist can reassure the child that it is okay to have fun and enjoy their time with the other parent. Sometimes that child may feel fear and anxiety about repercussions from the time-sharing parent should the time-sharing parent learn that they are enjoying themselves, are happy, and/or having a good time with the non-time-sharing parent during sessions. The therapist can assure the child that they will assist the parents in understanding the importance of the child having a happy and positive relationship with the non-time-sharing parent, but that in the meantime, the therapist will hold in confidence their delight and excitement while playing or engaging with the non-time-sharing parent during sessions. It is important for the therapist to frequently transmit the message to children and both parents that the children are "fired" from their adult role and that they get to be kids and have an amazing childhood. The therapist informs the children that the therapist is replacing them in any responsibility for the parents, so the children are no longer pressed to be accountable for adult matters.

ACT can also be employed with the child to facilitate movement forward in the reunification process. While the acceptance component of ACT appears to be counterintuitive with resistant children who feel particularly powerless, the goal of assisting the child in choosing their own valued direction, also a component of ACT, can be highly motivating for them. For children, their valued direction includes who they wish to emulate when they grow up, and while often this focus may be self-serving and egocentric, it is incumbent upon the professional to identify those valued objectives that align with the goals of reunification therapy. For example, if a child identifies with a well-regarded and illustrious professional basketball player, this athlete's philanthropic attributes in serving those less fortunate can be highlighted as a core value. This core value is applied to the children's relationship with their own non-time-sharing parent. By child ownership of these core values and who the child wishes to become, the child's own self-validation in this regard appropriately empowers them to engage in adaptive decision making within many areas of their lives including reunifying with an estranged parent.

Siblings: A Double-Edged Sword

The scientific literature indicates that living with a sibling, step-sibling, or half-sibling during and after divorce can ameliorate the untoward effects of divorce and enhance psychological wherewithal in children during and after the process. Jacobs and Sillars (2012) observed that the availability and camaraderie of siblings were associated with enhanced adjustment of children to divorce, concluding that sibling relationships serve as a protective factor regarding the potential adverse effects of divorce. Others have surmised that while initially conflict may increase between siblings during divorce, an adaptive sibling relationship may neutralize the negative effects of marital dissolution (Bush & Ehrenberg, 2003). While sibling relationships appear to have a powerful effect with respect to adjustment to divorce, it is likely that these relationships can enhance the reunification process, as the siblings can provide support to one another as well as implicit permission to engage with the non-time-sharing parent. It would also follow that the reverse could be operative as well, with a reunification-resistant child exerting a direct as well as indirect negative influence on the sibling who may be initially positively oriented toward the process.

It is prudent of the therapist to assess early in the process the quality of the relationship between the siblings, the dynamics of the sibling relationship including sibling dominance (e.g., does one sibling assume a parenting role over the other sibling), the influence each has on the other, and the impact that one child who is desirous of reunifying with a parent has on the other children. Generally, but not always, older children have more influence and power over the younger children. Sometimes the younger child has more power within the family system than the older child, and hence the latter takes their lead with respect to reunification with the non-time-sharing parent. The assignment of power to a child has diverse trajectories, including a parent's identification with the child due to several factors including gender, birth order, and child temperament, as examples. Alternately, the assignment of power can be due to the interaction of the parents, including interparental conflict. Family system therapists proffer that the child may actually represent or communicate problems within the family system (Minuchin, 1974), and child symptoms are essentially a method by which to deflect conflict between the parents or other dyads within the family unit (Minuchin et al., 1975). Similarly, the relationship quality between mother and child has been correlated with sibling relationship attributes and is related to maladaptive parenting practices (Shumaker, Miller, Ortiz, & Deutsch, 2011); consequently, assessment of the parents' parenting skills can assist in determining the quality of the sibling relationship. Given that most of the parents who are referred for reunification therapy have limited, ineffective, and/or maladaptive parenting practices, it is highly probable that the sibling relationship has been adversely affected, in some capacity, as well.

While receptive siblings to the reunification process can facilitate reunification between hesitant, resistant, and anxious siblings and their non-time-sharing parent, the opposite has been noted as well, with the resistant child quelling other siblings' movements forward in their relationship with the parent. Particularly noteworthy are cases of two or more siblings with the eldest child permitted to decide whether they wish to forge a relationship with the non-time-sharing parent. Not only does this allow the eldest child to make their own parenting decision, potentially allowing this child to "poison the well," by defaming the non-time-sharing parent to the younger siblings, but there also becomes an implicit social status associated with being allowed to not time-share with a parent. The message is "I am the oldest and with being the oldest I get to make many cool powerful decisions for myself including whether I spend time with my parent." It is not unusual to hear younger siblings bemoan the fact that they are not allowed to make the decision to see their time-sharing parent, while their older brother and sister are allowed to have this choice. In extreme cases, these younger children often mark time until they perceive they will be of sufficient age to make such "grown-up" decisions about time-sharing with their estranged parent.

Alternatively, it has also been observed that older siblings believe that they need to time-share with the non-time-sharing parent in an effort to "protect" their younger siblings either from perceived untoward behavior on the part of the non-time-sharing parent or from adverse feelings (e.g., anxiety) they perceive their younger siblings may have about time-sharing with this parent. While in some cases, these concerns may be realistic, in other cases, this stance affords the eldest sibling a face-saving maneuver to engage in time-sharing with the estranged parent without having to admit that they wish to time-share with this parent despite the absence of any realistic concerns or problems.

Developing an In-Session and Out-of-Session Safety Plan

Since much of the hesitancy of a child to time-share with the non-time-sharing parent is shrouded in the belief of the presence of some form of danger, it is important to implement a safety plan, not only to directly ensure the child's safety, but also to demonstrate to the child that they are safe and to provide enhanced self-efficacy or control over a situation which may seem completely imposed on them. The safety plan gives the child a roadmap in the event that an untoward incident begins to occur. Cognitively, having a predetermined plan a child can readily effectuate can reduce anxiety. Research has elucidated that a child's problem-solving ability moderates the impact of worry and anxiety (Wilson & Hughes, 2011). Safety planning includes plans that delineate safe escape pathways from the home of non-time-sharing parents such as exiting the house through the backdoor, through the backyard gate to neighbor "Shelia's house," while dialing 911, for example.

The use of video cameras placed throughout the non-time-sharing parent's home affords both child and non-time-sharing parent with protection. While these cameras should not be placed inside private areas such as bedrooms and bathrooms, they should be strategically positioned to focus on the doorways (entrance and exit pathways) to these rooms, so people entering these spaces can be video-recorded. This protects the child in cases where abuse may have occurred and is undocumented, or in the cases where the abuse did not occur, but the child has been told it occurred and hence the child is unsure and anxious about contact with the non-time-sharing parent. Continuous recording of all spaces in the home also protects the non-time-sharing parent from false allegations of abuse. Initially adding trusted adults as potential witnesses or ancillary parenting resources when time-sharing with the estranged parents can afford another layer of protection to the child and non-time-sharing parent.

An additional feature to safety planning is child provision with electronic communication devices in the event of an emergency. While many children of divorced or separated parents have cell phones to facilitate their mobility regarding drop-off and pick-up from school, extracurricular activities, and parents' homes, as an example, these devices may also be incorporated into safety planning. Contingent on the maturity of the child, very young children may be instructed in basic cell phone usage for the purposes of emergency use. Complaints may be lodged that the non-time-sharing parent may take the children's phones from them during time-sharing, with time-sharing parents indicating this has occurred previously. Ground rules must be maintained such that the phones or other agreed-upon electronic communication devices remain with the children when they are time-sharing with the non-time-sharing parent so they can stay in touch with the other parent. Similarly, while rules for electronic use must be implemented for the children, consequences for violation of the rules should not be phone removal. Rather rewards or positively valanced reinforcers should be disseminated for adaptive phone and electronic behavior.

Assessing Resistance of Others and Determining Outside Influences

It is important to listen for communications made by all family members engaged in the reunification therapy that contain themes of resistance by others such as attorneys, step-parents, and extended-family members. Additionally, the therapist will have contact with others regarding the case, as a matter of course, including guardians ad litem and attorneys. With respect to the latter, while reunification therapy is often considered an alternate form of dispute resolution to litigation (Faust, 2009; Faust & Salter, 2009), and legal professionals are often interested in resolving high-conflict cases without litigation for a variety of reasons, including the perception that their high-conflict case is in an untenable position with a judge who has been overly exposed to, and grown weary of their case, on occasion, attorneys may desire continued litigation. This drive for continued litigation in these cases may emanate from a variety of factors such as financial, psychological, and personality variables. With respect to the first of these, successful resolution of a case obviously leads to revenue loss.

Psychological variables can include the attorney's overidentification with their client (Margulies, 1996); consequently, their need to align with their client's position may be driven by their own anxiety and client overprotectiveness, for example. In fact, on occasion, the attorney may have contributed to the unresolvable rift between the parents, exacerbating the problem or, rarer yet, contributing to the development of the relationship problem leading to reunification therapy. With respect to personality variables, the discharge of personal affect such as anger can be transferred or sublimated by the attorney through the litigation of high-conflict cases (Gilson & Mnookin, 1994; Wolfram, 1979; Silver, 1999).

The undue influence of others in thwarting the relationship between non-time-sharing parent and child can be discerned when step-parents or significant others of the time-sharing parent have their own agendas and concerns about the reunification process. The therapist should listen to any themes related to these individuals to determine the extent to which the other adult is exerting undue influence on the child, thereby thwarting the reunification process.

For example, children who wish to adopt the parent's new partner as a replacement parent, instead of as an adjunctive special caretaker, may have been subjected to direct efforts of the time-sharing parent's significant other's actions or the collusion between time-sharing parent and their new partner. Children's communications such as "I am a Smith" (referring to the step-father and mother's new married name) "and not a Jones" (non-time-sharing father's name and child's legal surname); or "There is no reason to see my mom because I already have a mom (referring to time-sharing father's wife), and it is just a waste of time." Or "David proposed to my mom and me, and we are going to be a family, I am part of this family and not my Dad's." Similarly, children who refer to their biological parent's partner as Mom or Dad are also indicating such a campaign to relegate the non-time-sharing role to a subordinate one and promote the step-parent/partner as the principal parent.

In the language of time-sharing parents, one can discern similar messages. For example, a mother may convey, "her step-father has been more of a parent to this child than my ex-husband was or ever could be." "Anita knows that her step-mother is a real mother, and her own mother has never been there for her." Subcontexts regarding redirecting the child toward the step-parent as parent, and blocking the non-time-sharing parent from reunification, may be an indication that the step-parent is attempting to fulfill their own needs and desires as a parent by assuming the direct parent role. These step-parents or ancillary caretakers may also wish to assume the role of primary parent in an attempt to move closer to their partner (time-sharing parent) by aligning with the children and becoming a super dad or super mom, to work through issues (e.g., jealousy, anger, irritation, or frustration) with the non-time-sharing parent, "adopting" the children in an attempt to mend their own relationship with the time-sharing parent, and to address financial issues, including attempts to reduce child support paid to the non-time-sharing parent or increase the child support payment to the time-sharing parent.

When it has been determined there exists an underlying motivation or agenda of a time-sharing parent's significant other to thwart the relationship between time-sharing and non-time-sharing parents, there are a number of ways for the therapists to intervene. The therapist can begin with explaining the socioemotional impact this may have on the child, including causing significant confusion, in addition to trivializing or marginalizing the non-time-sharing parent's relationship with the child. Additionally, in many cases, legal settlement agreements or adjudicated parenting plans specify that parents are to call only the legal parent "mom" or "dad." The therapist can use this leverage and express concern that the judge may view this in a negative light, which could potentially have a deleterious outcome for the time-sharing parent. Alternately, it is beneficial to validate the step-parent or other caretaker's role in the children's lives and to include them in family therapy, not only to address the potential issues listed above but also to enlist this adult's unique perspective and role in facilitating time-sharing between child and non-time-sharing parent.

Critical Collaboration With Other Case-Specific Professionals

One of the most difficult potential barriers to successful reunification between a parent and child is other professionals involved in the case. While some of these professionals can delimit or impede the therapy process, they may also have a significant utility in promulgating forward reunification therapy. With respect to the potential obstruction of these professionals to the process, this is derived from the very nature of a professional's specific role. For example, should the child have an individual therapist who has been working previously with them, as well as concurrently with the reunification therapy, such individual therapists serve as an advocate for their child patient, and as such they observe the child through a different lens from that of a reunification therapist. Advocacy requires, to some degree, the suspension of objectivity and has as its benefits enhanced opportunities to establish rapport and fortified working relationships between therapist and child. Individual therapies are child-driven in this regard, which in many cases places decision-making power in the hands of the child. It is not unusual for individual therapists to recommend to reunification therapists and to other case-involved professionals that the child should not spend time with the reunifying parent because the child has expressed their disinclination regarding time-sharing, and they believe the child's reunification preferences should supersede those of others. Individual therapists may also promote the child's decision-making power, or they may state they believe the veracity of the child's communications about child maltreatment. It is often quite concerning that the individual therapist may maintain a belief in the veracity of the child's allegations against the non-time-sharing parent, despite not considering all available data, such as information collected via a social investigation or custody evaluation, and despite the fact that they did not collect their own data or follow-up regarding the child's communications, or that they merely accepted the communications of the child or time-sharing parent without speaking with the non-time-sharing parent or others regarding facts pertinent to the case.

Children's Individual Differences and Special Abilities

It is important that the reunification therapist has specialty knowledge of child clinical psychology issues including working with children who have neurodevelopmental disorders. Unique features of the child's symptom presentation may require the therapist to approach therapy with consideration given to the child's unique features. Children with neurodevelopmental disorders often struggle with communication and prosocial exchanges (Coggins, Olswang, Carmichael Olson, & Timler, 2003; Greenway, 2000). For the non-time-sharing parent who may not know the child well, it will be important to assist in educating this parent about the child's diagnosis, including any symptoms and personal characteristics that may impact therapy. For example, a father who was completely estranged from his former wife and had no contact with his 14-year-old son since the child was 2-years-old, wondered if the child was "mentally retarded," because the child had been diagnosed with ASD. The father's orientation to the diagnosis was addressed, lest the father approach the child as if he was developmentally impaired; furthermore, the connotations that "mental retardation" engendered for this father were likely contributing to a negative orientation toward the child, which could have been disastrous for the reunification process, especially since the child was not developmentally delayed and was attending entirely advanced placement and international baccalaureate classes. In addition to educating the non-time-sharing parent about the idiosyncrasies of a child with ASD, the therapist also would likely change their reunification approach when working with the special needs of the child.

Children on the autism spectrum struggle with communication and interpersonal skills. In addition, they are often cognitively concrete, lack self-awareness, and do not pay attention to contextual cues (Ben-Itzchak, Abutbul, Bela, Shai, & Zachor, 2016; Ropar & Peebles, 2007). For example, a 16-year-old, very intelligent daughter had not seen her mother since she was 3-years-old. The mother brought her daughter a beautiful gold bracelet with a small, engraved heart to the first session. The daughter while initially excited, became anxious and said she was not confident she could accept the gift because her mother was a stranger, and she was not allowed to accept items from strangers. It was not until her father, the time-sharing parent, informed her that it was acceptable to receive the gift, that the daughter acquiesced and accepted the present. Similarly, children with ASD often have difficulty with transitions, which has the potential to create anxiety (Sullivan, Martens, Morley, & Long, 2017) as they anticipate moving between two different households and reunifying with the non-time-sharing parent. Allowances need to be made to accommodate transitional difficulties such as concrete advanced planning (use of tangible calendars) and incorporation of the child's special items, which should be transported between both time-sharing parents.

CHAPTER 6
Working With the Non-Time-Sharing Parent

Initial Therapy Considerations

In the beginning of treatment, initial intake sessions are held to gather background information from the non-time-sharing parent. After meeting with both parents individually, the therapist subsequently meets alone with the child or children. Information gleaned from the child sessions should be used in a follow-up individual session with the non-time-sharing parent to assist with effecting change.

While commitment to the reunification therapy process is generally less of an issue with the non-time-sharing parent than with the other family members, especially since it is typically the non-time-sharing parent who is seeking the reunification, periodically therapists will find themselves in the position of having to sell the process to the non-time-sharing parent to obtain a "buy-in." More problematic than the buy-in are a lack of parenting skills, of adaptive parenting behaviors, and of requisite coparenting skills observed in the non-time-sharing parent. There are data showing that the non-time-sharing parent may not have the necessary assertion skills to be able to motivate the other parent to comply with the parenting plan. They may also be intimidated by their child, due to their own guilt or fear of rejection, and unable to effectively set and follow through with limits. In many cases, these parents have children who run roughshod over their attempts to exert parenting authority; as a consequence, it is not unusual for non-time-sharing parents to respond with authoritarian parenting techniques, which has a cyclical effect of heightened child resistance. For example, a mother who was attempting to have an improved relationship with her daughter enticed her with surfing lessons. This had some degree of success, as the child would spend time with her mother three times a week, as the pair engaged in these lessons. The daughter was thrilled and excited with the surfing lessons; however, the dyad became embroiled in a discussion as to why the daughter would not spend the night with her, which had a chilling effect on the daughter's communication with the mother. Ultimately the mother threatened her with removal of the surfing lessons if she did not disclose her feelings and have a meaningful discussion as to why she did not wish to spend nights with her. The daughter refused to render herself vulnerable, the mother had no parenting leverage, and the father "rescued" the daughter by taking her to the surfing lessons himself.

A more extreme example of bartering for affection is often enacted via the legal system, such that the time-sharing parent requires a government or legal document from the non-time-sharing parent for verification of address for a school boundary, or the time-sharing parent seeks the non-time-sharing parent's signature on a passport application. Additionally, the time-sharing parent may petition the court for child support (or an increase in child support) given that they time-share with the child fulltime. In response, the non-time-sharing parent without parenting leverage counters these court motions by demanding more time with the child or in some cases merely the opportunity to meet the child. Unfortunately, in many such cases, especially with teenagers, the child is privy to the passport and school boundary issues and even the child support payment issue. Their knowledge of these sources of interparental conflict often exacerbates their own anger directed toward the parent without parenting leverage, the non-time-sharing parent.

At the commencement of reunification therapy, it is not unusual for the non-time-sharing parent to eagerly anticipate the reunification and place pressure on the therapist to have an immediate parent–child session after the initial intake of the children. The reunifying parent will typically drop their demand after being educated about the process and the need to approach the situation delicately; in some cases, reunifying parents are not satisfied with this explanation and continue to push for access, either directly or through their attorneys. Motivational interviewing techniques to facilitate understanding on the part of the reunifying parent may be helpful.

For example, the therapist can ask the reunifying parent what they believe will happen if there is an instantaneous therapy session or contact with the child. The reunifying parent's response often encompasses a diatribe regarding inequity and the injustices that have been inflicted on the reunifying parent. The therapist provides empathy and support, while maintaining a neutral stance, such as saying, "It is incredibly painful to not have been able to see your children." If the non-time-sharing parent cannot, or does not, answer the question about the perceived outcome of an instantaneous therapy session, the question should be repeated. If the question is repeated, then the parent typically responds that they do not know what would happen, or they might indicate an unfavorable outcome.

In addition to the use of motivational interviewing to address the client's wish for an immediate parent–child session, highlighting the impact of such a stance for the non-time-sharing parent by informing them that while the therapist has had great success in reunifying families and while they cannot necessarily guarantee success in reunification, they can virtually guarantee failure should the reunifying parent push the child in the process. This inevitably leads to a discussion about parenting leverage and the fact that because the non-time-sharing parent is the "odd person out" or a "persona non grata," they have minimal to no parenting power. This translates into the inability for the parent to make any demands on the child, even reasonable parent-oriented demands during the early treatment phase. Therefore, the therapist may utilize information from the initial interview and motivational interviewing techniques and Socratic questioning to enlighten the non-time-sharing parent as to the ineffectiveness of their demanding behavior, no matter how reasonable it may seem.

During the initial session, the therapist gathers data and evaluates the role the non-time-sharing parent had in the breach in the relationship with the child and disruptions in the relationship with the other parent, if applicable. Furthermore, the practitioner should assess any insights the non-time-sharing parent may have with respect to their role in the relationship disruption, given that all problems are co-created.

Even if the non-time-sharing parent's role was a marginal contributory factor, it was a factor nonetheless and must be addressed, lest the situation repeat itself, and problems recur in the parent–child relationship. Furthermore, a parent's level of insight can elucidate their orientation, not only to the reunification therapy process, but also toward parenting and interpersonal interactions with others which may be critical to relationship reparation and maintenance.

At the first follow-up session with the non-time-sharing parent, typically, the therapist will address with the non-time-sharing parent, the myriad of feelings the child is experiencing. It is important to relay to the non-time-sharing parent, the child's anxiety regarding reunification and the precipitant causes if known. The non-time-sharing parent should be informed as to the child's concerns that they will be angry with the child. This is a common apprehension of the child, and one that often elicits surprise from the non-time-sharing parent, who for the most part realizes the child is not at fault for the separation. For some non-time-sharing parents who feel victimized by the parent-child separation or lack significant empathy, they may actually struggle with not blaming the child for the derailment in their relationship. The language the non-time-sharing parent uses in describing the child is a clue to the degree to which the non-time-sharing parent blames the child. Words used to describe the children as manipulative, sneaky, entitled, and being "just like their mother or father" are indicators of the non-time-sharing parent's blaming the child.

Those who are healthier psychologically and realize that the child is an unwitting victim in the parents' dissolution or other adult decisions that have resulted in their inability to spend time with the parent, may struggle with not blaming the alternate parent. This denunciation of the alternate parent can easily seep into the non-time-sharing parent's communications with the child, which may appear initially innocuous but which directly pressure the child and indirectly blame them. These invidious communications are questions and statements that simultaneously transmit a message with a component of care, concern, love, and loss (missing them), which is the reason they appear innocuous. The care component may seem to justify their use, because they superficially transmit feelings of care and compassion. However, embedded in these communications are messages of quiet and subtle manipulation (e.g., pressure). The therapist should block non-time-sharing parent guilt inducers and other pressuring remarks (e.g., for the child to spend time with the parent) directly and through modeling of appropriate responses while communicating that the child is a victim, not a perpetrator.

Examples of these kinds of communication include:

- **Direct Guilt Inducers**
  - "Why haven't you called?"
  - "Don't you want to see me?"
  - "You know it was extremely difficult for me being over in the Middle East fighting the war. All I could think of was reuniting with you, and it kept me going."
- **Indirect Guilt Inducers**
  - "I missed you at Christmas."
  - "We had a birthday party for you, even though you weren't there."

  - In response to a child saying they were inducted into the National Honor Society: "I am so proud of you; I wish I could have seen your induction."
- **Guilt Inducers via a Third Party**
  - "Your grandmother is not doing well and is so sad not to have heard from you."
  - "Your dog sleeps on the bed, waiting for you to come home."
- **Non-Guilt-Related Pressure**
  - "When are you coming over to see me?"

This last question places the responsibility for time-sharing with the child, while any form of time-sharing is in fact a parent's determination, and not the child's. Furthermore, in highly contested cases, it is not feasible that a child could legally make a time-sharing determination. Also, children under the driving age cannot jump in a car and drive over to their non-time-sharing parent's house. When a non-time-sharing parent uses this form of pressure, a therapist's contextual statement can be useful, such as turning to the child and saying, "I bet you wish you could drive and get your own apartment and let the grown-ups worry about the grown-up stuff." This absurdity creates flexibility in thinking, while changing the tenure and tone of the non-time-sharing parent's communications.

It is useful to go over this list as well as generate other statements and questions specific to the case that could exert this form of pressure on the child.

Anger and Blame

It is important to explain to the non-time-sharing parent that the child is not at fault for the separation in any manner and that this must be communicated at the first conjoint session whether it occurs by telephone or face-to-face. The mileage in facilitating a relationship between parent and child can be significant once the child knows the non-time-sharing parent is not angry with them.

For example: Raphael Angelo Jr., a first-generation American citizen of Italian descent, has shared time with his parents, Mr. Angelo and Ms. Donatello, on a 50/50 time-sharing schedule since he was 2-years-old. Given their culture, the parent relationship was animated, and when disagreements arose at times, their communication was verbally volatile. Mr. Angelo's deep voice exacerbated his expressiveness, and in Ms. Donatello's Mediterranean culture, it was expected that mothers are the preferred parents to fathers, and first-born sons were to be revered (Emerson & Souza, 2008; Stavrou, 1999; Park & Cho, 1995). This latter parenting orientation contributed to the mother's enmeshment and over-attachment to the son, which included episodic periods of his co-sleeping with her, despite being in the fifth grade. Not surprisingly, shortly after his parents divorced, the parents engaged the services of a parenting coordinator (PC) to assist them when disputes arose regarding their time-sharing plan. The PC worked with the parents throughout Raphael's childhood, addressing issues regarding problems with the parents' communication, time-sharing exchanges, the timing of vacation, and the exchange of the child's belongings including school uniforms. Subsequently, for approximately a month while in the fifth grade, Raphael refused to visit his father. His mother asserted that he was afraid of his father, stating that Mr. Angelo screamed at him for not completing his homework. In contrast, the son reported that he did not know the reason for his fear of his father but admitted that he feared being apart from his mother, evidencing symptoms of separation anxiety. To the PC's credit, she had grave concerns about the length of time that had passed since the son had engaged in time-sharing with his father, and made an immediate referral for reunification therapy. During the initial individual sessions with Raphael, he could not specify his fear of his father but "just knew" that he did not want to spend time with him. He also discussed worrying that both parents would die and feared of his own death. He described scenarios such that if he did not receive a response from his texts or phone calls to his mother, he would become panicky, describing the possible circumstances that raced through his mind regarding the loss of his mother. After addressing his anxiety and incorporating methods of coping, as well as working with Ms. Donatello as to how to address the child's separation anxiety, Raphael tentatively agreed to a reunification session with his father.

It was arranged such that Mr. Angelo was to be situated in the therapy room first, and with mother and son arriving subsequently in the waiting room. In the waiting room Raphael appeared pale and trembling, breathing rapidly; consequently, he was brought into a separate treatment room, and relaxation techniques were employed. Given his observable distress, he was given a number of options, including talking to his father on the telephone from a separate room, or speaking to him "down the hall and between the walls," as there was no one else in the office suite, enhancing privacy and maintaining confidentiality. He was also given the option of attempting the session again later in the week.

He reassured the therapist that he was fine, but he needed a moment, and then asked her if she was sure that his father would not be angry with him for the separation.

Once he was reassured, he walked down the hall with the therapist to where the father was waiting with the door ajar; this writer exclaimed so the father could hear, "We are almost there, but Raphael is nervous that you are angry with him." The cue prompted Mr. Angelo immediately into action, and he exclaimed with an endearing voice, "Oh Raphael, I am so not angry with you. I miss you and love you." This gave Raphael the courage to walk through the door into the therapy room. Initially he was extremely quiet, an ice breaker game of Connect Four was played; approximately 10 minutes into the session, the father had to take an emergency phone call so he stepped outside of the therapy room. Raphael turned to the psychologist and whispered, "Can I go?" This writer asked, "Leave the session and go back home with mom?" He said, "No I want to start seeing my father again." He indicated he wanted to resume time-sharing immediately, and after the father returned to the session, a preliminary plan was made for the weekend, contingent on working out the details with both his parents.

Contemporaneous with anger is blame, and although the parent may not blame the child directly or indirectly, they may struggle with not blaming the time-sharing parent to the child. The impact of blaming the time-sharing parent to the child should be explored with the non-time-sharing parent. It is useful to ask this parent how they perceive disparaging the other parent to the child will affect the child and what they hope will evolve out of such censure of that alternate parent. Typical responses include: "They (the children) need to know the truth," "I have taken the high road which has not progressed anywhere" and "I must reprogram them."

In utilizing motivational interviewing techniques during an individual session with the non-time-sharing parent, one can enhance the parent's ability to understand that their wish for the child to perceive the situation differently is often fueled by their own anger and at times desperation. The following motivational interviewing questions may assist in moving the process forward: What is their hope for change by telling the child adult information to rectify the perceived wrong? What is their expectation of the child and the process, and what will their child gain by learning the adult "truth" from them? How will it help the parent obtain their ultimate reunification goal by expecting the child to change behaviors that only the time-sharing parent has the ability to change?

Children on some early level know that they belong to both parents via the powerful mechanism of attachment (Bowlby, 1989). Older children know that they are the by-product of the union between both parents and hence are part mother and part father. For one parent to denigrate the other parent to the child, devalues the part of the child that comprises that parent.

With respect to anger and blame, a rarer observation, but one that occasionally emerges, is a parent's directly expressed anger toward the child for refusal to time-share. This is especially perplexing when the non-time-sharing parent becomes angry with the child for this refusal in those circumstances where it is obvious the time-sharing parent is thwarting the process. An example of this can be discerned when a non-time-sharing parent yells at a child for missing the time-sharing event by going home after school with a friend, even when the estranged parent knows the time-sharing parent sabotaged the other parent's plan to transport the child from school.

Professionals have noted a non-time-sharing-parent's inability to empathize, which can arise through a number of different trajectories. Filial therapy is based on the premises of humanistic and client-centered therapy, which has had some promising results in working with parents and with children of divorce (Baggerly & Green, 2015). Through this approach, parents are trained in reflection and empathic responding that serves to validate the child's experiences and communicates to the child a higher level of understanding and empathy concerning the child. The instruction of parents in basic helping skills can facilitate empathic responding, and these skills include low levels of reflection and more advanced summaries of feelings and cognitive perceptions. Appendix C is an empathy training manual to use when working with both the non-time-sharing parent and the time-sharing parent in reunification cases.

Parents Who Have Been "Victimized" and/or Maintain Their Victim Role

Non-time-sharing parents who either do not accept responsibility for their contribution to the breach in the parent–child relationship or who have been vilified by the time-sharing parent or others, may have difficulty relinquishing their bitterness and acrimony directed toward those who they perceive responsible for their loss. With respect to victimization or persecution, research has demonstrated that incarcerated offenders who externalize blame for their antisocial acts are more likely to respond negatively to intervention programs than those who take responsibility for their maladaptive criminal behavior (Jackson, Lucas, & Blackburn, 2009). Consequently, to render reunification therapy effective, the non-time-sharing parent accepts responsibility for their role in the relationship disruption and for taking action to make required changes to advance reunification, without blaming or holding others responsible. ACT reduces the parent's externalization of self-perceived vilification, enabling acceptance of responsibility and effectuating concomitant change of interfering relationship behaviors through identification and acceptance of thoughts and feelings, choosing their own valued path, and taking action in accordance with this valued direction. Encouraging the parent to identify all feelings regarding the parent–child situation as well as their core values generally, and parenting specifically, and elucidating a cognitive and behavioral pathway that supports these core values will assist in the reunification process.

Parents Without Parenting Leverage

As stated above, the non-time-sharing parent cannot be the disciplinarian or exert authority over the child, at least initially in the reunification process. It is actually good to be a "Disney World" mother or father in these cases, both figuratively and literally. The benefit of being the fun parent in this process is threefold: (1) It heightens pleasant events and exchanges between the non-time-sharing parent and the child, which research supports from a behavioral activation perspective and operant conditioning. (2) It alleviates any chance of a negative exchange or power struggle, (3) and in the cases of estrangement by the time-sharing parent, it removes the child from the time-sharing parent's "home field advantage," by removing the child from the time-sharing parent's residence to a different locale such as a theme park. This is particularly important in cases where a parent is estranging the children from the non-time-sharing parent. In many cases, when the non-time-sharing parent is able to facilitate even a mini weekend trip out of town with a fun activity planned, both non-time-sharing parent and children frequently report positive interactions with their children.

Temporary Abdication of Parenting

In cases of temporary abdication of parenting, the non-time-sharing parent surrenders their time-sharing without direct pressure from the time-sharing parent. These parents believe it is better for the child to take a break from time-sharing, and they relinquish their opportunity to time-share with the child. Occasionally, this is motivated by a sense of helplessness, anger to punish a child for their resistance to time-share, or fear of the child and/or the time-sharing parent. This temporary abdication of time-sharing often exacerbates the child's initial resistance and subsequently balloons into staunch refusal to see the alternate parent, making it more difficult for the child to resume their time-sharing with the non-time-sharing parent. It is important for professionals from all realms, including attorneys, guardians ad litem, and therapists, to prevent the abdication of time-sharing when it is occurring. The earlier the therapist can intervene to prevent finalized abdication of time-sharing, the better the chances of eventual reunification success. Strategies to assist in the prevention of complete relinquishing of time-sharing include educating parents regarding the adverse impact of abdication of their time-sharing, as well as building initial child–parent contacts that are enjoyable for the child. The Disney World parent as described above, when used as a specific intervention, may be facilitating in these circumstances. So in other words, if the mother has relinquished her time-sharing for several weeks, and the child has increased resistance about resuming time-sharing, the first contact and cluster of overnights may include a mini or weekend vacation or day trips that are considered special for that child. The message should be clear during this time that the time-sharing is merely for fun and not for discussing the problems at hand, as that will be reserved for another time with the treating therapist. Collateral damage to the parent–child relationship when the non-time-sharing parent temporarily abdicates their relationship with the child, includes not only the child's feelings of rejection and abandonment as well as fears of future abandonment, but also the time-sharing parent's disfavor, which they may feel a need to express to the child either out of anger or in a misguided fear of protecting the child. These reactions typically only serve to further estrange the child from the non-time-sharing parent and reinforce a breach of trust which is arduous to overcome.

Parents Without Adequate Parenting Competencies and Self-Confidences

It is not unusual for non-time-sharing parents to have deficient or inappropriate parenting skills. Some non-time-sharing parents have laissez-faire or authoritarian parenting styles, neither of which, as demonstrated in the literature, is an effective parenting approach (e.g., Okorodudu, 2010). With respect to the former, the laissez-faire parenting approach affords the child an opportunity to obtain their own predetermined reinforcers from the environment, often enabling them to obtain the parenting power in the parent–child relationship. This does not bode well for the parent who will need to be able to set appropriate child limits, and for the non-time-sharing parent, ultimately their parenting leverage and power are eroded. Alternately those non-time-sharing parents who are authoritarian, exhibit harsh, punitive, and inconsistent parenting practices, place themselves at risk for further distancing their children from them if their parenting style is not addressed in reunification treatment. The incorporation of parent training skills as described in the chapter on working with children (Chapter 5) will assist the non-time-sharing parent who lacks adequate parenting competencies.

Fear of Rage, Retaliation, and Rejection of the Child and the Alternate Parent

Related to laissez-faire parenting style is a passive parenting style that is acquired due to the anxiety of the parent. This anxiety is generated in response to fear of the child and/or the time-sharing parent's rage and/or fear of their retaliation. Furthermore, the non-time-sharing parent may also fear rejection or abandonment by the child, which is ironic given that there already has been a rejection or loss of the child in these reunification therapy cases. Jacobson (1978) identified the non-time-sharing parent's passivity as a correlate in those parents who have been excluded from the child's life. It is incumbent on the professional to empower the non-time-sharing parent through education and cognitive restructuring. With respect to the latter, many of these passive parents are of the conviction that they are powerless and do not have the right to ensure the child has a respectful relationship with them. Their powerlessness in its most extreme form includes communications regarding resignation and elopement from reunifying with their child.

Ground Rules for Non-Time-Sharing Parents

When Interacting With Children During Reunification Sessions

To create a therapeutic environment that will effectuate reunification, non-time-sharing parent parameters or ground rules should be implemented.

Fundamental Ground Rules

The following is a list of the fundamental ground rules that should be observed by the non-time-sharing parent:

- No touching including hugging the child unless cleared with clinician and child first;
- No pressure for the children to explain themselves regarding the lack of contact;
- No presenting their (non-time-sharing parent's) "side of the story";
- No pressure on the child to say "I love you";
- No questioning of the child about the other parent;
- No speaking poorly of the time-sharing parent or their extended family;
- Control of emotions (The parent may have tears, but not openly cry, and should excuse themselves if they do not believe they can control their emotions).

Based on the specifics of the case, other ground rules are likely to apply. In fact, the therapist will need to meet individually with the non-time-sharing parent after meeting with the child, to brief the non-time-sharing parent on the ground rules and expectations regarding the first interactive encounter with the child. Additionally, the therapist should give the non-time-sharing parent some parenting and communication strategies to use when meeting with the child initially. It is not unusual for the child to worry that the non-time-sharing parent will not validate their experiences; therefore, it is very important to teach the non-time-sharing parent how to validate the child. This includes reduction of defensiveness by the non-time-sharing parent and implementation of validating skills via empathy training (see Appendix C).

CHAPTER 7
Working With the Time-Sharing Parent

Establishing a solid working relationship with the time-sharing parent is critical to the success of forging a relationship between child and the reunifying parent. For too many practitioners, the intervention focus is placed primarily on the reunifying parent and child, and much of the work with the time-sharing parent is neglected. While practitioners are painfully aware that they need to address issues of the residential parent, much of the time, therapy focuses on the resistance of this parent; consequently, the practitioner is often putting out fires as they arise from this resistance, and a truly collaborative relationship is not forged.

Resistance Versus Intentional Interference

During the initial session with the time-sharing parent, the therapist must not only obtain important background information including child development and the history of the parents' relationship and concomitant conflicts, but also attend to this parent's story, as it may contain significant information regarding resistance and interference with the reunification process. The residential parent's story contains many different themes, and the practitioner must listen for (1) the current theme, (2) the historical theme with respect to the other parent, (3) themes about the child and their different relationships, and (4) the intrapersonal theme including the parents' own perception of relationships and their psychological demeanor.

The Current Theme

A primary current theme that permeates the time-sharing parent's communications and orientation to the process is related to child support and money. It is notable that states calculate child support based on a formula that includes a percentage of time the child spends with the parents (e.g., Office of Child Support Enforcement, 2015; originally 2002). To avoid the painstaking efforts of calculating time-sharing hour by hour or minute by minute (and the interparental conflict this likely would engender), states calculate time by the number of overnights the child spends with each parent. Examples of the current prevalent concerns about finances and child support include time-sharing parents' statements regarding not having sufficient funds to pay their required share of the reunification therapy costs, and even in some cases when the non-time-sharing parent is solely responsible for session payment, the time-sharing parent may assert that they do not have requisite funds to pay for travel to and from the therapy sessions. Time-sharing parents may not wish for the children to have overnights with the non-time-sharing parent, because once the child feels comfortable with overnight time-sharing, there is a concern that this will become the norm, thereby reducing the amount of child support the time-sharing parent receives, or for some cases, that the time-sharing parent subsequently will be required to pay the non-time-sharing parent child support.

A pervasive current reunification theme observed in therapy includes reunification concerns by the time-sharing parent that are within the historical theme. The overt concern generally revolves around the safety or danger to the child when in the presence of the non-time-sharing parent. It may also include the overt worry of the parent that somehow the child will be psychologically injured or harmed by the non-time-sharing parent. This worry includes a myriad of concerns including violent or potentially abusive proclivities of the non-time-sharing parent, the non-time-sharing parent's parenting ability, including their potential for supervisory neglect, the non-time-sharing parent speaking poorly about the time-sharing parent to the child, and worry that the non-time-sharing parent has limited or other poor parenting skills and/or poor judgment. Occasionally these concerns are legitimate – although, generally not to the degree projected by the time-sharing parent. Just as the child's anxiety is reinforced through avoidance, a time-sharing parent's anxiety and worry can increase with physical and emotional distance from the non-time-sharing parent, as in many cases the time-sharing parent has been previously exposed to stressors or trauma associated with the non-time-sharing parent. Hence through principles of operant conditioning and information processing theory, this parent's anxiety also increases. It is necessary to address the time-sharing parent's concerns and fear periodically throughout treatment.

During the initial treatment stage, the therapist must be alert to communications made by the child that are indicative of the transmission of fear by the time-sharing parent or of the child's originating the fear. Unfortunately, given children's developmental status, children often equate their fear to their time-sharing parent's fear about having to see or establish a relationship with the non-time-sharing parent. They believe that because of this fear and/or the events that transpired to cause the breach in time-sharing, that they do not have to see the parent. This is a legitimate premise and is simplistically realized through the concrete operational stage of development for elementary school–aged children who tend to exhibit black-and-white thinking as well as a concrete conceptualization of social justice (Piaget, 2000). So for example, children typically know that if they have an injury then the parent will take care of it, or if they break a rule, there will be consequences; their sense of causality is linear during this developmental stage (Piaget, 2000).

Similarly, adolescents may also have the presumption that they are the ones who decide whether or not time-sharing will occur with their parent. Adolescents in the formal operational stage of thought are egocentric and can imagine and consider possibilities that may not exist in the real world; hence they are often perplexed as to why they cannot make decisions for themselves and are often under the mistaken impression that at age 12, 13, or 14 years, they are able to decide with which parent they will reside. However, not only is there research to indicate that children's brains are developing at this age and often they do not have sufficient maturity to make such important decisions as to who will finish raising them, but also in many states, the law recognizes that children are to be raised by both of their parents until the age of majority.

It is important to periodically assess the child's orientation to time-sharing and custody throughout treatment, and this may require recurrent discussions addressing this perspective during the therapy sequence. Additionally, the first line of problem resolution in this regard *may not* be through the child, who is often very loyal to the time-sharing parent or at least trusts that parent immensely and hence their beliefs about whether or not having to establish a relationship with the non-time-sharing parent are derived in part (or whole) from this parent, but rather the therapist should address these perceptions and beliefs with the time-sharing parent directly. Reminding the time-sharing parent that therapy is for reunification purposes and that it will not be helpful if the child believes that if they are afraid enough or resistant enough (voicing that they do not wish to spend time with the non-time-sharing parent), then they will not have to have a relationship with that parent.

In family law cases, it is also important to delineate the fact that the power regarding reunification decisions in all probability resides with the judge, and that if the judge determines that the child is to have time-sharing with the non-time-sharing parent then that will occur. It will be important to highlight how the parents and the therapist can redirect some of that power away from the judge and make the best decisions for the family with respect to reunification. It is useful to explain that judges typically have hundreds to thousands of cases, and they do not have the time to learn the nuances of their particular family and will rule according to the law, without necessarily being able to know or weigh all of the variables in a case. It is important to explain that if, parents and therapist retain control over the reunification process, then the possibility of establishing a smooth and healthy transition is maximized without court involvement.

To reduce the time-sharing parent's anxiety, it is best to reiterate that this is a methodical process not a sink-or-swim outcome, that safety plans will be devised whether or not they are needed for real or imagined security needs, and the therapist can explain that once the core of the reunification process is over, follow-up maintenance sessions can be scheduled monthly, every 2 months, or semiannually, as examples. The continued involvement of the reunification therapist often provides additional security to the time-sharing parent knowing that there is continued monitoring of the process. The time-sharing parent's assistance is solicited in reorienting the child to the likely possibility that they will be required to reestablish a relationship with the parent. The therapist empathically relays to the time-sharing parent that they may unwittingly increase the child's anxiety and distress if they implicitly (or explicitly) inform the child that they are able to decide or have a voice regarding spending time with the non-time-sharing parent. Additionally, it is relayed to the parent that the child's anxiety is likely magnified if, despite their opinion against time-sharing, the judge rules for reunification without reengagement in reunification therapy, because it had been previously attempted unsuccessfully.

Reducing the time-sharing parent's anxiety concerning the safety of the child when they spend time with the alternate parent is extremely important for several reasons. Not only will the reduction of the time-sharing parent's anxiety assist in the child reunifying with the other parent, but it will also reduce the child's own anxiety about time-sharing because the time-sharing parent can transmit their anxiety to the child through the social learning process of modeling (Hirshfeld-Becker & Biederman, 2002). The experience of tension that anxiety generates can be extremely unpleasant as well as have potential health risks; consequently, it is important to reduce the experience of distress for parent and child. Frequently, the therapist may inadvertently overlook the degree to which the time sharing parent is experiencing anxiety, as anxiety is often masked by the overt anger they are projecting outward, typically toward the reunifying parent.

The Historical Theme

With respect to the historical theme, some typical examples of these that may be inherent in the time-sharing parent communications include rejection by the non-time-sharing parent, which typically comprises feelings of hurt, anger, and sadness. It is imperative for the clinician to listen to the time-sharing parent's vocabulary and phraseology when referencing the non-time-sharing parent and the family problems. Some communication examples of rejection include "She left us and therefore does not deserve to have a relationship with Keisha"; "He chose his other family over us; he should just go on and be with his new family"; or "He abandoned us." Additionally, it is not unusual for the hurt and rejected parent to use the word or synonyms for *distrust.*

Methods to address the time-sharing parent's feelings of hurt and rejection involve working initially with the non-time-sharing parent to assist them in apologizing to the residential parent for the hurt that the individual has caused them. Additionally, the non-time-sharing parent is instructed in validating the time-sharing parent's feelings through reflection and the acknowledgement of those feelings, assuming the responsibility for causing the hurt and the pain for the dissolution of the relationship. This is accomplished via a session that includes both parents together, without the child. The therapist facilitates the building of trust by inviting the time-sharing parent to express their feelings of distrust, while having the non-time-sharing parent validate those feelings through acknowledgment of the pain they have caused the parent.

At this juncture, the therapist requests the time-sharing parent to divulge those actions and communications with which the non-time-sharing parent would need to engage to rebuild their trust. The therapist assists the non-time-sharing parent in demonstrating their trust-building ability and has this parent relay these actions to the time-sharing parent. It is important to prepare the non-time-sharing parent in advance for this session. These acts of trust building can be as simple as increased communication about the children when time-sharing, such as writing an e-mail summary of what transpired, after the time-sharing is completed. More complicated trust-building demonstrations include the non-time-sharing parent's random alcohol and drug testing, telephone or video conferencing communications with the time-sharing parent during the initial outings of the non-time-sharing parent and child, or inclusion of the time-sharing parent in initial extrasession activities between the non-time-sharing parent and the child.

Child and Different Relationships Themes

It is critical for the clinician to understand the time-sharing parent's needs, concerns, and beliefs concerning the relationship that is to be forged between the non-time-sharing parent and the child. This includes the parent's own developmental history and family of origin history, including cultural identity, psychological problems the parent has experienced in the past and currently, the residential parent's beliefs about family structure and the roles each parent has in relationship to child rearing. It is not unusual for a time-sharing parent to recreate family processes from their family of origin, either as an attempt to master early conflicts and familial problems or as their operating knowledge base of family functioning. For some families and cultures, the pervasive belief that the mother is the only competent parent is operative. These mothers are often surprised to learn that American culture and law dictate otherwise and that they illuminate the importance of both parents in children's upbringing.

In some cases, parents with unresolved or untreated child abuse histories "observe" their abuser in the non-time-sharing parent, despite the lack of any evidence that the alternate parent has ever engaged in child maltreatment. For example, a father who was abused by his emotionally constricted step-mother through isolation and rejection, levied objections regarding the mother time-sharing with the children, accusing her of emotional abuse of the children. Despite the lack of evidence of emotional (or physical) maltreatment by the mother, he lamented, "I feel like every time I drive the children to see their mother, I am taking them to the barren fields of Siberia in winter time." Over the course of therapy, it became clearly evident that his orientation to his former wife was embedded within his own childhood history.

The Intrapersonal Theme

The fourth theme, the intrapersonal theme, including parents' own perception of relationships and their psychological functioning, influences the time-sharing parent's orientation toward reunification. Some time-sharing parents have widely discrepant parenting views from the alternate parent, which contributes to the derailment of interparental cohesiveness. For example, an overprotective time-sharing parent who may infantilize a child and prevent the child from seeking relationships other than the one with the time-sharing parent, will typically be resistant to sharing the child with the non-time-sharing parent.

In a recent study, the level of acrimony the parents had for one another during family law litigation predicted child adjustment (Ko, Faust, Painter, & Hoefling, 2015). It would not be surprising that the time-sharing parent's acrimony regarding the other parent could adversely affect reunification and the child's adjustment. Similarly time-sharing parents with their own mental health issues, including those with thought disorders, personality disorders, and mood and anxiety disorders, are also likely to struggle with the reunification process. Additionally, research indicates that parents' problem-solving ability during family law litigation impacts children's adjustment, and the parents' locus of control predicted child internalizing disorders (Faust, Greenhawt, & Ko, 2015; Faust, Ko, Alexander, Painter, & Hoefling, 2015).

For time-sharing mothers, another intrapersonal theme includes the belief that mothers are innately the preferred parent, and/or that the children are inherently attached to mothers over fathers, which is sometimes culturally influenced, and therefore, the mother should have sole or the majority of time-sharing. Another related theme includes that of parental prerogative in the case of a parent with a life-threatening disease, irrespective of whether or not this is overtly communicated. These time-sharing parents may not have the insight to understand their motivation to sequester the non-ill time-sharing parent from the children is an attempt to acquire as much time as possible with the children in the context of their own life-threatening illness.

Enhancement of Time-Sharing Parents' Engagement in Reunification Therapy

Direct methods to enhance the collaboration of the time-sharing parent with the reunification process include providing the time-sharing parent with research that delineates the social, emotional, and academic benefits of the children establishing a healthy relationship with the other parent. Relevant references cited in the Chapter 2 section "Why Does the Need Exist for Reunification Therapy?" may be distributed and discussed with the time-sharing parent in order to increase the understanding and acceptance of this parent to the reunification process. Similarly, the research that demonstrates adverse impact of interparental conflict on the child can also be disclosed. While the time-sharing parent may indicate that there is no conflict with the non-time-sharing parent, because they do not speak to the time-sharing parent, it is important to inform the time-sharing parent about how *not* speaking is also a form of communication. Williams, Shore, and Grahe (1998) observed that those who were the recipients or the disseminators of the "silent treatment" perceived it as punishing, and it adversely impacted children's self-esteem. Children are aware that the use of silence as a form of communication is actually a conflictual communication. Additionally, Liu and Roloff (2015) did not observe the silent treatment to be a form of passive withdrawal but rather saw this behavioral act as punitive. In fact, children as young as 5 years who observed adults to engage in the silent treatment and not to resolve arguments, perceived these adults as being more angry and unhappy than those who directly resolved disagreements. They also reported greater negative emotions and discontent with those engaged in these withdrawal communication strategies contributing to unresolved conflicts (Reiter & El-Sheikh, 1999).

A more indirect method than the dissemination of information in establishing an effective working relationship with the time-sharing parent is to appeal to their empathy regarding the child's loss and feelings of missing the other parent, as well as the non-time-sharing parent's feelings regarding the loss of the child. Loss is a universal phenomenon that individuals experience from the beginning of life. While some loss is more direct, as is the case with the death of a parent, other losses are more subtle and yet have a powerful impact on human beings, such as leaving attachment figures to attend school or leaving the birth home to live in a new house. Since loss is universal and engenders painful feelings for most individuals, time-sharing parents can relate to the experience of loss in a significant emotional manner. To access the time-sharing parent's empathy regarding the separation of child from the non-time-sharing parent, the therapist may need to have the time-sharing parent recount a particularly painful event that involved the loss of someone important to them.

Chloe Madanes (1990), highlighted the healing importance of a heart-felt, sincere apology from the incest perpetrator to their child survivor. She advised in order to obtain a genuine apology from the perpetrator, it is important to engender empathy in this previously abusive family member. Madanes (1990) indicated that to do so one must access an extremely painful memory that the incest perpetrator had for that child, not only to access their own painful feelings regarding that child but also to generate the perpetrator's empathy for the child's painful experiences.

Time-Sharing Parents Require Empathy and Support Too

Time-sharing parents experience a myriad of emotions including fear, anxiety, sadness, grief, emotional pain, and anger. At times they may be misguided in their perspective of not wishing for their child to be reunified with the non-time-sharing parent; however, their perspective is genuine for them and must be validated. Additionally, it is important for the therapist to express genuine concern for the residential parent's having to be monitored by the court and potential outcomes of this judicial monitoring. Not only does this communicate genuine empathy and regard, but it may also contribute to a time-sharing parent's reconsidering their role in thwarting the reunification process.

With respect to the time-sharing parent's anxiety regarding the child's safety, it is not unusual to observe this parent operating through a valence that indicates they view their child as being at a much younger developmental level than the child's chronological age. This distortion emanates from a number of antecedents, including the age of the child the last time they had contact with their non-time-sharing parent, the age of the child when the time-sharing parent had the most significant conflict with that parent, and early non-time-sharing parenting errors when the child was extremely young. It is important for the therapist to assist the parent with identifying their young-child valence as they express their concerns, to demonstrate for the parent the older child's knowledge regarding cell phone usage (e.g., calling 911), and to effectuate a safety plan, for example. It is not unusual for these parents to have an "ah-ha" moment and respond, "You're right, Sammy isn't a little child anymore."

Closing Parenting Loopholes

There are a number of potential loopholes that need to be addressed when working with the time-sharing parent and the child. In some cases, children attempt to do an "end run" around the time-sharing parent in an attempt either to directly thwart addressing their relationship with their non-time-sharing parent or to engage in an activity that they prefer over sharing time with the parent. This is particularly true of adolescents, who developmentally shift their focus from parent interactions to peer socialization (Harris, 2011). This will need to be anticipated and addressed with the time-sharing parent, who may have ineffective parent management skills. For example, these children may not make themselves available for either the reunification session or the time-sharing outing with the non-time-sharing parent. Eliciting the time-sharing parent's own creative problem solving not only enhances the probability of successful problem resolution but also empowers the parent via self-efficacy, thereby increasing the probability of general future problem resolution when issues emerge. Data suggest that people are more likely to follow through with a plan of action or problem resolution if they have generated the plan themselves or contributed to its development (Meierding, 1993). The self-reinforcing properties of successful outcomes based on the impact of one's own behavior further promulgate the probability of engaging in that behavior in the future.

Common time-sharing parent messages that generate the parenting loopholes for the child and interventions to address these include:

1. **Messages of Powerlessness and Helplessness**
   - "I can't make him go."
   - "He is too big to carry into the car."
   - "What if she runs away?"
2. **Reverse Prioritizing Messages**
   - "He refuses to go, and it is his choice."
   - "She has soccer on Mondays and Wednesdays, tutoring on Tuesdays, ballet on Thursdays and Hip Hop on Fridays, and Saturday mornings are soccer games. I don't know how we can possibly schedule a reunification therapy session."
   - "He is a teenager and is old enough to decide whether or not he sees his mother."
3. **Messages With the Accent on the Wrong Syllable or Misdirected Motivational Emphasis**
   - "I am not going to punish him for not seeing his father."
   - "Reunification is moving too fast, and Jennifer isn't ready."

4. **Messages That the Time-sharing Parent Is the Psychological Expert**
   - "He is extremely hurt and angry and needs intensive therapy before reunifying with mother."
   - "Mother needs to apologize in (therapy) session for her absence, and once she does so, I am sure daughter will time-share."
5. **Loophole Messages That Are Entrenched in Culture**
   - "In our family, Mother knows best and Father may be able to visit one day, but the children shouldn't spend overnights."
   - "Fathers just don't know how to take care of children."
6. **Parent's Fear of Child Retaliation**
   - "Now when I insist that we need to come to session to see his mother or talk to her on the telephone, he is becoming angry with me. I don't want him to hate me."

With respect to messages of powerlessness and hopelessness (1), it is first important to determine how the time-sharing parent motivates their children and obtains compliance. One way to obtain this information is to ask how they intercede if the child refuses school attendance or to take medicine. It is not unusual for parents to relay that this does not occur with them, and if the therapist asks what would they do if in the future this does transpire, they typically respond with "it would never happen." To free-up their thinking in this regard, it may be useful to ask, hypothetically, what they would do in the event their child innocently fell in with the wrong crowd and was unduly influenced to skip school. Typically, the parent relays that they will take action, as failing school is unacceptable.

This is often successfully addressed by the therapist by discussing how children and teenagers have both privileges as well as responsibilities, and the former is tied to the latter. The therapist assists the parent in identifying the children's responsibilities in the family. Typically families identify a cluster of chores, and for those families who do not have specific chores for their children, they may be stymied to some degree when attempting to identify child obligations. The therapist may help expand their repertoire of these responsibilities by asking the parent if homework is one of the expected responsibilities of the child. Parents typically respond with "of course, this is a given." Consequently, the therapist assists the parents in identification of core responsibilities that are so firmly entrenched in family operations that parents do not necessarily consider them chores, jobs, or responsibilities, because they are fundamentals woven into the fabric of the family.

This discussion may facilitate cognitive flexibility for parents to explore other child responsibilities that are so inherently integrated into the family's process that the parent may have overlooked well-integrated child duties. The therapist explores such inherent responsibilities by asking the parent about core family values. Typically, therapists encourage parents to discuss respect if they do not spontaneously identify respect as a family core value, which can also be identified as a responsibility for children. Respect as a core value is discussed in the context of the child's current rejection of the non-time-sharing parent, and the child's abject rejection of this family value is addressed with the time-sharing parent.

Once these responsibilities are identified, then the therapist assists the parent in identifying the children's current privileges, and those that they may wish to earn for the future. While at first glance, it may seem much easier for parents to identify child privileges, millennials may actually have privileges that appear to be integrated with routine life, such as cell phone access. In these cases, the child's "privilege" may in effect be the parent's convenience, such that instead of having to park the car and search physically for the child at school, a movie theater, or the beach, as examples, the parent merely calls or texts the child to meet them at a designated place upon the parent's arrival. Furthermore, some privileges are connected to a myriad of life functions including a child's social life, academic life, and recreational life; computer usage with Internet access is a prime example of this type of privilege. The goal is to attach the child's privileges to the responsibility for forging respectful positive relationships with both parents.

Similarly, using a grab bag for younger children to spend undistracted, fully engaged telephone or electronic face time with the non-time-sharing parent can be a useful motivator such that the time-sharing parent sets a timer for a requisite period of time, and if the child meets the terms of the agreement, then they receive a grab bag or treasure box reward. The agreement or mini-contract can be as simple as "Jordan if you stay on the phone and talk with your mother for 5 minutes, you get a grab bag prize."

Time-sharing parent resistant statements regarding implementation of a behavioral plan to heighten compliance and increase motivation, whether it is a complete behavioral contract or grab bag, can be discerned in statements such as "I don't need a behavioral plan for Jessica; she behaves perfectly with me and does what

I tell her to do"; "I am not bribing my child"; "There is nothing that my child will work towards or for; she doesn't like anything"; and "I have tried these before, and they don't work." With respect to the first example, the therapist explains that while they are delighted that Jessica behaves well with the time-sharing parent, the non-time-sharing parent does not have parenting leverage, so parenting strategy modifications need to be implemented. Concerning the last three communications of resistance, it is often useful to inform the parent that every child or adolescent has a price, and even adults work for rewards (e.g., a paycheck). It requires exploration to determine specific motivators for some children. Discussion often ensues with respect to secondary generalized reinforcers, such as money, which has universal appeal for older children and adolescents. Similarly, the therapist can explain that behavioral contracting is an art and that together with the parents, the therapist will create a very specific behavioral contract for the child to enhance compliance, and the therapist can virtually guarantee that it will work if the parents implement the contract as specifically directed by the therapist. The therapist can discuss the art of contracting and that at times the contract may need to be tweaked to maximize its effectiveness.

Regarding reverse prioritizing messages (2), it is important for the therapist to assist the time-sharing parent to place reunification therapy and time-sharing with the estranged parent in its appropriate context. One method to do this is to discuss hypothetical situations that involve role reversal with the time-sharing parent being unable to spend time with the children and the parent's concomitant feelings regarding this situation. Through this role reversal, the therapist may highlight for the time-sharing parent potential feelings of rejection and sadness if they experienced a similar rejection by their child. Additionally, the therapist may query the time-sharing parent regarding their beliefs concerning action they believe the other parent should take if the children suddenly refuse to see them. Similarly, the therapist may desire to engage the time-sharing parent in empathy training, as delineated in Appendix C, in order for them to develop empathy for the non-time-sharing parent's loss of the children and relegation to a low priority position (below extra-curricular activities) with the children. Frequently, the time-sharing parent will have disclosed their beliefs that the non-time-sharing parent is a passive, inept parent and this perspective can be utilized to motivate the time-sharing parent to avoid a similar parenting style by allowing the children to choose to refuse to visit with their other parent.

With respect to messages with the accent on the wrong syllable (3), when the time-sharing parent believes reunification therapy is moving too fast and the child is not ready to reunify with the other parent, it may be useful to remind the time-sharing parent that while the therapist appreciates their concern and protection of the child, the child has not seen their non-time-sharing parent for a very long time, so in effect a significant amount of time has already passed. Additionally, explaining to the parent that waiting a long time in anticipation of seeing the non-time-sharing parent creates additional anxiety for the child, and anxious children often ruminate or catastrophize. Additionally, for those parents who believe that the therapist is suggesting that they should punish their children for not time-sharing with the estranged parent, it is important to explain that enhancing motivation through positives (e.g. rewards) is suggested as the recommended parenting strategy. For those families who are in active litigation, it is also useful to explain to the parent the importance of moving forward with reunification in a safe therapeutic manner in contrast to allowing the legal system to impose a time-sharing schedule that may be more extensive and immediate than a reunification plan developed via therapy. The therapist may discuss with the time-sharing parent the importance of the family maintaining control over the process by both parents cooperatively working together in therapy to creatively design the reunification process as opposed to relinquishing control over reunification to a judge who generally will not have the time to work with the parent in the manner parents typically desire or require. The outcome of judicial intervention is risky with respect to parents achieving their desired outcome of litigation since the judge is a third party without having the degree of knowledge the parents have about their own family.

Messages that the time-sharing parent is the psychological expert (4), often contain covert communications or motivations that are designed to restrict the non-time-sharing parent's power in the situation. The time-sharing parent who believes the child is in need of intensive psychotherapy often desires to enlist the services of an individual therapist for the child in an attempt to align with this therapist to thwart the family reunification therapist and therapy. Likewise, the requirement imposed by the time-sharing parent of an apology from the non-time-sharing parent for the child may place the non-time-sharing parent in a bind because many times when the non-time-sharing parent apologizes, the time-sharing parent maintains the apology is not sufficient or that the non-time-sharing parent must repeat the apology (no matter how many times the non-time-sharing parent has apologized to the child, which generally happens outside of the presence of the time-sharing parent). Furthermore, frequently the events for which the time-sharing parent wishes the non-time-sharing parent to apologize are actions that are not of this parent's doing and may in fact be due to the actions of the time-sharing parent. In these cases, it is important for the therapist to have the non-time-sharing parent apologize to the child for the adverse feelings the situation caused the child. Additionally, the non-time-sharing parent may express to the child their wish to have prevented the situation or to have them express the wish that the child could have been spared the associated emotional pain. Furthermore, it is often beneficial at this juncture for the non-time-sharing parent to apologize to the time-sharing parent (without the child present) for the pain the events have caused the time-sharing parent. If the child engages in individual psychotherapy, it is critical that this individual therapist and the reunification therapist establish an effective working relationship to prevent triangulation of both therapists by the time-sharing parent and sabotage of the family reunification therapy.

Loophole messages that are entrenched in culture (5), require the therapist to engage in a delicate balance of communicating to the time-sharing parent validation of their beliefs and cultural principals while concurrently providing information regarding legislative and judicial perspectives of the importance of both parents having meaningful relationships with the child. Occasionally, the therapist may refer the parent to their attorney for specific legal information regarding this issue or encourage the attorney to provide this information to the client. Additionally, the reunification therapist may identify, for the time-sharing parent, universal core values such as respect for parents and elders in an attempt to alter the time-sharing parent's cultural perspective and resistance regarding the child's engagement with the non-time-sharing parent. Capitalizing on respect, an important universal value, may reinforce the time-sharing parent's adherence to this significant value and, in turn, cognitively strengthen the parent's moral resolve to be an upstanding member of their cultural community. As a result, the time-sharing parent is likely to encourage a meaningful relationship between the child and non-time-sharing parent.

Regarding the parent's fear of retaliation (6), one of the significant reunification challenges is when the time-sharing parent is fearful of the child's anger. At times this fear is embedded in loss of control of a child's acting-out behavior or worry that the child may reject the time-sharing parent. This parental fear of the child's anger, potential retaliation, and abandonment is extremely resilient. It is likely that the time-sharing parent has considered their angered child will join forces with the non-time-sharing parent and reject the time-sharing parent, which is extremely frightening for the parent, as they have observed the repercussions of the non-time-sharing parent's rejection. Other antecedents of the time-sharing parent's worry regarding a child's anger include the parent's own psychological make-up, family of origin issues, and misguided parenting practices. The instruction of parent effectiveness skills to increase a child's compliance not only modifies a child's maladaptive behavior but through this change the parent is reinforced to apply these new skills. The parent subsequently interprets the successful resolution of children's maladaptive behavior to their own skill, and, as a result, the parent's self-confidence increases and their fear of the child's potential for retaliation diminishes. Furthermore, messages of safety and empowerment, both in the context of historical information about the parent's family of origin as well as their current family structure, can be transmitted to the fearful time-sharing parent. For example, the therapist may remind these parents that their children's adolescence is very different from their own adolescence, which may have included two parents who were unavailable or abusive.

The Buy-In

Establishing a solid working relationship with the time-sharing parent is critical to the success of forging a relationship between the child and the reunifying non-time-sharing parent. For many practitioners, the intervention focus becomes so emphatically placed on the reunifying parent and child that much of the work with respect to the residential parent is neglected. Worse yet, parents and sometimes officers of the court refer children for individual therapy to address the child's reunification issues with the non-time-sharing parent. Typically judges, attorneys, guardians ad litem, and some time-sharing parents make an individual therapy referral for the child in these situations, unknowingly and innocently. Other time-sharing parents seek the assistance of an individual therapist for their child as a clandestine ally in their legal proceedings. Unfortunately, many therapists do not have sufficient training or experience in reunifying children and parents, and they will view the client to be the child instead of the entire family system with many moving parts.

It is important to begin the process of a collaborative working relationship with the time-sharing parent by meeting alone with the residential parent prior to meeting with the child and to beginning the joint sessions with child and reunifying parent. If more than one individual session is required with the time-sharing parent prior to beginning reunification sessions, it is highly recommended that the practitioner accommodate this plan, as time invested at the forefront of the process will not only save time and money but can increase the probability of success. It is important to clarify in the contract for reunification services that every session has as part of it the ultimate goal of establishing or reestablishing a relationship between parent and child; consequently, the division of session time between parents cannot be calculated as separate and apart from the reunification process. So for example, the practitioner may need to address complaints from one of the parties who is bearing more of the burden of treatment costs regarding an unfair distribution of service. At times these individuals will request or demand that the other party pay for the additional sessions.

Subterfuge

In some cases, the time-sharing parent's resistance is at such a level that, despite the therapist's best efforts, the resistance cannot be neutralized, and in fact, the time-sharing parent's agenda includes as its goal the eradication of the reunifying parent from any aspect of the child's life. These parents are somehow empowered to believe that they will prevail in court and obtain or retain sole custody without any time-sharing on the part of the reunifying parent. While typically misguided, many of these parents are astute enough to know that their approach to blocking the reunification must transpire surreptitiously. One such method is the time-sharing parent's insistence on an individual therapist for the child, typically one with whom they have had some contact either through a previous professional or personal relationship (e.g., they know them through contacts at a synagogue) or who they have interviewed in advance of the request for an individual therapist to be assigned to the case. In more extreme cases, the individual therapy has continued unbeknownst to the non-time-sharing parent and others involved in the case. The time-sharing parent attempts to solicit a collaborative relationship with this child's individual therapist and to convince them that reunification of parent and child is not in the child's best interest. Unfortunately, many naïve, unsuspecting, and/or untrained therapists will succumb to the time-sharing parent's campaign of denigration of the other parent. This subterfuge may either have a chilling effect on the reunification process, or it will stymie reunification completely.

Therapist at Risk of Being Thrown Under the Bus

Whether with calculated intent to block the reunification therapy, or as a by-product of the parent's anxiety regarding reunification, it is important for the therapist to be aware of the time-sharing parent attempts at sabotaging the therapist–child relationship. Some parents who do not wish to be considered the "bad guy" by the child will deflect the children's resistance and any anger levied towards them, by blaming the therapist. An example of this is a father who had a permissive parenting style, and struggled with obtaining compliance from the children to see their mother at reunification therapy. To obtain agreement from the children to enter the car to drive to the session, he told them, that the therapist would call the police and have him arrested if they did not comply with session attendance. Some time-sharing parents are less subtle, blaming the therapist directly for the child having to engage in the reunification process and connecting with the non-time-sharing parent.

These children often mimic the time-sharing-parents' blame of the therapist by accusing the therapist of impartiality. For example, they may allege that the therapist works for the non-time-sharing parent or is the non-time-sharing parent's therapist.

CHAPTER 8
Conjoint Sessions and Effecting Change

I wonder if what makes a family isn't doing everything right all the time, but, instead, giving a second chance to the people you love who do things wrong.

Jodi Picoult (2012, p. 356)

Initial Non-Time-Sharing Parent–Child Contact

Prior to the first conjoint session, the therapist allows the children some control and power in the reunification process by having the children select where they would like to sit, and the activity in which they would like to engage for the session, for example. In some cases, an in-session safety plan is implemented irrespective of the reality of a potential threat by the non-time-sharing parent, to heighten the child's sense of security. For cases where, despite the case being demarcated as ready for reunification, the therapist is not completely confident the parent is in good control of their feelings, particularly anger, the therapist may wish to inform the child in one of the individual sessions: "If I tell you to go, please leave the session, and go to therapy room B or the waiting room." A similar directive may be addressed to the non-time-sharing parent within their individual session, such that the non-time-sharing parent will be instructed to leave the therapy room upon an agreed directive or code phrase such as "please go retrieve the documents from the car."

Initial in-person contact between the non-time-sharing parent and the child often engenders anxiety in a child who has not spent time with a parent in recent weeks, months, or years (or ever). As stated previously, this anxiety may emanate from different sources. Irrespective of anxiety generated from the child's previous relationship with the non-time-sharing parent, children often become anxious in response to the separation. It is not uncommon for children to worry that the non-time-sharing parent is angry with them for the separation. This is not surprising given children's egocentric view of the world, their difficulty in understanding the motivations of others, and their difficulty in holding different feelings simultaneously for the same target (e.g., Harter, 1986).

Furthermore, if the time-sharing parent has attempted to collude with the child against the non-time-sharing parent, the time-sharing parent may attempt to place a negative spin on the reunification of the child, which may also heighten the child's anxiety. The initial sessions with the child individually and the non-time-sharing parent alone should address the child's concerns about this parent's anger; subsequently, at the first conjoint session, the child's fears regarding the non-time-sharing parent's potential for anger should be dispelled. It also may be helpful for a trusted neutral adult other than the time-sharing parent to bring the child to some of the earlier sessions with the non-time-sharing parent. A child's demeanor and receptivity to the process is often more inhibited when in the presence of the time-sharing parent than with neutral others, particularly if the child is concerned about the time-sharing parent's feelings regarding the other parent. As the time-sharing parent becomes more receptive to the process and the parents repair their relationship, the time-sharing parent is better able to facilitate transportation of the child to therapy sessions and out-of-session homework assignments. As delineated in Chapter 3 (see the section "Systematic Desensitization and Exposure-Based Therapy: Interventions Based in Classical Conditioning"), it is often helpful to conduct systematic desensitization with the child. For very anxious children and teens who have not seen the non-time-sharing parent for a while, the child may be shown pictures of the parent as an initial step, leading to writing letters, texts, or e-mails between parent and child, and then phasing in a phone conversation with the non-time-sharing parent during initial sessions. Subsequently a face time and then an in-person session may be effectuated. On occasion, resistant children are better able to avoid communication with the non-time-sharing parent than audio-only telephone contact. This is because they can use their facial expressions and body movements to communicate, without experiencing as much motivation to communicate verbally as they would via audio communication methods. If the therapist observes this to be happening, then they should switch from face-time communication methods to verbal ones until greater gains are made in the reunification process.

With respect to phone contact or if starting with in-person session time, the content of the session should be lighthearted or "chit-chatty" with the addition of board games to take the pressure off the child and create a warm and engaging atmosphere. At times, the therapist will need to give the child "permission" merely to listen to the parent without any pressure to speak. Occasionally, some children will initiate discussing the emotionally laden issues at the first session, even if they had not anticipated broaching these topics. It is important to have prepared the non-time-sharing parent for potentially affectively charged discussions and to have developed strategies for this parent to effectively address these dialogues, which include reflective listening and empathic communication, prior to the first conjoint session. It is essential for the non-time-sharing parent not to defend or offer explanations as to the choices they made, since this defensive stance can impede communication and alignment of the child with the parent.

Low-key initial contact to reduce pressure on the child and to develop a warm and engaging atmosphere within the conjoint sessions often includes the non-time-sharing parent bringing photo albums to the initial sessions. These albums should include the non-time-sharing parent with the child from previous years. This communicates several different messages: First, it validates for the child their importance to the non-time-sharing parent, which may also send a different message from the one they have been receiving from the time-sharing parent. Additionally, it demonstrates to the child that the non-time-sharing parent cares for the child to such a degree that they have kept pictures readily available of that child. Finally, these photographs almost always depict happier times in the family's life than currently.

Another useful initial activity for non-time-sharing parent and child is to develop a family tree which includes immediate and extended-family members. The non-time-sharing parent can provide interesting and perhaps unknown (to the child) information about the family members. The tree demonstrates to the child a sense of belonging and connectedness to the non-time-sharing parent. It also communicates to the child that they have biological or historical ties (if they have been adopted) to the non-time-sharing parent. Finally, the family tree may indirectly dispel family myths communicated to the child from the time-sharing parent and/or their family.

When information is presented to the child in these conjoint sessions that contradicts information that has been previously conveyed by the time-sharing parent and others, the child can become confused. It is extremely important for the therapist and the non-time-sharing parent to not place any subtle or direct blame on the time-sharing parent, but rather to normalize the discrepancy as a miscommunication or misunderstanding with no one at fault. Also, the therapist shifts the focus to encouraging the child to be a child and to allow the adults to address adult issues and problems.

Staying Present-Focused

Don't let yesterday use up too much of today.

Cherokee Proverb

Inherent in the field of behavior therapy is that the focus of intervention is on effectuating change in the present. To some degree this was true of the early cognitive behavior therapists as well; however, in recent years, cognitive behavior therapists have included an examination not only of core belief systems but their origins as well (Beck, 2011). For the most part, family reunification therapy is based on the present and attempts to repair current relationships. Reviewing the past may only serve to reinforce and strengthen the position of the child not wishing to have contact with the target parent and may justify the time-sharing parent's resolve to maintain the divide between target parent and child. Parents and children alike are often focused on reviewing past tribulations, and the therapist must block the temptation to "go to the past." The therapist can state, "I wish we could go to the past and fix XYZ," or "I wish we could go back in time and both your parents could have handled some things differently, but unfortunately we cannot go to the past to fix these things," and, further, "The goal is to help you and your parent do things differently now and to make changes."

It is prudent to demonstrate to the child that the focus is on assisting the non-time-sharing parent with learning different parenting strategies and doing things differently, as opposed to having that person change, since the child's mantra is often that "he or she will never change, and I have given him (or her) thousands of chances." The word *change* is often a trigger for this mantra, which can become an endless feedback loop with the conviction that the target parent "will never change."

Instructing Parents Not to "Take the Bait": Children's Attempts at Triangulating Parents

One of the common communication tactics of children and adolescents is to provide different information to each parent about the same event. Typically these events are emotionally charged and/or symptomatic of the conflict inherent in the parents' relationship. Motivation to present different information to each parent or caregiver arises from a number of different sources, including attempts to obtain reinforcement and to escape punishment. Furthermore, research suggests that children engage in biased contextual disclosures of information to their parents to obtain power within the family system and to maintain previously assigned roles, which feel more comfortable for the child. For example, if the adolescent has been given the power to make their own parenting decisions such as whether or not they go to school on specific days when with the time-sharing parent, they are going to be disinclined to spend time with the non-time-sharing parent who enforces school attendance. Similarly, children may engage in these differential disclosures to parents in response to loyalty pressures, such as telling the time-sharing parent they had a miserable time or that they were bored with the non-time-sharing parent, when the children were actually observed to engage in upbeat and energetic play as well as spontaneous affection with the non-time-sharing parent.

While there is less available data regarding specific parent–child communicative exchanges during divorce and other familial disruptions, there is research that indicates parents may disclose their thoughts and feelings about the other parent and the couple or family disruption directly to the child (Afifi, 2003; Afifi, McManus, Hutchinson, & Baker, 2007). In fact, some research indicates that parents may disclose their dissolution-related stress, which has the potential to bind the parent and child closer while simultaneously, creating greater stress or maladjustment for the child. In some cases, this disclosure creates a loyalty bind for the child. This in turn can create emotional pressure, sometimes wittingly induced, and on other occasions, unintentionally induced.

Presenting a Unified Front

Met with mom and met with dad. The only thing they have in common is a son named Dallas, and I am not even sure it's the same kid.

Colby Schepps, Doctoral Student

Contingent on the circumstances of the particular reunification therapy case, the therapist may include the time-sharing parent in a number of the conjoint sessions with the non-time-sharing parent and child. The reasons for incorporating the time-sharing parent are to address specific family issues and enhance communication so that everyone is "on the same page" and for the parents to model a unified front for the reunifying child. Not only does the inclusion of coparenting sessions close the loopholes that youths often attempt to create to obtain whatever they want by playing parents against each other, but also children can learn adaptive problem solving via observation or modeling. Bandura (1969) was one of the first scientists to suggest individuals learn vicariously through demonstrations by others. A child refusing contact with the non-time-sharing parent due to loyalty to the time-sharing parent may be able to dismantle this loyalty stance when they observe the time-sharing parent interacting amicably with the non-time-sharing parent. In fact one adolescent girl was observed to refer to her mother as a traitor when mother was positively communicating with the non-time-sharing father. Initially, the girl perceived her mother had betrayed her. Over time, her anger disappeared and she reunified with her father.

In fact, it is important that before the therapist includes both parents together in-session with the child, the therapist works initially with both parents without the child present. Not only does this format lend itself to the instruction of new coparenting and communication skills, but it also allows the therapist to assess the level of conflict and acrimony between the parents, which should be addressed prior to placing the child in a session with both parents together, lest the parents engage in open disagreement or strife in the presence of the child. Research demonstrates that parental conflict in the presence of the child impacts them adversely; in fact, interparental conflict drives children's psychological adjustment during parents' dissolution proceedings over and above time-sharing schedules, especially once a child reaches the age of 4 years (e.g., McIntosh, Smythe, & Kelaher, 2013; McIntosh, Smythe, Kelaher, Wells, & Long, 2011). Furthermore, the parents' acrimonious feelings toward each other often drive parent–child estrangement; consequently, therapists may find themselves in the position of primarily repairing the co-parenting relationship, which then has a positive cascading effect on the parent–child relationship. In these circumstances, once the parents' relationship is positively addressed, improvements in parent–child relationships are noted with minimal parent–child intervention.

Additionally, during these coparenting sessions, the therapist may assist the parents in implementing a parenting behavioral plan (contract) as described in Chapter 5, to reduce the child's resistance to time-sharing with the parent, and/or for those children who are time-sharing with the non-time-sharing parent, to enhance the child's positive behavioral exchanges during parent–child interactions.

"More Is More"

Frequent spurts of between-session contact between child and non-time-sharing parent can reduce anxiety and increase the propensity for contact between the child and non-time-sharing parent. This is particularly important for younger children, who have a restricted conception of time. However, irrespective of the child's age, frequent contact units can promulgate reunification. Phone contact is useful in facilitating episodic contact. In these cases, the time-sharing parent can set a kitchen timer for discrete periods of time such as for 5 minutes so the child knows when they have met the five-minute phone call criterion. The timer also enables the time-sharing parent to extricate themselves from the child and non-time-sharing parent's telephone interaction, since the timer serves as the time monitor and not the time-sharing parent. Between session live contact with child and parent is effectuated through homework assignments.

Homework: A Necessary Tool

The ability to transfer training and the acquisition of skills to a more natural environment is best observed in a realistic setting apart from the therapy session. After the parent and child have had an opportunity to interact in sessions, the child's anxiety is abated, their resistance tempered, and new communication and parenting skills are obtained, then the parent and child are assigned various homework assignments with increasing amounts of contact. For example, initial, low-level-contact homework assignments include attending movies or theater productions. These types of assignments are encapsulated in discrete periods of time and with a low level of pressure for direct interaction. Moderate-contact homework assignments include those that require some direct interaction, are bound by the structure of the activity, and often have a demarcated end goal, such as miniature golf and bowling. A higher level of moderate contact homework assignment includes those that are time-limited and activity-focused, with direct interaction, such as eating a meal at a restaurant. Finally, high-level contact activities are those that require a significant amount of interaction between parent and child, which are not bound by the structure of an activity, nor have a specific end goal. Generally, the length of these assignments increases within each level domain and with each exposure. If the child cannot decide on, or is hesitant to select, homework activities, Appendix B includes examples of activity sheets that can be photocopied, cut-up, and placed in a container. The child blindly draws one of the activities from the receptacle. Possible outings should be ones that both non-time-sharing parent and child endorse, and ones that do not require the affirmation of the time-sharing parent. As an example of the latter, if a 12-year-old wished to learn scuba diving, the non-time-sharing parent would have to obtain assent from the time-sharing parent, given the inherent risk involved in the activity.

In some cases, ancillary individuals are incorporated into the homework assignments to enhance compliance and reduce anxiety. For cases incorporating adjunctive adults into the extra-session assignments, the successfulness of these projects is maximized when selecting these adults as a function of treatment goals, family system dynamics, and child and parent variables. For example, in cases where historically the time-sharing parent has interfered during time-sharing exchanges, the therapist should recommend that the time-sharing parent not be involved in the transition for the homework assignments and further that, should a third party be needed in such a case, a family member close to the time-sharing parent should not be selected either as this ancillary adult. The use of independent professional supervisors is often useful in this regard, as their neutrality can counterbalance the tenor of the interpersonal climate, allowing the child to have the freedom to interact with the non-time-sharing parent without direct or indirect pressure from the time-sharing parent or their relative or friend. The supervisor becomes an impartial observer, providing valuable feedback to the therapist. On occasion a neutral supervisor may be recommended for initial visits to protect the non-time-sharing parent from false allegations levied by an estranging time-sharing parent.

When assigning non-time-sharing parent and child activities, the therapist may request that the child keep a journal or generate notes regarding "what worked" and "what needs work" in the parent–child interaction, at the completion of the outing. These notes are subsequently used in reunification therapy sessions to affect change. By assigning this tracking task, the child is also appropriately empowered in the process to collect data for therapy, with an adaptive present and future focus.

Utilizing Interparental Electronic Communications to Effectuate Change

As discussed previously, telephone and audiovisual interactions, as well as text, e-mail, and other electronic communication means are useful methods to slowly reintroduce children to a non-time-sharing parent. Additionally, once children and non-time-sharing parents commence their interactions, telephone, and audiovisual (e.g., face time) contact are employed to facilitate dyadic contacts, between reunification sessions. Electronic communication is extremely important for parent and child in cases where they live significant distances from each other, which often prevents frequent real-time contact.

Obstacles During Family Treatment

It is not unusual for adverse blowback from the time-sharing parent after sessions where progress is made toward the reunification goal. This negative fallout can take a number of forms including difficulty in scheduling continued therapy sessions, complaints by the time-sharing parent that the process "is not working" or the child is suffering ill effects (despite evidence to the contrary), and/or motions filed with the court to have either the reunification therapist removed or reunification therapy ceased all together. Furthermore, during family treatment, it is not unusual for resistant time-sharing parents to up-the-ante during the process by expressing concerns the child may run away, commit suicide, or fail school (purposefully or as a concomitant of the process). Attempts to insulate the process to avoid these adverse repercussions include reinforcing the child for their maturity and excellent communication skills, as well as reinforcing the time-sharing parent for effective parenting and strength in the face of their self-perceived adversity. Assisting either the child or the time-sharing parent with identifying areas of the process where they do have control while simultaneously reaching the end goal of reunification can propel the therapy forward.

Elements of strategic family therapy such as Jay Haley's ordeal therapy (Haley, 1984) are often useful for the resistant time-sharing parent who is delaying the scheduling of or even canceling the scheduled sessions. The implicit message from the time-sharing parent is one of resistance to the process. The ordeal underscores the therapist's message of the importance of the reunification process. So, for example, in these cases, the therapist may express concern about the lapse in treatment and schedule two or more sessions for the same week, or require the time-sharing parent to participate more frequently in the therapy than previously.

The non-time-sharing parent may become impatient with the process, especially in cases where this parent feels the breach in the child–parent relationship was completely unjustified. They may communicate with the therapist that they wish to abdicate the process and that they will leave the decision up to the child to return to the relationship when they reach the age of majority. Educating the non-time-sharing parent about the lack of research to support the viability of spontaneous reunification and the risks inherent in waiting it out, is critical. The use of motivational interviewing and instruction in problem-solving methodologies is helpful in reengaging the non-time-sharing parent in the process. At times, it may be useful to contact the extremely resistant parent's attorney to have them assist the parent in engaging or reengaging in the process. Although it is generally best to have, as a rule, both parties' attorneys present during phone conferences, to prevent splitting, there are some specific occasions when it may be more prudent to speak with only one side's attorney, to prevent the other party's attorney from prematurely overreacting, thereby disrupting the reunification process. When one parent is demonstrating interfering resistance during treatment, the therapist may not necessarily wish to have both parents' attorneys at an initial conference regarding this difficulty, as it could create an unnecessary problem should the nonresistant parent and their attorney learn of the other parent's potential disengagement from treatment and reunification in general. However, when all efforts have been exhausted to move the treatment forward, and the process has stalled, having both attorneys in a phone or in-person meeting will ultimately be necessary.

Including Other Professionals in the Process to Effectuate Change

The Guardian Ad Litem

For family law cases, a guardian ad litem is often the one who makes recommendations to the judge regarding the best interests of the child. The guardian ad litem collects information from multiple sources, including neutral and subjective collaterals, home visits, parent–child interaction observations, and documents such as medical and academic records. As a result of the need of the guardian ad litem to accrue a significant amount of information to formulate recommendations regarding time-sharing, they require information about reunification therapy progress and each individual's response to treatment. In fact, in many cases, it is the guardian ad litem who may have initiated the reunification process via the recommendation to the attorneys and/or court for the reunification therapy. There are a number of ways a guardian ad litem can be helpful to reunification therapy and its outcome.

Guardian Ad Litem as Observer

The reunification therapist can provide meaningful information to the guardian ad litem, which they will want to consider in making recommendations about time-sharing and access to the court. While therapists are typically protective of the boundaries between the legal profession and psychotherapy, as stated previously, in family law cases, this intervention is forensic in nature and hence the process and procedure is often distinct from that of traditional psychotherapy, including the abatement of confidentiality. However, this does not allow for the boundary to be entirely eradicated, as lack of complete trust between therapist and the parties will prevent the forging of a working relationship necessary to effect change. Alternately, given the training models of most psychotherapists, the tendency is to set rigid boundaries between the client and others, and hence the therapist may find themselves inadvertently excluding the use of others in the process, due to the entrenched limitations of privacy and confidentiality. The conduit of information between the guardian ad litem and therapist is blocked, hence not only does the therapist block the flow of information to the guardian ad litem, but also the therapist is not forthcoming with information either. With respect to the latter situation, family law cases often turn on the outcome of reunification efforts; hence the provision of information regarding reunification therapy progress to the guardian ad litem is crucial.

Reunification therapy information is provided to the guardian ad litem through a number of mediums. Typically, therapists and guardians ad litem communicate by telephone; however, one such conduit of this information is to include the guardian ad litem in sessions to observe the contact between child and the non-time-sharing parent, between the non-time-sharing parent and the time-sharing parent, and in the interaction between both parents simultaneously with the child. The effect of observing children run into a non-time-sharing parent's arms and beg to be held upside down by this parent, for example, is much more impactful than describing a positive interaction on the telephone, particularly when the time-sharing parent has spoken at length with the guardian ad litem as to how fearful the children are of the non-time-sharing parent and/or how scary the target parent is. The impact of direct observation on the guardian ad litem is particularly evident for those non-therapist guardians ad litem such as attorneys and lay people, and as such carries notable sway.

Guardian Ad Litem as Good Cop/Bad Cop

The guardian ad litem is able to assist with therapist leverage to effectuate reunification when there is child or time-sharing parent resistance. In these instances, the guardian ad litem positions themselves as the "bad cop" and discusses with the time-sharing parent potential ramifications should the child not engage in the prescribed contact with the non-time-sharing parent. This can commence at the beginning of treatment when even minimal contact between the child and non-time-sharing parent is prescribed (e.g., phone conversation), and can continue throughout treatment including when out-of-session in vivo contact is prescribed. By the guardian ad litem becoming the "bad cop," the contrast with the reunifying therapist heightens therapist affability in the time-sharing parents' eyes and often leads to the parent as well as the child selecting the path of least resistance, opting to work with the therapist to effectuate change in order to avoid possible adverse consequences.

Guardian Ad Litem and Therapist Mirroring the Parenting Dyad

At times it is useful for the guardian ad litem and therapist to mirror the ambivalence and approach–avoidance stance of the parenting dyad. The confusion this ambivalence engenders can also be highlighted. For both parents and child, a child's approach to this presentation cannot only yield useful information for the guardian ad litem but it can also be used to highlight the struggles the child is experiencing in their relationship with both parents. This demarcation not only serves to enhance the child's insight into the conundrum in which they are placed, but also functions as a vehicle by which to effectuate the selection of alterative problem-solving strategies, thereby enabling the child to extract themselves from the middle of their parents' conflict.

Guardian Ad Litem and Therapist as a Team

Another potential therapeutic practice which includes the guardian ad litem is to work together as a team with the therapist in support of the child. The team, together, empathizes with the child's taxing position and offers their support in assisting the child in overcoming the hurdles necessary to develop a positive relationship with their estranged parent. Both therapist and guardian give explicit directions to the child to remove themselves from the middle of their parent's conflict, to relinquish adult decision making, and to enjoy their childhood. The team also informs the child that they will address the problems with the parents and run interference between parent and child in an attempt to insulate the child from adult problems and interparental conflict. Children are given permission to contact the team should they need assistance in negotiating their parents' impediments that interfere in the children's ability to enjoy their childhood, extricate themselves from their parents' conflict, and abdicate their pseudo–adult decision-making role.

Children Who Cannot Separate From the Time-Sharing Parent for Reunification Therapy

In a small minority of cases, children may struggle to separate from their time-sharing parent and join the therapist in the therapy room. A useful technique to address this form of separation anxiety is based in the principles of shaping and graduated exposure, by having the time-sharing parent sit in the hallway outside of the therapy room door and to have the door completely open. As the child becomes more acclimated to the therapy room, the door is slowly closed, which may occur during the session as well as across sessions. An alternative to this approach is to have the door remain open and the parent slowly move their chair down the hall. One must consider privacy and confidentiality when engaging in these strategies, such that in some cases the topics of conversation with the therapist and child will be limited contingent on the degree of privacy available.

Other techniques include the use of reinforcement of adaptive behaviors regarding separation behaviors, such as giving stickers or small rewards for every 10 to 15 minutes of the session the child is able to cope effectively with being apart from the time-sharing parent. If the separation anxiety is related to the anticipated reunification with the non-time-sharing parent, it is extremely important to reassure the child that the non-time-sharing parent is not present at these initial sessions and to tell the child that the therapist will not surprise the child by including the non-time-sharing parent in the session without previously informing them. The therapist informs the child that they will always be informed as to when this parent will join the session.

Similar strategies can be used to assist the child in separating from the time-sharing parent to join the therapist with the non-time-sharing parent in the session. If the level of acrimony can be controlled between the parents, then the time-sharing parent may join initial sessions with the non-time-sharing parent and the child, to reduce the child's separation anxiety. Over time the time-sharing parent can be faded out from the therapy sessions, as the child becomes comfortable with the separation from this parent as well as relaxed with the non-time-sharing parent.

There are occasions after successful daytime time-sharing has been established where separation anxiety may prevent a child from overnight time-sharing with the non-time-sharing parent even once reunification has been successful. Addressing the anxiety through cognitive behavior principles including the instruction of coping strategies and systematic desensitization is recommended (Clementi & Alfano, 2014). Having the child remain with the non-time-sharing parent for longer periods of time in the evenings over time can diminish anxiety and enhance the child's comfort level with spending evening time with the non-time-sharing parent. On occasion, children may succumb to the natural consequences of a delayed departure by falling asleep or feeling too tired to make the trip back to the time-sharing parent's home.

Additionally, utilizing positive incentives for adaptive coping and spending the night with the time-sharing parent can enhance successful overnight time-sharing. For example, one parent may devise a treasure hunt for the child while the child is asleep so that in the morning they may search for treasure hidden by the non-time-sharing parent. Alternately, the non-time-sharing parent can schedule a fun night or movie night, for which the child may select an activity such as consecutively watching several movies, with the instruction that they can stay up all night and not go to sleep, and therefore they are not sleeping overnight. Once the child stays through the night, the negative mystery surrounding spending the night becomes obsolete, and they will have experienced success thereby diminishing anxiety and increasing self-efficacy. Finally, pets that travel with the child to the non-time-sharing parent's home may also reduce separation anxiety.

In cases where a child has never met their non-time-sharing parent and may not ever have known them, having both parents or a trusted caretaker in session with the child and non-time-sharing parent in the room for the initial session can be beneficial. These initial sessions should be light in tenor and fun in action; the time-sharing parent can eventually be faded-out from the sessions.

Use of Ancillary Strategies to Enhance Contact

To maximize the beneficial effects of, and outcomes for, reunification therapy, it is important to examine the child's inner and external environment for significant and meaningful stimuli and processes. There is a lengthy historical literature that highlights the importance of animals for children; in fact, in 1949, Leopold Bellak and Sonia Bellak discussed the shortcomings of the Thematic Apperception Test (TAT) in its use with children. They believed that children would more freely identify with animals, enhancing the probability of obtaining more meaningful material from children than that generated by the TAT; hence the Children's Apperception Test was created (Bellak & Bellak, 1949).

More recently, health care professionals have considered the use of animals not only as pet service animals but also in addressing a myriad of disorders including physical health issues (e.g., reducing blood pressure) and enhancing children's social and emotional functioning (e.g., Krause-Parello & Kolassa, 2016; Lee, Dakin, & McLure, 2016; Satiansukpong et al., 2008). Animal-assisted therapy has not only included domestic house pets such as dogs, cats, and birds, but even larger animals including horses and elephants. Lee et al. (2016) reviewed qualitative, experimental, and quasi-experimental research of animal-assisted therapy and concluded that there is demonstrated effectiveness of equine therapy in assisting adolescents with their communication and relationship skills as well as initial evidence for its utility in heightening children's and adolescents' emotional, social, and behavioral adjustment.

While the incorporation of a program of equine therapy or other structured animal therapies may be too time consuming and costly when conducting reunification therapy, since it is an additional expense, a modified use of animals in assisting the reunification process is viable. Non-time-sharing parents' pets known to the children and which have not had contact with the children because of the disruption in the parent–child relationship may be useful icebreakers and actually bridge the gap in the relationship between parent and child. In other cases, the child may bring their own pet from the time-sharing parent's home as a positive distraction from the looming issues of the time-sharing. For example three teenage boys' blatant resistance about visiting their father was a passive-aggressive attempt to punish him for leaving their mother. The boys had not had contact with their father for 10 months, and in fact, their 5-year-old Labrador had gone through her own distress at the loss of her three favorite playmates. At the first reunification session with the father he brought the dog, Madea, who was extremely excited to see the boys. This completely disarmed the sons, and they rolled around on the floor with her, asking their father many questions as to Madea's exploits in their absence.

Reunification therapists have also set up initial parent–child contacts at pet stores, riding stables, and the Humane Society. Additionally, once time-sharing resumes, the movement of the family pet with the child between homes can enhance transitions and give additional comfort to the child. For example, parents of a child struggling with particularly notable separation anxiety agreed to have his three cats move back and forth between the parents' residences during time-sharing exchanges, which facilitated a smooth transition during the resumption of time-sharing.

Developing New Traditions

Extended-Family Systems: Grandmother, Grandfather, and Others

Once sufficient progress has been made with respect to the reunification of the non-time-sharing parent with the child, it likely will be necessary to add to the process other important family members related to the non-time-sharing parent. This would include spouses and partners of the non-time-sharing parent as well as their children. Additionally, grandparents who might hold ancillary caretaking roles (e.g., assist in babysitting for the non-time-sharing parent) or those grandparents who have been eliminated from the child's life as part of the collateral damage in the divorce or family law litigation may also need to participate in the reunification therapy. At the very least, the reunification therapist may need to instruct the non-time-sharing parent as to how they should address their own parents in the reunification process. It is not unusual for grandparents to be hurt and angry about their grandchildren's refusal to time-share with their son or daughter, and with good intentions, they may attempt to intervene with their grandchildren's time-sharing refusal. Unfortunately, these non-time-sharing grandparent interventions are likely to fail, and the child may perceive the grandparent as aligning with the non-time-sharing parent.

The reintegration of grandparents and other relatives or close family friends may include the development of new traditions and family activities, while relying on historically embedded ones. For example, a mother and a father while married had staged a piñata for the children and prepared tamales on Christmas Eve with the grandparents in the marital home. Once divorced, the father and children changed the tradition to a beach volleyball tournament party, with relatives, and they included a piñata, tamales, and grilled hamburgers at the beach. The celebration was held either Christmas Eve Day or Christmas Day contingent on which day of the year the father was celebrating the holiday with the children per the parents' parenting plan. This became the newly reintegrated family's yearly holiday tradition.

Enhancing Attachment: Photography and Video Recording

When a parent has been separated from a child for many years, or when a father has never met his son or daughter, it is important to consider the attachment orientation of the parent to the child. Development of a family tree can enhance the cognitive integration of the child into the non-time-sharing parent's life; the tree also gives the child contextual meaning regarding belonging and identity with the non-time-sharing parent. Family photographs and audiovisual recordings are also vehicles to facilitate family contextual identity development and parent–child cohesion. In a longitudinal study by Main, Kaplan, and Cassidy (1985), the parent's internal model of attachment was significantly associated with the security of infant attachment over 5 years. These researchers also observed that early secure maternal attachment was associated with a child's emotional receptivity when viewing a family photograph. Behrens, Bahm, Li, and O'Boyle (2011) also perceived a link between maternal quality of attachment orientation and responsivity to their children's photographs. Furthermore, research indicates that those who have experienced loss of a loved one through death seek to maintain memory connections through photographs and other stimuli. Maintenance of a connection to the absent loved one can be self-validating and soothing (Moss, 2004). Photographs and video recordings of a child with their non-time-sharing parent help to bind the relationship and facilitate reunification.

In many cases, the child's hesitancy about accepting a photograph or recording of the child–parent interaction during reunification therapy and associated homework is evident due to a concern that their time-sharing parent will be hurt or angry. The therapist can intervene with the time-sharing parent to assist with the child's acquisition of these items. It is also important to inform the parents in the statement of understanding that photographs and audiovisual recordings are routinely collected for the purposes of facilitating the parent–child relationship.

Planned Termination of Reunification Therapy

For many reunifying groups including reunifying military parents, incarcerated parents and children, medically hospitalized parents, and parents of adult children, treatment is completed when the family together with the therapist agree that reunification goals have been met. In many cases, a similar resolution is obtained within family or dependency court. With agreed planned termination, parents and therapist may schedule follow-up sessions for maintenance of treatment gains. In highly contested and conflictual family law and dependency court cases, it is important to notify both parents' attorneys and the guardian ad litem that reunification therapy is completed and the child has been reunified with the parent(s). This serves as a signal for the legal professionals to finalize a time-sharing plan or the concluding elements of the case.

CHAPTER 9
Legal Processes During and After Treatment

While it is important to educate attorneys about the process and procedures of reunification therapy prior to treatment, it is not unusual for counsel to attempt to glean information from the reunification therapist *during* treatment. In fact, an attorney may attempt to subpoena the reunification therapist midtreatment for deposition. Similarly, it is not unusual for attorneys to wish to hold a conference with the reunification therapist at the very beginning of the process even prior to the therapist having held all initial sessions with the family members at the commencement of treatment. The attorney's motivation may be to advocate for their client with integrity, to posture in an attempt to obtain an attorney-perceived advantage with the therapist over opposing counsel, to demonstrate to their client their prowess and case aggressiveness, to attempt to add billable hours without a specific agenda, and/or to work through their own psychological schemas through their client's case.

It is extremely prudent of the therapist to have both parties' attorneys present, whether on the telephone or in person, when having discussions with either side. This prevents the risk of the therapist being triangulated by one attorney and party in the case; it also prevents the conferencing attorney from misconceptions and using the information against the therapist in legal proceedings as well as providing information out of context in the case. Furthermore, it communicates a stance of neutrality in the case on behalf of the therapist, leading to clearer objective evaluations regarding the process. With neutrality, there is a tendency toward heightened trust in the reunification therapist by both parents. As discussed previously in Chapter 8, on extremely limited occasions, the reunification therapist will benefit from a circumscribed communication with one party's attorney but only in an attempt to enlist the assistance of this partner's attorney in helping their client drive the reunification therapy forward without illuminating the problem to the other side which could have the potential to derail the reunification therapy process. Such circumscribed topics to be shared with one attorney include addressing a parent's resistance if multiple attempts have proven futile during treatment to enlist the cooperation of the parent, as well as ensuring that one parent who is in need of individual therapy is attending their own individual therapy or making a new recommendation that this particular parent receive treatment. This may be particularly important in situations where a therapist is not receiving a return call from a parent's individual therapist. Any reunification therapist's third-party communication should have as its primary, if not only, goal the propelling forward of the reunification therapy and thereby reunification of the child with the parent. The therapist should be attuned to the possibility that at times an attorney assisting with motivating their client may use information imparted by the therapist to posture their case and either directly or indirectly sabotage reunification therapy.

The therapist must caution the attorneys that should they be deposed or called to court to testify while the therapy is in progress, there is a chance that the reunification therapy will be rendered ineffective. This is because information disclosed at deposition or court may be directly or indirectly imparted to the child as well as breach the therapeutic relationship between parent or parents and therapist. With respect to the former, an angered residential parent may inform the child directly what was disseminated to others or use the information disclosed in deposition to coach the child. For example, if the reunification therapist describes a happy and excited child at non-time-sharing parent–child meetings and this bodes well for reunification but runs counter to the residential parent's plans, the time-sharing parent may tell the child that the therapist is an advocate for the non-time-sharing parent, or they cannot demonstrate happiness in the target parent's presence while in therapy, because this may be perceived that the child wants to be reunified with the non-time-sharing parent.

For example, a 9-year-old boy informed his reunification therapist, completely out of context of their immediate discussion, that the only reason he acts happy in the presence of his reunifying mother is because he is worried that his mother will be angry if he does not "fake happiness." Despite a solid working relationship between the child and the therapist, he could not delineate to the therapist, even in private, why he believed his mother would be angry, how she would express it, and why the reunification therapist would be ineffective in protecting him from her anger. Furthermore, his statement of concern about his mother's anger and faked happiness ran counter to the observations gleaned in-session, of spontaneous enjoyment and excitement during the parent–child interactions. Unfortunately, the therapist had previously testified at a hearing regarding the child's apparent genuine happiness when interacting with his mother. Given the timing and presentation of the child's disclosures regarding his faked happiness, it was highly probable that information disclosed by the therapist at the hearing was relayed to the child.

Similarly, another 8-year-old boy with his 10-year-old brother arrived at a session with his hair unusually meticulously coifed with hair product applied to hold his hair in place. After 10 minutes of play in the office with his father, he became very self-aware of his hair and with wide eyes, agitation, and notable anxiety, he attempted to smooth his hair. Despite the therapist's reassurance and his subsequent reengagement in play, approximately 30 minutes into the session the child departed from direct session interaction to a corner in the room requesting a mirror from the therapist, as his brother continued to play with the father. The therapist asked him about his concern regarding his hair and if there was a reason for his notable attention to grooming that day, such as plans for post-session. He replied that he merely preferred to be neat and clean. Yet, he concurrently prided himself in being an extremely active and athletic boy, responding with pride about being "rough and tumble" and when asked about the frequent bruising on his limbs, he would recount each wound as if they were badges of honor. When the psychologist told him "it was okay;" that he was allowed to have fun with his father, he relaxed and abandoned his tidiness concerns. Ultimately he disclosed that he "was not allowed to have fun" with his father because his mother would "lose in court." Evidently, his mother chastised him for appearing to have enjoyed the session with father, given his disheveled appearance, animated affect, and behavioral excitement.

In addition to the impact the deposition or other testimony has on the child and the potential for sabotage, testifying in family court during the reunification process can engender conflict between, and distrust by, the non-prevailing party for the reunification therapist. Hence, it becomes difficult to recover working relationships with that parent once the therapist has provided testimony. The reunification therapy contract should specify that if the therapist testifies, then they may no longer be able to serve as the reunification therapist. This is not always the case; however, the clients should be notified that this could be a potential outcome.

Translucent Legal Agendas (AKA Not-So-Transparent Agendas)

It is not unusual for the non-time-sharing parent to desire the elimination of the reunification therapist from the case when this parent perceives that the reunification therapist is not aligned with their own treatment goals and that the contact between child and non-time-sharing parent is insufficient, or is moving at a rate slower than that perceived to be necessary by this parent. The reunification therapist has a specified rationale for the designated contact and the rate of this contact. If the non-time-sharing parent is resistant to the plan, they may petition the court for a replacement therapist, which is sometimes not unexpected.

Also fairly common is when the non-time-sharing parent who has previously not been spending time with the child *is* pleased with the process, its rate, the observable outcomes, and the therapist, and yet the *time-sharing* parent petitions the court for a replacement reunification therapist, pleading to the court that reunification therapy is not working. Intuitively, if not explicitly, it would seem that if the reunification therapy was not working, then the one wishing to be reunified with their child would be the one campaigning to eliminate the reunification therapist, not the one who has all of the time-sharing and in effect does not want the time-sharing to occur. This is a red herring in order for the court to obtain a new therapist, one who hopefully will co-sign the resistant time-sharing parent's agenda of eliminating or reducing contact between the non-time-sharing parent and child.

"Less Is More"

Mental health practitioners are trained in a wide array of effective communication strategies that use both verbal and nonverbal modalities and are implemented for different therapeutic purposes, including assessment and evaluation (initial, ongoing, and after treatment), establishment and maintenance of therapeutic relationships, and dissemination of information (informed treatment). The "helping profession" tenor of the field orients the mental health practitioner toward assisting others in any way they can, which often includes provision of information via explanation. This is further compounded by the offensive (i.e., nondefensive) positions that attorneys often assume, given their profession, thereby placing others including the therapist on the defensive. Once positioned on the defensive, a common communication strategy is to overly provide information. Unfortunately, by excessively disseminating information to attorneys, one may unwittingly and innocently provide information that may be taken out of context and used against the therapist and the therapy. The more information provided, the greater the risk for therapists to unwittingly deliver a legal arsenal to the attorney. *Less information* provided to nonclient third parties, particularly legal personnel, is often rewarded with *more therapeutic benefit* for the family.

CHAPTER 10
Special Topics

Preparing Children When Reunification Is Not Possible

As the therapy progresses, there are cases where it becomes clear that the reunification process is not possible due to concerns regarding the non-time-sharing parent's and/or the time-sharing parent's situation and/or mental health. With respect to the latter, issues related to anger management, substance abuse, undocumented major mental illness, or known mental disorders that are not sufficiently managed, are examples. Related or not to these potential issues, there are occasions when the non-time-sharing parent abandons their legal case and terminates treatment and occasionally abates an anticipated relationship with the child.

Despite a child or adolescent claiming that they do not wish to have a relationship with the non-time-sharing parent, the magnitude of the impact of a parent relinquishing their relationship with a child cannot be overstated. In very extraordinary circumstances, a child is relieved or satisfied with the loss of a parent in this manner. But most feel discarded, abandoned, and deserted; the impact on their self-esteem can have untoward effects. It further validates the child's belief that the non-time-sharing parent never really cared (a message that may have been erroneously perpetuated by the estranging time-sharing parent) or is confirmation that the time-sharing parent is a horrendous parent and/or mentally ill. Ironically, while the child feels despair and other painful feelings, the non-time-sharing parent is bewildered and stunned when learning of these feelings, as that knowledge runs counter to the child's expressed wishes of never wanting to see that parent again. When a non-time-sharing parent abdicates their relationship with the child, it is important to work with the child and, in many cases, with the time-sharing parent in addressing this impasse and also with the child's individual therapist, if not contraindicated.

In the most extreme cases, a serious psychopathology of the time-sharing parent, who has engaged in extreme interference or estrangement of the child from the non-time-sharing parent in an attempt to thwart the non-time-sharing parent's relationship with the child, may have a deleterious effect on the child, notwithstanding intervention by the therapist or the court. Despite exhausting all efforts to reunite a parent with a child, in some of these cases, the reunification may be unsuccessful, and to continue with the process, the child could be damaged further by the estranging parent who has serious psychopathology, which drives their efforts at sabotaging the relationship between non-time-sharing parent and child. Also, in these particular circumstances, it is critically important to work with the child and, in many cases, with the child's individual therapist.

In cases where the parent has abdicated their parenting role, the abandonment of the child will need to be addressed in treatment, with a primary cognitive emphasis on the fact that the child is not responsible for that parent's desertion. Should this parent surreptitiously leave treatment and the child, there is a tendency for well-meaning caretakers and other adults to lie to the child about the whereabouts of that parent, in an attempt to protect the child's feelings. While this attempt at sparing the child from painful affects is seemingly innocuous, it may have potentially deleterious consequences, as children typically learn the truth via the direct communication "slippage" of others, by reading nonverbal cues and synthesizing seemingly incongruous communications or facts delivered in the lie, and by learning the truth via inadvertent or intentional eavesdropping.

The consequences of the child learning the truth in one of the aforementioned ways can be ruinous for a number of reasons. First, the trusted time-sharing parent may cause a fissure in their own trustworthiness with the child, thereby weakening the child's security and sense of stability with typically their only accountable parent. Second, the vehicle for the lie can contribute to the child's anxiety and fear or aversion regarding the replacement event for the parent's absence. For example, it is not unusual for parents to tell their children that their incarcerated or absent parent is sick or away on business. Hence, it places the child at risk of equating illness or work with a painful loss.

In cases where children were prepared for a temporary loss of their parents due to military deployment, or reunification plans were initiated in anticipation of the parent's return, the parent's death during deployment can have deleterious effects. Cohen and Mannarino (2011) found that most children who have lost a military parent to death have grief reactions, and some have traumatic grief reactions. They suggest that traumatic reactions to a military parent's death likely emanates from the unique features of the death, including the child being unprepared for the possibility of loss of life at deployment, the notable rate of suicide concomitant with the parent's PTSD, military rituals and funerals, viewing body disfigurement or medically related interventions when visiting the parent in the hospital, political protests, and notification via uniformed officers approaching the residence, and for divorced military parents, the child learning of the death from third parties or via the media. These researchers advocate for the use of trauma-focused CBT to assist these children (Cohen & Mannarino, 2011). The shift in focus of therapy includes grief work with the child and their other parent.

Similarly, the death of psychiatrically or medically ill parents, including those with addiction problems, can have similarly detrimental effects for the child. It is not unusual in these cases for the reunification therapist to be the last person associated with that parent and the parent–child relationship, and therefore, the therapist becomes associated for the child with the deceased parent. Due to this association, the child often elevates the therapist to a special status, considering that the therapist was the only one to understand the mother and father and the unique issues in their relationship. In effect the therapist belongs to a small club of two after the parent's death. It is imperative for the therapist to engage with the children to determine the impact of the death (e.g., grief vs. traumatic grief) and to assist in clarifying and delineating the feelings the children are experiencing, including not only sadness and pain but also anger and guilt. The latter two are emotions particularly evident in parent suicide (Cohen & Mannarino, 2011) but have also been observed in those children whose parents have died due to drug overdose. In these cases, the child believes that they are responsible for not intervening in a manner that would have saved the parent's life.

Reunifying children may express guilt for their resistance in reestablishing a relationship with their now deceased parent. Many children will spontaneously report that they were happy if not relieved to have had the opportunity to reunify with their estranged parent prior to their death, while some will experience anger regarding it being "too little, too late." It is important to use the strategies in this book based in cognitive behavior, client-centered, and family system therapies to assist the children with the myriad of feelings they have when their parent dies. The therapist can discuss methods to memorialize that parent for the child, including utilizing the photographs taken in reunification sessions and outings to create a new special book of photographs.

Three teenage boys who had been reunifying with their morbidly obese mother, spoke openly and angrily about her eating disorder, which contributed to her being several hundred pounds overweight; they worried she would die prematurely. When she learned that their anger masked fear and pain, her defensiveness about her weight decreased, and she began to take serious action to manage her health, including weight loss. While the boys and mother made significant gains in therapy, ultimately she had a stroke and initially lost her mobility and communicative skills. All three boys were relieved they had mended their relationship with her and were actively engaged in assisting in her care in an appropriate manner (as teenagers and not adults). Eventually she regained much of her functioning, and the boys and mother re-established adaptive mother–son relationships, which was particularly important as the children were all anticipating imminently leaving home for college, signifying another breach in the parent–child relationship, despite it being a developmentally appropriate separation.

Reunification Therapy With Other Primary Caretakers

In an ever-changing society, children may have more than two primary caretakers, and while the law may not allow for the time-sharing of additional caretakers such as step-parents and grandparents, there may be circumstances in which the inclusion of other caretakers is necessary for the child's health and well-being. The reunification therapist may have an opportunity to address this in reunification therapy. In fact, the inclusion of step-parents and step-siblings may be a necessary, if not required, component of the reunification process, since the child may include these individuals in the non-time-sharing parent's camp and reject them as well, or alternatively, a child may never have met these other family members. Integration of these others in the child's life through a therapeutic setting is critical prior to the child establishing regular time-sharing with the non-time-sharing parent.

Step-parents may not understand the reunification process as thoroughly as the biological parents, nor have the same affinity for the child as the biological parent, which can contribute to a step-parent's impatience. Just as the non-time-sharing parent does not have leverage in parenting the child, a step-parent not only does not have parenting leverage but may also be an odd-person-out. They have less power than the biological parents, particularly if they are partnered with the non-time-sharing parent. Step-parents should be the fun-time parents and should not be involved in any adversity with the step-children, including discipline.

Non-time-sharing parents' relatives and significant others may show anger toward the child (and their time-sharing parent) for the perceived emotional toll they have taken on the non-time-sharing parent. It is important to educate these individuals regarding the process, as well as the impact their own behavior may have on the child. Blaming the child and the time-sharing parent will only serve to facilitate further estrangement. Unfortunately, many of these relatives will have already learned the consequences of their behavior from their own experiences of being rejected by the child. Explaining and demonstrating to the relatives that the child is a victim can greatly assist in adaptively reorienting the blaming relatives. Therefore, conjoint sessions between the non-time-sharing parent and their relatives and/or significant others are critical prior to including the children in the interaction with these ancillary family members.

Reunification Therapy When Physical Distance Is a Factor

It is not unusual for physical distance to have been a factor in the breach of a parent–child relationship, whether this was a result of hospitalization, incarceration, parent's job, military deployment, or the nature of the parents' relationship. Parents who endure relative lengthy hospitalizations for unique physical conditions or specific mental health treatments that require relocation out of the child's accessible community fall within this domain. Not only does the nature of the condition and the treatment often prevent easy access of child to parent, but the physical distance is a barrier as well. In these cases, bridging the gap with telephone voice or electronic voice and face communications can facilitate the maintenance of the relationship; however, for some medical patients and many mental health patients, family contact is often restricted or prohibited in totality. The absence of the parent from the child's life is addressed individually with the child as well as with the child and time-sharing caretaker together; furthermore, the caretaker, often together with the therapist may work with the hospital or treatment facility regarding scheduling of electronic parent–child contact. In some cases, the child, contingent on their age, may be included on the telephone in reunification sessions or mental health sessions with the non-time-sharing parent.

Similarly with incarcerated parents, the distance of the facility may render it extremely difficult for children to visit their parents. The therapist together with the caretaking adult can develop a visitation plan with the facility, as many have family visitation days that are geared toward the inclusion of children. The caretaker can post a calendar for the children, so they can predict when they will be visiting with their incarcerated parent. It is also useful for the caretaker to assist the children in assembling photo albums of the absent parent. Honesty about the reason for the incarceration is critical lest the child learn through family gossip, social media, the Web, or "thin walls," information that is ostensibly the truth about the incarceration, which may differ from information relayed by the primary caretakers. The potential for a child's adverse response and poor adjustment to the incarceration is heightened via a breach of trust by the child's residential caretaker.

In some cases, fathers first learn that they have fathered a child when the mother files a motion with the court for child support. While the mother has attempted to conceal the knowledge of the child's existence from the father, she is often unaware that once the court is petitioned for child support, the father is legally notified with respect to the child support motion; subsequently, the existence of the child is no longer concealed. Alternately, mothers who file for public assistance are required to name the father on the application, and government agencies will generally contact the father. Once contacted, the father in these cases frequently counterpetition the court for time-sharing, access, and decision-making rights.

For other cases, the dissolution of the parents' partnership may include one parent relocating to another state, and with this relocation, abandonment and other strong feelings emerge for the child. Once these feelings have been addressed by the therapist, they must also be addressed immediately with the non-time-sharing parent and child together. The reunification therapist prepares the non-time-sharing parent for this joint session by imparting information concerning the child's feelings. Travel costs may limit the frequency of in-person reunification sessions. Typically, the first initial session with the physically distant non-time-sharing parent and therapist is held by telephone given the physical distance. Initial contact with child and parent is graduated from letters sent between parties but through the therapist initially, to in-session telephone screen face contact, and finally in-session live contact.

Immersion Interventions: Workshops and Retreats

In recent years, retreats, camps, and workshops have evolved to assist parents and guardians in repairing the parent–child relationship. These programs include primarily the non-time-sharing parent and children, but for some programs, the time-sharing parent is also included. Some programs are held in a group format including multiple families simultaneously, while other retreats are held with the individual family only. Many of these residential programs typically are 4 to 7 days in length. Controversy has arisen regarding lengthier programs that remove the child completely from the time-sharing parent for weeks and months at a time. According to Dallam and Silberg (2016), for many children who have been abused or traumatized, removing them from their time-sharing parent can have further traumatizing effects. This is particularly pertinent in cases where adequate assessment and treatment of traumatized children have not been rendered and reunification therapy includes the perpetrator (Dallam & Silberg, 2016).

According to Dallam and Silberg (2016) these immersion programs, while often claiming efficacy, also maintain that they are not treatment programs but rather educational centers, thereby circumventing the ethical requirements of treatment. It is evident that some of the programs are led by non-professional volunteers, but there are also reputable programs professionally managed that have demonstrated some scientific efficacy, with treatment gains maintained across time (e.g., Reay, 2015). Despite promising results with respect to some immersion programs, for many families the costs of these programs are untenable, because the expense is not limited to the service itself but also includes travel and time off work.

Despite the limitations with retreats, a reunification therapist may cluster reunification sessions to be held locally and daily (after school and work) on an out-patient basis to facilitate cost-effective reunification therapy, which is particularly appealing to those parents who travel great distances (e.g., across continents) for reunification and reunification therapy. However, if the child has significant anxiety and oppositionality problems, the clustering of sessions is contraindicated, because the child will not have had a sufficient opportunity to practice the copings skills and cognitive behavior interventions necessary for anxiety reduction and effective coping, nor will the parent have had an opportunity to practice parent training strategies to address resistance.

Reunification of Infants and Very Young Children With Their Parents

For many of the cases of reunifying infants and very young children with their parents, reunification is in actuality a *unification,* in the sense that the child may never have had a relationship or contact with the non-time-sharing parent. Initial contact for very young children and babies should include relatively brief but frequent interactions with the non-time-sharing parent. Frequent contact is necessary given the underdeveloped memory traces in a young child's development (Piaget, 2000). The timing and length of contact at these meetings should be determined by the child's temperament and individual needs. For example, for a child who requires more sleep than a typical infant, the scheduling and length of the visits with the non-time-sharing parent should be adjusted accordingly.

Given the frequency of contact between parents in these cases, as well as the likelihood of heightened protection by the time-sharing parent over a very young and essentially vulnerable child, it becomes particularly incumbent on the clinician to reduce the conflict between the parents and/or inoculate the parents against negative engagement that can occur in the child's presence. Research has demonstrated that even very young babies (and in fact even those in utero) can absorb environmental stressors, including interparental incendiary disagreement (Merlot, Couret, & Otten, 2008). Sessions that include both the non-time-sharing parent and young child held daily or several times a week initially can heighten attachment and assist with reunification. In fact, the American Academy of Matrimonial Lawyers' Child-Centered Residential Guidelines (2015) for parenting plans for infants indicate frequent parent–child contacts as important to facilitate attachment and healthy relationships between the child and both parents.

For very young children who have receptive language skills, explanations that take into account the child's developmental age, regarding the relationship of the reunifying parent to the child may be needed in many cases. For example, a 3-year-old girl, through the variety of her mother's romantic partnerships, believed that she had two fathers including her current step-father and the mother's previous and absent boyfriend with whom she developed an attachment. Unfortunately, the mother's solution to dissolving her relationship with that absent boyfriend was to completely eradicate him from both her and the child's life, leaving the girl to grieve. Subsequently, reunification was initiated with the biological father and daughter, whose understanding was then that she had three different fathers (mother's boyfriend, step-father, and biological father) with three different names, all versions of "father." The absence of the first father known to the child was addressed in the context of family therapy with both parents and child, to assist the child with her grief and to inoculate the daughter from worry that her reunifying biological father would also disappear.

CHAPTER 11
Fundamental Treatment Plan

This chapter presents a fundamental treatment plan, which, while structured for parents dissolving their relationship, can be modified for other groups, including incarcerated, institutionalized, or military parents.

Reunification Therapy for Dissolved Parental Relationships

Pretreatment

For family law and dependency court cases: At initial contact, it is important to request and obtain a court order for the reunification work. Furthermore, the statement of understanding, as delineated in Chapter 4, can be sent either via e-mail or by fax to the parties. At this telephone screening, it is important to ascertain clearance for participation in the reunification process. The process of family reunification therapy, including lack of confidentiality, should be explained at this screening.

Treatment Sessions

Week 1

Session 1 (intake session), with the estranged parent or caretaker: In addition to the information garnered for a general intake, the therapist also gathers general background information and information specific to the history of the couple's relationship, the birth of the child, the child's functioning (as they know it – but they may have limited knowledge in this regard), the course of their relationship, and factors regarding the dissolution of the parents' or caretakers' relationship. Information is gathered concerning the targeted parents' perspectives of the barriers to the parent–child relationship and their perceptions of the other parent's or caretaker's roles, their own role, and the children's role in the development and maintenance of the barriers to the relationship. This often includes undue influence by others such as step-parents, romantic partners of the parents, grandparents, and other extended-family members. If the estranged parent has had some minimal contact with the child recently, the composition of the contact, including what type of contact (e.g., over the phone or face to face), the content (what is discussed, what did they do), frequency, and quality, is addressed as well as the strengths and weaknesses of this contact. The impact of any cultural diversity variables is also addressed, such as in the case, for example, of a child who is a first-generation Asian Indian American, and who may have struggles with their non-time-sharing parent that are culturally based, and these issues may be a potential barrier to the relationship.

At this session, the therapist should have the parent sign a release of information for the therapist to be able to speak with appropriate collateral sources. If the child and the non-time-sharing parent employ individual therapists, the reunification therapist must speak to both of these individuals prior to having the parent and child interact together. It is best to speak to these other therapists as soon as possible. If available, the time-sharing parent's therapist should also be consulted early in the process. It is also imperative for the therapist to speak with the guardian ad litem early in this process, if one has been assigned to the case. When there is family law litigation occurring for these reunifying families, in some states, neither the parties nor the therapist can waive confidentiality of the child's privileged information (e.g., from therapy). In these states, only the judge can waive confidentiality.

The therapist should also spend time delineating for the parent the composition of reunification therapy, including the general plan and its components. The therapist should also cover the limitations of the therapist's role such that while time-sharing can occur at some point in the process, as instructed by the therapist for homework assignments, this does not mean the therapist can recommend specific time-sharing schedules for a parenting plan either used as part of a marital settlement agreement or for court. The statement of understanding is reviewed at this session.

Session 2 (intake session), with the residential parent or caretaker: In this session, the therapist gathers the same information as was gathered from the estranged parent, but this time from the time-sharing parent or caretaker. The therapist gathers information concerning the time-sharing parent's perspectives regarding the barriers to the parent–child relationship and their perceptions of the other parent's or caretaker's roles, their own role, and the children's role in the development and maintenance of the barriers to the relationship. This often includes undue influence by others such as stepparents, romantic partners of the parents, grandparents, and other extended-family members.

The therapist should delineate for the time-sharing parent or caretaker the composition of reunification therapy, including the general plan and its components. The therapist should also cover the limitations of the therapist's role, such that, while time-sharing may occur at some point in the process as instructed by the therapist for homework assignments, this does not mean the therapist can recommend specific time-sharing schedules in a parenting plan used as part of a marital settlement agreement or for court. The statement of understanding is reviewed at this session.

As is the case with the non-time-sharing parent, the therapist has the parent sign a release of information for the therapist to speak with appropriate collateral sources.

Session 3: The therapist meets with each child living at home (even if they are not the target child for reunification) as an initial session. The therapist must establish a relationship with the child via reflection and validation, while gathering information from the child. The therapist commences with topic areas that are important to them, as gleaned from the previous parent sessions, such as their school activities, extracurricular activities, social activities, and pets. The therapist listens for the topic of discussions the child divulges to assess their anxiety about the process, or whether or not they are being unduly influenced not to see their estranged parent. It is important to ask the child if they know who the therapist is and what they do. Listen for hidden agendas. Then ask them, "What did your parent tell you about coming today?" Also clarify the therapist's role, informing the child that the therapist is to assist their family so they can have "good relationships with both parents," and if appropriate, one of the goals is "to help their parents get along better."

Most children grow weary of (at the very least), and are adversely affected (at worst) by, being triangulated by their parents' conflict, even if they are aligned with the time-sharing parent. One of the goals of therapy is the child's removal from their parents' conflict (i.e., to get them out of the middle) and to allow the parents to address their own problems with each other. It is likely that the therapist will have to address the child's ambivalent feelings about being shielded from their parents' problems, such that, while they would very much desire to be shielded from their parents' conflict and their parents' problems, they are drawn to desiring to know all that is being contemplated and discussed between their parents. This is likely a coping device to reduce anxiety by heightening predictability (if one knows what is to occur, then one can better prepare for it).

By the end of the first week, the therapist should have consulted with the guardian ad litem, if there is one assigned to the family. Also, the child's and the non-time-sharing parent's therapists should be consulted, hopefully by this time, if not, then by the end of the second week.

Week 2

Session 4: At this session, the therapist should again meet with each child living at home. They should continue to establish a working relationship with the child or children, working with them individually at first. The therapist decides whether to include multiple siblings together for a segment of the session. Sometimes the segregation of the siblings from each other can be beneficial in assisting the therapy to move forward, as often the most resistant child can attempt to stage a campaign for the other siblings to thwart reunification therapy.

In this phase, the therapist assesses the child's anxiety levels. Anxiety may be specific to the reunification process, in that children typically worry that their target parent is angry with them for not having seen them. Alternately, children may be anxious because they want to see or spend time with the non-time-sharing parent and are fearful of the impact reunification will have on the time-sharing parent. Or the child's anxiety may be related to the parent–child relationship prior to the divide in the relationship. In some cases, anxiety can be a function of all three sources. The therapist develops a hierarchy of triggers for the anxiety and assesses the origins and stimuli and events that are maintaining the anxiety. Additionally, the therapist assesses the child's coping skill set so that this can be addressed appropriately. If the child already has an individual therapist, the reunification therapist calls the individual therapist to ascertain the issues being addressed in individual therapy, to coordinate treatment, and to prevent duplication of services.

Week 3

Session 5: The therapist again works with each child individually, assisting with anxiety reduction as needed, and if not already being addressed in their individual therapy. This may include teaching PMR with guided imagery, deep breathing, imaginal systematic desensitization, and/or cognitive restructuring with the implementation of specific adaptive self-statements.

The therapist develops a list with the child with respect to what they would like the alternate parent to know about themselves and what they would like to know about the other parent. This serves two purposes. With respect to the former, the child has an opportunity to be heard and validated by the other parent for the person they are. With respect to the latter, this forces the child to step outside of themselves and to consider the other person's perspective, thereby creating greater flexibility in their thinking. It also can help dispel erroneous beliefs about the non-time-sharing parent that may cause the child anxiety.

For example, a mother was arrested in the presence of her 6-year-old for driving with her daughter while under the influence of alcohol. Despite being discharged from jail within 48 hours, after making bond post arraignment, she was not allowed to have contact with her child. She entered drug rehabilitation as part of her plea bargain and did not serve any jail time (other than two nights after her initial arrest, prior to bonding out of jail). Due to the reason for her arrest and vigorous family law litigation, she was prevented from seeing her child or speaking with her child even in a supervised setting for 2 years. It was not until this session when therapist and child were developing a list of questions for the mother that it was revealed that the child assumed her mother was in jail for the entire 2 years, because the last time she saw her, she was being led away by police in handcuffs.

Additionally during this session, therapist and child together develop a separate list of concerns the child would like to address with the parent, including behaviors the parent previously demonstrated that caused them emotional pain and anxiety. The therapist explains to the child that this last segment of the list is typically not covered on the same day as the first session with the child and non-time-sharing parent. Additionally, the therapist and the child develop a list of fun things they would like to do with the parent and fun things they previously did with the parent. The purpose of developing these lists of activities is twofold. First, as an assessment it can help the therapist delineate the level of resistance regarding contact with the non-time-sharing parent. So for example, if the child relays that their non-time-sharing parent never did anything fun with them and were not ever capable of engaging in fun activities, the therapist has a greater understanding of the child's cognitive orientation to the process.

The second purpose of developing the list of potential fun activities is so the therapist can determine the child's preferences regarding activities to engage in with the non-time-sharing parent. Such preferential knowledge can assist in treatment planning and, in particular, for the between-session contact homework assignments that will be assigned to the non-time-sharing parent and the child.

In this session, a plan of action needs to be discussed in the event the child feels uncomfortable in the initial telephone session with the non-time-sharing parent. Furthermore, in anticipation of future sessions, the therapist and child should discuss a safety plan for sessions (sit near the door, get up and leave, etc.). Similarly, a basic outline of a safety plan for the future when time-sharing resumes outside of session is discussed. These safety plans can assist the child cognitively to reduce their anxiety even if there is no immediate plan for the child to engage in time-sharing outside of the sessions. Similarly, in order to reduce the child's potential anxiety, the therapist communicates to the child that rules of no touching and no demands by the estranged parent for a hug or a kiss, as well as other primary rules, are in place for the non-time-sharing parent.

Session 6: The therapist meets with the time-sharing parent, who is instructed in reducing the exposure of the child to the antecedents of the anxiety response (e.g., eliminate negative descriptions about the time-sharing parent) and not modeling anxiety for the child. Educating the parent about social learning paradigms of transmission of anxiety (e.g., modeling) to the child is important. This parent is instructed in parent effectiveness training to assist the child in compliance. Specifically, instruction is given regarding behavioral contracting, including child compliance with engaging in rebuilding a relationship with the target parent. This cluster of behaviors can include compliance with attending therapy sessions in an adaptive manner, engaging in the therapy process through talking on the phone in session with the alternate parent, engaging in phone contact between sessions, and attending the outings, which are homework assignments.

The therapist must work earnestly to build a working relationship with the residential time-sharing parent. The therapist needs to validate the concerns of the residential time-sharing parent and to attempt to problem solve with the parent regarding their concerns. Often there is at least a kernel of reality in the concerns the parent has about the alternate parent having contact with the children, even if it is the relatively noninflammatory fact that the child and parent have not seen each other in many years, and the child may feel uncomfortable. The therapist reassures the time-sharing parent that as long as the therapist is involved in the case that they will be available to monitor the situation. Frequently, the time-sharing parent will catastrophize about the future when the therapist is no longer involved in the case. At this time different therapist involvement paradigms can be presented to the time-sharing parent for when reunification therapy is mostly completed, such as relatively lengthy treatment fading into monthly sessions or sessions every 2 months, for follow-up.

The therapist should prepare the time-sharing parent for the first phone or other initial contact between the non-time-sharing parent and child. They should also review the general plan for reunification therapy with the time-sharing parent.

Session 7: The therapist meets alone for a second time with the non-time-sharing parent and reviews with them the child's concerns. The therapist instructs the parent in adaptive communication and how to address the child's complaints without being defensive. The therapist pre-briefs the non-time-sharing parent about the content of the first contact session and the likely questions that they will be asked by the child, as well as assists with questions that they wish to ask their child. With respect to the latter, the therapist assists the parent in weighing the pros and cons of their questions and how to deliver the questions in a helpful manner.

At this session, the therapist implements parent effectiveness training, including instruction in behavioral contracting. The therapist reviews the primary initial session rules, including no touching and no demands for a hug, a kiss, or a statement of "I love you" to be made by the estranged parent.

Week 4

Session 8: The therapist meets with the child and the non-time-sharing parent face to face or on the telephone. For some children, the telephone is less threatening, as it affords more distance, while for other children, face time is less threatening because they "need to see," which may afford them some much-needed control. These two different perspectives dovetail with their sensitizer-repressor copying styles when children are confronted with anxiety-provoking situations. Additionally, some children prefer to engage in face time contact because they are simply curious, especially when they have not seen their parents in awhile. During a telephone session, the therapist encourages the child to ask preferred questions of the parent. Additionally, the therapist gives the child the option of asking the parent directly the questions or having the therapist deliver the questions for them while validating the children's engagement in the phone call with the estranged parent.

At the completion of the telephone session, the therapist holds a debriefing with the child. During the debriefing, the therapist asks the child what worked well in that session. The therapist also asks the child if at any time they felt uncomfortable, and if so, what did the child do to address their discomfort (examine the use of adaptive coping skills).

Session 9: The therapist holds the first face-to-face session 2 or 3 days after Session 8 (later in Week 4). For this first direct session, the therapist may hold the session down the hall and between the walls. For some children and families, it may be useful for the therapist to have the non-time-sharing parent sit in one room, while the child sits or stands in the hall outside of the parent's session room, if the office space supports the requisite level of privacy for this session structure, or the child may sit in a different therapy room. The child then speaks to the parent through a cracked door or over the telephone.

At the first direct, face-to-face in vivo session, the therapist should use icebreakers to reduce any anticipatory anxiety. Level 1 icebreakers include having the parent bring a pet to the session and/or playing a lively game or engaging in a craft activity. The goal of this session is to enhance comfort in the session by making the contact as neutral as possible and by engaging in non–emotionally laden material (other than delight regarding a pet or a play activity).

Level 2 icebreakers include family photos and photo albums, making a family tree, or starting a scrapbook. If the non-time-sharing parent has photographs of themselves with the children, have the parent bring those to the session or enlist the help of the time-sharing parent in this regard. Alternately, the therapist may have the time-sharing parent supply photo albums that include pictures of the non-time-sharing parent with the children.

If the therapist believes the session went well and that increased contact should occur, adding in some face time or telephone contact and/or a brief outing between this session and the next session should occur. The therapist will need to spend part of the session alone with the time-sharing parent, to debrief them about the session, to plan the homework assignment prior to the next session, and to discuss the next therapy session. Consequently, arrangements will need to be made in advance for another adult (not the non-time-sharing parent) to supervise young children while the therapist meets with the time-sharing parent.

The therapist will need to assist the parents in planning the logistics of the contact, such as date and time as well as place and transportation to and from the site, if the contact is to be in vivo. If the parents can tolerate being together in the same room to work out the details, then this should occur; otherwise the therapist works with the parents separately.

Regarding the initial rules of no touching by the estranged parent and no demands for a hug or a kiss: If it appears the child would like to hug their parent or runs into their arms, the therapist facilitates and does not block the interaction. The therapist can assist the child in asking the parent for a hug, if it is apparent that this is the child's preference. If the parent asks in the child's presence if they can hug the child, make it clear to the child that it is completely their decision and that they may decline the request.

Crying: It is not unusual for the non-time-sharing parent to cry at the first meeting. While some tearing is perfectly fine, if the parent looks as if they are going to lose control, the therapist should have them step outside the therapy room. It can frighten children to observe their parents, caretakers, or other adults cry; it can also have an insidious effect of exerting undue pressure on the child, such that the child may feel guilty or sorry about the parent's emotional state. For some children, parental crying can trigger feelings of anger, which in turn can heighten resistance toward the non-time-sharing parent.

Please note that in some cases the process can and should be speeded up! Time is often critical to successful reunification. If the therapist can conclude all of the initial sessions during the first week, and work with the child and parents separately the second week, by the third week some contact between parent and child is initiated. In some cases, particularly when the reunifying parent lives a notable distance from the child, these 14 sessions can be compressed into 1 week, with daily meetings for blocks of time upon the child's contingent emotional state.

Week 5

Session 10: The therapist may wish to meet initially alone with each parent for a few minutes to obtain an update regarding the outcome of the homework assignment from the previous week. The therapist should also continue to disseminate parent training interventions and problem solve areas of difficulty in this regard. If no homework was assigned, then obtain the non-time-sharing parent's assessment of the child's reaction to the last session. The therapist should be prepared for push back from the time-sharing parent, especially in cases where there have been direct attempts to estrange the child from the parent. This resistance will need to be addressed through problem solving, motivational interviewing techniques, validation of the parents' concerns, and emotional support. Sometimes the inclusion of the guardian ad litem at this session may be necessary.

The therapist then will meet with the child alone or with the child and non-time-sharing parent together, depending on whether or not they have had contact between sessions and how well that appears to have evolved. The therapist should use motivational interviewing techniques (see Appendix A) to assist in this regard.

In this session, the therapist may wish to continue with icebreakers including the use of pets, games, and photo albums or family tree development. Problems and concerns in the parent–child relationship should be addressed with both parent and child. The therapist should refer to the list of problem areas and concerns that was developed by the child and therapist earlier on in treatment.

Increased contact between child and non-time-sharing parent should be the goal of the session, adding in some face time or telephone contact *and* an outing between this session and the next session. The therapist will need to spend part of the session alone with the other parent (time-sharing parent), to debrief them about the session, to plan the homework assignment prior to the next session, and to discuss the next therapy session. Consequently, arrangements will need to have been made in advance for another adult (not the non-time-sharing parent) to supervise younger children while the therapist meets with the time-sharing parent.

The therapist assists the parents in determining the logistics of the contact, such as date and time as well as place and transportation to and from the site, if the contact is in vivo. If the parents can tolerate being together in the same room to work out the details, then this should occur; otherwise the parents will have to work with the therapist separately.

The treatment approach in this session is the same as that described for Session 9.

Week 6

Session 11: The therapist follows the steps as delineated in Session 10.

Session 12 (conjoint parent session): At this point in the treatment, it is often useful for the therapist to hold a parent session in an attempt to assist the parents with communication and problem solving in order to facilitate reunification therapy and the building of a solid co-parenting relationship. In addition to enhancing adaptive communication and problem solving, it is helpful to assist both parents in the rebuilding of trust.

Week 7

Session 13: The therapist should initially meet alone with each parent for a few minutes to obtain an update regarding the outcome of the homework assignment from the previous week (as in Session 11). In this session, the same steps are followed as in Session 9. Although co-parenting therapy as described in Session 12 may assist in inoculating against the time-sharing parent's resistance or push back often observed in these cases, the therapist should inform the time-sharing parent that they understand their concerns and explain how these are being addressed in the treatment with child and non-time-sharing parent. This resistance will need to be addressed through problem solving, motivational interviewing techniques, validation of the parents' concerns, and emotional support. Sometimes the inclusion of the guardian ad litem at this session may once again be necessary.

The therapist then will meet with the child alone or with the child and non-time-sharing parent together, depending on whether or not they have had contact between sessions and how well that appears to have evolved. The therapist should use motivational interviewing techniques (see Appendix A) to assist in this regard.

In this session, the therapist may wish to continue with games and play activities and photo album or family tree development; however, greater emphasis is placed on addressing the issues in the parent–child relationship and the instruction of more advanced communication skills and techniques. The therapist should be attuned to the struggles the target parent may be having during the parent–child outings as well as communication difficulties overtly evidenced during session.

At this point in treatment, if reunification has been realized, the therapist will need to spend part of the session alone with each parent or, if sufficient progress has been made with the co-parenting relationship, both parents together. The therapist should debrief the parents not only about the session, but also about the future time-sharing plan; consequently, arrangements will need to have been made in advance for another adult to supervise young children while the therapist meets with the parents.

If the parent and child have at this point been reunified in the estimation of the therapist, the therapist should discuss this with the guardian ad litem (if there is one on the case), and schedule a telephone conference with both attorneys together, after this session and before the next session (the termination session). At this point in treatment, should the parent–child dyad not be reunified and further work is warranted then the therapist should consider the barriers to treatment and address these as described in Sessions 9 through 11. If the barrier to treatment is the child's anxiety, then the protocol utilized in Sessions 5 and 6 should be followed to assist the child. If the barrier to successful reunification is the coparenting relationship, then additional sessions that address further reparation of the parents' relationship should be effectuated as discussed in Session 12. Finally, while this treatment plan is a typical model, therapists may need to adjust the speed at which they cover session material so that some families will need additional time to cover session material while others may move more rapidly through this material.

Session 14 (termination and future-planning session): The non-time-sharing parent and child should spend part of the session together reviewing their progress in therapy and their relationship. The therapist should highlight relationship strengths and address preventative measures lest problems emerge in the future. Additionally, the therapist should discuss taking a break from therapy to allow the dyad to continue to develop their relationship outside of session. Both parents should meet alone together with the therapist to discuss future time-sharing plans. Both parents should be positively acknowledged for their commitment and dedicated work on the process, and the therapist should discuss co-parenting communication and problem solving to reinforce the co-parenting dyad. The therapist should schedule a follow-up family therapy session, with timing of the session (e.g., 1 month, 3 months and 6 months) to be determined jointly by parents and therapist.

Important Notes

1. The rate of movement through these sessions may vary given the needs of the children and the family unit. For example, for anxious children, the therapist may have to increase the number of sessions to adequately assist in anxiety reduction and heightened coping strategies.
2. The involvement of step-parents, grandparents, other extended-family members, and parents' significant others should be considered for some cases. When appropriate, the therapist should allow for additional sessions to include these other family members in the treatment. The therapist should obtain additional written consent from both the parents, as well as assent from the guardian ad litem (if one exists) to add additional family members to treatment. The therapist should ensure that the parents have briefed their attorneys regarding the inclusion of these additional parties and, if there are any legal concerns, that these are addressed before incorporating other adults into the process.
3. Should the time-sharing parent cancel a session or wish to wait 2 weeks to schedule a session due to their alleging they have time constraints and cannot attend session the following week, then schedule *two* sessions for the following week. This is to prevent too much time elapsing in the process, thereby potentially derailing treatment, as well as to counter the resistance, with increasing the *ordeal* by the parent's having to attend two sessions in 1 week.
4. As indicated above, it is often useful, to schedule follow-up check-in sessions on a monthly basis, initially, and this should be discussed with the parties, the attorneys, and the guardian ad litem at the time of case termination.

References

American Academy of Matrimonial Lawyers. (2015). *Academy of Matrimonial Lawyers' Child-Centered Residential Guidelines*. Chicago, IL: Author.

Adshead, G., & Bluglass, K. (2001). Attachment representations and factitious illness by proxy: Relevance for assessment of parenting capacity in child maltreatment. *Child Abuse Review, 10*(6), 398–410. http://doi.org/10.1002/car.723

Afifi, T. D. (2003). "Feeling caught" in stepfamilies: Managing boundary turbulence through appropriate communication privacy rules. *Journal of Social and Personal Relationships, 20*(6), 729–755. http://doi.org/10.1177/0265407503206002

Afifi, T. D., Huber, F. N., & Ohs, J. (2006). Parents' and adolescents' communication with each other about divorce-related stressors and its impact on their ability to cope positively with divorce. *Journal of Divorce and Remarriage, 45*(1/2), 1–30. http://doi.org/10.1300/J087v45n01_01

Afifi, T. D., McManus, T., Hutchinson, S., & Baker, B. (2007). Inappropriate parental divorce disclosures, the factors that prompt them, and their impact on parents' and adolescents' well-being. *Communication Monographs, 74*(1), 78–102. http://doi.org/10.1080/03637750701196870

Agllias, K. (2015). Difference, choice, and punishment: Parental beliefs and understandings about adult child estrangement. *Australian Social Work, 68*(1), 115–129. http://doi.org/10.1080/0312407X.2014.927897

Agllias, K. (2016). Disconnection and decision-making: Adult children explain their reasons for estranging from parents. *Australian Social Work, 69*(1), 92–104. http://doi.org/10.1080/0312407X.2015.1004355

Alfano, C., Lau, S., Balderas, J., Bunnell, B., & Beidel, D. (2016). The impact of military deployment on children: Placing developmental risk in context. *Clinical Psychology Review, 43*, 17–29. http://doi.org/10.1016/j.cpr.2015.11.003

Al Gharaibeh, F. M. (2015). The effects of divorce on children: Mothers' perspectives in UAE. *Journal of Divorce and Remarriage, 56*(5), 347–368. http://doi.org/10.1080/10502556.2015.1046800

Allen, S. M., & Hawkins, A. (1999). Maternal gatekeeping: Mothers' beliefs and behaviors that inhibit greater father involvement in family work. *Journal of Marriage and the Family, 61*(1), 199–212. http://doi.org/10.2307/353894

Alvarez, A., & Booth, A. E. (2016). Exploring individual differences in preschoolers' causal stance. *Developmental Psychology, 52*(3), 411–422. http://doi.org/10.1037/dev0000085

Amato, P. R. (2000). The consequences of divorce for adults and children. *Journal of Marriage and Family, 62*(4), 1269–1287. http://doi.org/10.1111/j.1741-3737.2000.01269.x

Amato, P., & Anthony, C. (2014). Estimating the effects of parental divorce and death with fixed effects models. *Journal of Marriage and Family, 76*(2), 370–386. http://doi.org/10.1111/jomf.12100

Amato, P., & Cheadle, J. (2005). The long reach of divorce: Divorce and child well-being across three generations. *Journal of Marriage and Family, 67*(1), 191–206. http://doi.org/10.1111/j.0022-2445.2005.00014.x

Amato, P. R., & Fowler, F. (2002). Parenting practices, child adjustment, and family diversity. *Journal of Marriage and Family, 64*(3), 703–716. http://doi.org/10.1111/j.1741-3737.2002.00703.x

Amato, P. R., & Gilbreth, J. G. (1999). Nonresident fathers and children's well-being: A meta-analysis. *Journal of Marriage and the Family, 61*(3), 557–573. http://doi.org/10.2307/353560

Amato, P. R., & Sobolewski, J. M. (2001). The effects of divorce and marital discord on adult children's psychological well-being. *American Sociological Review, 66*(6), 900–921. http://doi.org/10.2307/3088878

American Psychiatric Association. (2013). *Diagnostic and statistical manual of mental disorders* (5th ed.). Arlington, VA: American Psychiatric Publishing. http://doi.org/10.1176/appi.books.9780890425596

American Psychological Association. (2002). *American Psychological Association ethical principles of psychologists and code of conduct*. Washington, DC: Author.

American Psychological Association. (2010). Guidelines for child custody evaluations in family law proceedings. *The American Psychologist, 65*(9), 863–873. http://doi.org/10.1037/a0021250

American Psychological Association. (2013). Specialty guidelines for forensic psychology. *The American Psychologist, 68*(1), 7–19. http://doi.org/10.1037/a0029889

Arkes, J. (2015). The temporal effects of divorces and separations on children's academic achievement and problem behavior. *Journal of Divorce and Remarriage, 56*(1), 25–42. http://doi.org/10.1080/10502556.2014.972204

Aronson, E. (2000). Cognitive dissonance. In A. Kazdin (Ed). *Encyclopedia of psychology* (, p. 141). Washington, DC: American Psychological Association.

Attorney ad Litem for D. K. v. Parents of D. K., 780 So. 2d 301 (4th D. C.A., 2001).

Ayoub, C. C., Deutsch, R. M., & Maraganore, A. (1999). *Emotional distress in children of high-conflict divorce, Family Court Review, 37*(3), 297–315.

Axline, V. M. (2013). *Play therapy: The inner dynamics of childhood*. Worcestershire, UK: Read Books.

Backhaus, S., Neumann, D., Parrot, D., Hammond, F. M., Brownson, C., & Malec, J. (2016). Examination of an intervention to enhance relationship satisfaction after brain injury: A feasibility study. *Brain Injury, 30*(8), 975–985. http://doi.org/10.3109/02699052.2016.1147601

Baggerly, J., & Green, E. (2015). Play-based family counseling for children in divorced or blended families. In E. J. Green, J. N. Baggerly, A. C. Myrick (Eds.), *Counseling Families: Play-Based Treatment* (pp. 127–144). London, UK: Rowman & Littlefield.

Bandura, A. (1969). Social-learning theory of identificatory processes. In D. Goslin (Ed), *Handbook of Socialization Theory and Research* (pp. 213–262). Skokie, IL: Rand McNally & Company.

Barber, M.A., & Davis, P.M. (2002). Fits, faints, or fatal fantasy? Fabricated seizures and child abuse. *Archives of Disease in Childhood, 86*(4), 230–233. http://doi.org/10.1136/adc.86.4.230

Barth, R.P., Gibbons, C., & Guo, S. (2006). Substance abuse treatment and the recurrence of maltreatment among caregivers with children living at home: A propensity score analysis. *Journal of Substance Abuse Treatment, 30*(2), 93–104. http://doi.org/10.1016/j.jsat.2005.10.008

Bastaits, K., & Mortelmans, D. (2016). Parenting as mediator between post-divorce family structure and children's well-being. *Journal of Child and Family Studies, 25*(7), 2178–2188. http://doi.org/10.1007/s10826-016-0395-8

Bateson, G., Jackson, D.D., Haley, J., & Weakland, J. (1956). Toward a theory of schizophrenia. *Behavioral Science, 1*(4), 251–264. http://doi.org/10.1002/bs.3830010402

Bauserman, R. (2002). Child adjustment in joint-custody versus sole-custody arrangements: A meta-analytic review. *Journal of Family Psychology, 16*(1), 91–102. http://doi.org/10.1037/0893-3200.16.1.91

Beck, J.S. (2011). *Cognitive behavior therapy: Basics and beyond.* New York, NY: Guilford Press.

Beckerman, N.L., & Shepherd, L. (2002). Couple therapy: Identification of conflict areas. *Family Therapy, 29*(2), 77–87.

Behrens, K.Y., Bahm, N.I.G., Li, Y., & O'Boyle, M.W. (2011). Electroencephalographic responses to photographs: A case study of three women with distinct adult attachment interview classifications. *Psychological reports, 108*(3), 993–1010. http://doi.org/10.2466/02.07.09.21.PR0.108.3.993-1010

Bellak, L., & Bellak, S. (1949). *Children's Apperception Test.* Grace Station, NY: Consulting Psychologists Press.

Ben-Itzchak, E., Abutbul, S., Bela, H., Shai, T., & Zachor, D.A. (2016). Understanding one's own emotions in cognitively-able preadolescents with autism spectrum disorder. *Journal of Autism and Developmental Disorders, 46*(7), 2363–2371. http://doi.org/10.1007/s10803-016-2769-6

Bernstein, D.E. (2001). Frye, Frye, again: The past, present, and future of the General Acceptance Test. *Jurimetrics, 4*(1), 385–407.

Bersoff, D.N. (2003). *Ethical conflicts in psychology.* Washington, DC: American Psychological Association.

Black, B., Ayala, F.J., & Saffran-Brinks, C. (1993). Science and the law in the wake of Daubert: A new search for scientific knowledge. *Texas Law Review, 72*(4), 715–743.

Borkovec, T.D., Alcaine, O., & Behar, E. (2004). Avoidance theory of worry and generalized anxiety disorder. In R.G. Heimberg, C. Turk, & D.S. Mennin (Eds.), *Generalized anxiety disorder: Advances in research and practice* (pp. 77–108). New York, NY: Guilford Press.

Bornovalova, M., Blazei, R., Malone, S., McGue, M., & Iacono, W. (2013). Disentangling the relative contribution of parental antisociality and family discord to child disruptive disorders. *Personality Disorders: Theory Research and Treatment, 4*(3), 239–246. http://doi.org/10.1037/a0028607

Bowlby, J. (1989). The role of attachment in personality development and psychopathology. In S. I. Greenspan & G.H. Pollock (Eds.), *The course of life, Vol. 1: Infancy* (pp. 229–270). Madison, CT: International Universities Press.

Brockman, C., Snyder, J., Gewirtz, A., Gird, S.R., Quattlebaum, J., Schmidt, N., ... Zettle, R. (2016). Relationship of service members' deployment trauma, PTSD symptoms, and experiential avoidance to post deployment family reengagement. *Journal of Family Psychology, 30*(1), 52–62. http://doi.org/10.1037/fam0000152

Brown, A., Creswell, C., Barker, C., Butler, S., Cooper, P., Hobbs, C., & Thirlwall, K. (2017). Guided parent-delivered cognitive behaviour therapy for children with anxiety disorders: Outcomes at 3-to 5-year follow-up. *British Journal of Clinical Psychology, 56*(2), 149–159. http://doi.org/10.1111/bjc.12127

Burelli, D.F., & Miller, M.A. (2013). *Military parents and child custody: State and federal issues (Report R42091).* Congressional Research Service. Retrieved from https://fas.org/sgp/crs/misc/R43091.pdf

Bush, J.E., & Ehrenberg, M.F. (2003). Young persons' perspectives on the influence of family transitions on sibling relationships: A qualitative exploration. *Journal of Divorce & Remarriage, 39*(3–4), 1–35. http://doi.org/10.1300/J087v39n03_01

Byng-Hall, J. (1998). *Rewriting family scripts: Improvisation and systems change.* New York, NY: Guilford Press.

Cal. Family Code § 3047 (2011). *Division 8: Custody of Children; Chapter 2: Matters to be Considered in Granting Custody.*

Carr, K., Holman, A., Abetz, J., Kellas, J.K., & Vagnoni, E. (2015). Giving voice to the silence of family estrangement: Comparing reasons of estranged parents and adult children in a nonmatched sample. *Journal of Family Communication, 15*(2), 130–140. http://doi.org/10.1080/15267431.2015.1013106

Carter, S.B., & Sanders, D. (2001). Anatomy of a child custody evaluation. *The Florida Bar Journal, 75*(6), 89–94.

Catley, D., Harris, K.J., Mayo, M.S., Hall, S., Okuyemi, K.S., Boardman, T., & Ahluwalia, J.S. (2006). Adherence to principles of motivational interviewing and client within-session behavior. *Behavioural and Cognitive Psychotherapy, 34*(1), 43–56. http://doi.org/10.1017/S1352465805002432

Chaffin, M., & Friedrich, B. (2004). Evidence-based treatments in child abuse and neglect. *Children and Youth Services Review, 26*(11), 1097–1113. http://doi.org/10.1016/j.childyouth.2004.08.008

Chandra, A., Lara-Cinisomo, S., Jaycox, L.H., Tanielian, T., Burns, R.M., Ruder, T., & Han, B. (2010). Children on the homefront: The experience of children from military families. *Pediatrics, 125*(1), 16–25. http://doi.org/10.1542/peds.2009-1180

Cheung, H., Siu, T. S. C., & Chen, L. (2015). The roles of liar intention, lie content, and theory of mind in children's evaluation of lies. *Journal of Experimental Child Psychology, 132*(1), 1–13. http://doi.org/10.1016/j.jecp.2014.12.002

Child Trends Data Bank. (2015). *Births to unmarried women.* Retrieved from http://www.childtrends.org/?indicators=births-to-unmarried-women

Choi, S., Huang, H., & Ryan, J. P. (2012). Substance abuse treatment completion in child welfare: Does substance abuse treatment completion matter in the decision to reunify families? *Children and Youth Services Review, 34*(9), 1639–1645. http://doi.org/10.1016/j.childyouth.2012.04.022

Clementi, M.A., & Alfano, C.A. (2014). Targeted behavioral therapy for childhood generalized anxiety disorder: A time-series analysis of changes in anxiety and sleep. *Journal of Anxiety Disorders, 28*(2), 215–222. http://doi.org/10.1016/j.janxdis.2013.10.006

Clever, M., & Segal, D.R. (2013). The demographics of military children and families. *The Future of Children, 23*(2), 13–39. http://doi.org/10.1353/foc.2013.0018

Coggins, T.E., Olswang, L.B., Carmichael Olson, H., & Timler, G.R. (2003). On becoming socially competent communicators: The challenge for children with fetal alcohol exposure. *International Review of Research in Mental Retardation, 27*(2), 121–150. http://doi.org/10.1016/S0074-7750(03)27004-X

Cohen, J.A., & Mannarino, A.P. (2011). Trauma-focused CBT for traumatic grief in military children. *Journal of Contemporary Psychotherapy, 41*(4), 219–227. http://doi.org/10.1007/s10879-011-9178-0

Cohen, J.A., Mannarino, A.P., Berliner, L., & Deblinger, E. (2000). Trauma-focused cognitive behavioral therapy for children and adolescents: An empirical update. *Journal of Interpersonal Violence, 15*(11), 1202–1223. http://doi.org/10.1177/088626000015011007

Cohen, L.J., Tanis, T., Bhattacharjee, R., Nesci, C., Halmi, W., & Galynker, I. (2014). Are there differential relationships between different types of childhood maltreatment and different types of adult personality pathology? *Psychiatry Research, 215*(1), 192–201. http://doi.org/10.1016/j.psychres.2013.10.036

Coughenour, J.C. (1995). Separate and unequal: Women in the federal criminal justice system. *Federal Sentencing Reporter, 8*(2), 142–144. http://doi.org/10.2307/20639877

Coyne, L.W., McHugh, L., & Martinez, E.R. (2011). Acceptance and commitment therapy (ACT): Advances and applications with children, adolescents and families. *Child and Adolescent Psychiatric Clinics of North America, 20*(2), 379–399.

Dallaire, D.H., Zeman, J.L., & Thrash, T.M. (2015). Children's experiences of maternal incarceration-specific risks: Predictions to psychological maladaptation. *Journal of Clinical Child and Adolescent Psychology, 44*(1), 109–122. http://doi.org/10.1080/15374416.2014.913248

Dallam, S., & Silberg, J.L. (2016). Recommended treatments for "parental alienation syndrome" (PAS) may cause children foreseeable and lasting psychological harm. *Journal of Child Custody, 13*(2–3), 134–143. http://doi.org/10.1080/15379418.2016.1219974

Darnall, D., & Steinberg, B.F. (2008). Motivational models for spontaneous reunification with the alienated child: Part II. *American Journal of Family Therapy, 36*, 253–261. http://doi.org/10.1080/01926180701643230

Definitions, Tex. Family Code Ann. § 153.701 (2009).

De Grauwe, S., Swain, A., Holcomb, P.J., Ditman, T., & Kuperberg, G.R. (2010). Electrophysiological insights into the processing of nominal metaphors. *Neuropsychologia, 48*(7), 1965–1984. http://doi.org/10.1016/j.neuropsychologia.2010.03.017

DeJong, M., & Davies, H. (2013). Contact refusal by children following acrimonious separation: Therapeutic approaches with children and parents. *Clinical Child Psychology and Psychiatry, 18*(2), 185–198. http://doi.org/10.1177/1359104512444629

Dempsey, J., McQuillin, S., Butler, A.M., & Axelrad, M.E. (2016). Maternal depression and parent management training outcomes. *Journal of Clinical Psychology in Medical Settings, 23*(3), 240–246. http://doi.org/10.1007/s10880-016-9461-z

Digiorgio-Miller, J. (2002). A comprehensive approach to family reunification following incest in an era of legislatively mandated community notification. *Journal of Offender Rehabilitation, 35*(2), 83–91. http://doi.org/10.1300/J076v35n02_06

Dillman Taylor, D., Purswell, K., Lindo, N., Jayne, K., & Fernando, D. (2011). The impact of child parent relationship therapy on child behavior and parent-child relationships: An examination of parental divorce. *International Journal of Play Therapy, 20*(3), 124–137. http://doi.org/10.1037/a0024469

Doherty, W.J. (1998). Responsible fathering: An overview and conceptual framework. *Journal of Marriage and the Family, 60*(2), 277–292. http://doi.org/10.2307/353848

Dorrance Hall, E., & McNallie, J. (2016). The mediating role of sibling maintenance behavior expectations and perceptions in the relationship between family communication patterns and relationship satisfaction. *Journal of Family Communication, 16*(4), 386–402. http://doi.org/10.1080/15267431.2016.1215316

Emerson, P.M., & Souza, A.P. (2008). Birth order, child labor, and school attendance in Brazil. *World Development, 36*(9), 1647–1664. http://doi.org/10.1016/j.worlddev.2007.09.004

Emery, R.E., Laumann-Billings, L., Waldron, M.C., Sbarra, D.A., & Dillon, P. (2001). Child custody mediation and litigation: Custody, contact, and coparenting 12 years after initial dispute resolution. *Journal of Consulting and Clinical Psychology, 69*(2), 323–332. http://doi.org/10.1037/0022-006X.69.2.323

Fabricius, W.V. (2003). Listening to children of divorce: New findings that diverge from Wallerstein, Lewis, and

Blakeslee. *Family Relations, 52*(4), 385–396. http://doi.org/10.1111/j.1741-3729.2003.00385.x

Famularo, R., Kinscherff, R., & Fenton, T. (1992). Parental substance abuse and the nature of child maltreatment. *Child Abuse & Neglect, 16*(4), 475–483. http://doi.org/10.1016/0145-2134(92)90064-X

Faust, J. (1996). *Trauma-focused cognitive-behavioral treatment manual for abused children with posttraumatic stress disorder and anxiety symptoms*. Unpublished manuscript.

Faust, J. (2000). Integration of family and cognitive behavioral treatment for treating sexually abused children. *Cognitive and Behavioral Practice, 7*, 361–368.

Faust, J. (2009). *Parent coordination: Conflict resolution alternatives to traditional litigation practice*. Paper presented at the Florida Bar Legislative Update, Naples, FL.

Faust, J. (2010). Parent-child reunification therapy in family law cases: Recommendations and suggested guidelines. *The Florida Bar Family Law Section Commentator, 24*(4), 11–13.

Faust, J., Gold, S., Nelson, S., Brosbe, M., Hoefling, K., & Ko, C. (2014). *Treatment outcomes for children and adolescents following intra vs. extra-familial sexual abuse.* Paper presented at the 122nd annual meeting of the American Psychological Association, Washington, DC.

Faust, J., Greenhawt, S., & Ko, C., (2015). *The impact of time-sharing plans, length of litigation and parent's behavior on children's adjustment during family law litigation.* Paper presented at the Broward County Bar Association Matrimonial Luncheon, Fort Lauderdale, FL.

Faust, J., & Ko, C. (2016). *Gender matching and child psychological adjustment after divorce.* Paper presented at the meeting of the American Psychological Association, Denver, CO.

Faust, J., Ko, C., Alexander, A., & Greenhawt, S.F. (2017). Parent–child gender matching and child psychological adjustment after divorce. *Journal of Child Custody, 14*(1), 1–10. http://doi.org/10.1080/15379418.2017.1312658

Faust, J., Ko, C., Alexander, A., Painter, K., & Hoefling, K. (2015). *Parental problem solving abilities and locus of control in family litigation: Impact on children.* Paper presented at the 123rd annual convention of the American Psychological Association, Toronto, Canada.

Faust, J., Ko, C., Alexander, A., Tarver, S., & Gibson, K. (2016). *Treatment effects for abused children with externalizing and internalizing symptomology.* Paper presented at the 124th annual convention of the American Psychological Association, Denver, CO.

Faust, J., & Salter, S. (2009). *Parenting coordination: Enhancing conflict resolution and child adjustment.* Paper presented at the Bench and Bar Conference, Fort Lauderdale, FL.

Festinger, L. (1957). *A theory of cognitive dissonance* Evanston, IL: Row, Peterson.

Filippova, E., & Astington, J.W. (2010). Children's understanding of social-cognitive and social-communicative aspects of discourse irony. *Child Development, 81*(3), 913–928. http://doi.org/10.1111/j.1467-8624.2010.01442.x

Flood, W.A., & Luiselli, J.K. (2016). Home-based in vivo desensitization treatment of bathroom avoidance in a child with autism spectrum disorder. *Clinical Case Studies, 15*(6), 476–483. http://doi.org/10.1177/1534650116670512

FLS-50/50 time-sharing bill (SB 668) (2016).

Foa, E.B., & Kozak, M.J. (1986). Emotional processing of fear: Exposure to corrective information. *Psychological Bulletin, 99*(1), 20–35. http://doi.org/10.1037/0033-2909.99.1.20

Foa, E.B., & Rothbaum, B.O. (2001). *Treating the trauma of rape: Cognitive-behavioral therapy for PTSD.* New York, NY: Guilford Press.

Foa, E.B., Steketee, G., & Rothbaum, B.O. (1989). Behavioral/cognitive conceptualizations of post-traumatic stress disorder. *Behavior Therapy, 20*(2), 155–176. http://doi.org/10.1016/S0005-7894(89)80067-X

Forehand, R., Jones, D.J., & Parent, J. (2013). Behavioral parenting interventions for child disruptive behaviors and anxiety: What's different and what's the same. *Clinical Psychology Review, 33*(1), 133–145. http://doi.org/10.1016/j.cpr.2012.10.010

Forehand, R.L., & McMahon, R.J. (1981). *Helping the noncompliant child: A clinician's guide to parent training.* New York, NY: Guilford Press.

Frazier, B.N., Gelman, S.A., & Wellman, H.M. (2009). Preschoolers' search for explanatory information within adult–child conversation. *Child Development, 80*(6), 1592–1611. http://doi.org/10.1111/j.1467-8624.2009.01356.x

Frye v. United States, 293 F.1013 (D.C. Cir. 1923).

Furstenberg, F.F., Jr. (2010). On a new schedule: Transitions to adulthood and family change. *The Future of Children, 20*(1), 67–87. http://doi.org/10.1353/foc.0.0038

Garber, B.D. (2015). Cognitive-behavioral methods in high-conflict divorce: Systematic desensitization adapted to parent-child reunification interventions. *Family Court Review, 53*(1), 96–112. http://doi.org/10.1111/fcre.12133

Gardner, R.A. (1999). Differentiating between parental alienation syndrome and bona fide abuse-neglect. *American Journal of Family Therapy, 27*(2), 97–107. http://doi.org/10.1080/019261899261998

Gardner, R.A. (2003). The judiciary's role in the etiology, symptom development, and treatment of the parental alienation syndrome (PAS). *American Journal of Forensic Psychology, 21*(1), 39–64.

Gilson, R.J., & Mnookin, R.H. (1994). Disputing through agents: Cooperation and conflict between lawyers in litigation. *Columbia Law Review, 94*(2), 509–566. http://doi.org/10.2307/1123202

Ginn, N.C., Clionsky, L.N., Eyberg, S.M., Warner-Metzger, C., & Abner, J.P. (2017). Child-directed interaction training for young children with autism spectrum disorders: Parent and child outcomes. *Journal of Clinical Child & Adolescent Psychology, 46*(1), 101–109. http://doi.org/10.1080/15374416.2015.1015135

Givertz, M. (2016). Parenting Styles/Discipline. In C. Berger, M. Roloff, S. Wilson, J. Dillard, J. Caughlin, & D. Solomon (Eds.), *The International Encyclopedia of Interpersonal Communication* (Vol. 1, pp. 1–9). Hoboken, NJ: Wiley-Blackwell.

Goldsmith, D.F., Oppenheim, D., & Wanlass, J. (2004). Separation and reunification: Using attachment theory and research to inform decisions affecting the placements of children in foster care. *Juvenile and Family Court Journal, 55*(2), 1–13. http://doi.org/10.1111/j.1755-6988.2004.tb00156.x

Goldstein, N.E., Arnold, D.h., Rosenberg, J.L., Stowe, R.M., & Ortiz, C. (2001). Contagion of aggression in day care classrooms as a function of peer and teacher responses. *Journal of Educational Psychology, 93*(4), 708–719. http://doi.org/10.1037/0022-0663.93.4.708

Gottman, J.M., & Driver, J.L. (2005). Dysfunctional marital conflict and everyday marital interaction. *Journal of Divorce & Remarriage, 43*(3–4), 63–77. http://doi.org/10.1300/J087v43n03_04

Gottman, J.M., & Levenson, R.W. (2000). The timing of divorce: Predicting when a couple will divorce over a 14-year period. *Journal of Marriage and Family, 62*(3), 737–745. http://doi.org/10.1111/j.1741-3737.2000.00737.x

Gover, A.R., & Bosick, S. (2011). Family deviance. In C. Bryant (Ed.), *The Routledge handbook of deviant behaviour* (pp. 329–335). New York, NY: Routledge.

Green, S., Ralph, M.A. L., Moll, J., Deakin, J.F., & Zahn, R. (2012). Guilt-selective functional disconnection of anterior temporal and subgenual cortices in major depressive disorder. *Archives of General Psychiatry, 69*(10), 1014–1021. http://doi.org/10.1001/archgenpsychiatry.2012.135

Greenberg, L.R., Doi Fick, L., & Schnider, R. (2012). Keeping the developmental frame: Child-centered conjoint therapy. *Journal of Child Custody, 9*(1–2), 39–68. http://doi.org/10.1080/15379418.2012.652568

Greenway, C. (2000). Autism and Asperger syndrome: Strategies to promote prosocial behaviours. *Educational Psychology in Practice, 16*(4), 469–486. http://doi.org/10.1080/713666112

Greif, G.L. (2009). The long-term aftermath of child abduction: Two case studies and implications for family therapy. *American Journal of Family Therapy, 37*, 273–286. http://doi.org/10.1080/01926180902754711

Gritzer, P.H., & Okun, H.S. (1983). Multiple family group therapy. In B.B. Wolman, G. Stricker, J. Framo, J.W. Newirth, M. Rosenbaum, & H.H. Young (Eds.), *Handbook of family and marital therapy* (pp. 315–342). New York, NY: Springer.

Guardia, A.C. L., & Banner, A.T. (2012). The goal of reunification: An Adlerian approach to working for therapeutic change within the foster care system. *The Family Journal, 20*(4), 361–368. http://doi.org/10.1177/1066480712452390

Guralnik, D. (1986). *Webster's new world dictionary*. New York, NY: Prentice Hall.

Haight, W.L., Black, J.E., Workman, C.L., & Tata, L. (2001). Parent-child interaction during foster care visits. *Social Work, 46*(4), 325–338. http://doi.org/10.1093/sw/46.4.325

Haley, J. (1960). *Direct study of child-parent interactions: Workshop*, 1959: 3. Observation of the family of the schizophrenic. *American Journal of Orthopsychiatry, 30*(3), 460–467.

Haley, J. (1984). *Ordeal therapy*. San Francisco, CA: Jossey-Bass.

Harris, J.R. (2011). *The nurture assumption: Why children turn out the way they do*. New York, NY: Simon and Schuster.

Harris, R. (2009). *ACT made simple: An easy-to-read primer on acceptance and commitment therapy*. Oakland, CA: New Harbinger.

Harter, S. (1978). Effectance motivation reconsidered: Toward a developmental model. *Human Development, 21*(1), 34–64. http://doi.org/10.1159/000271574

Harter, S. (1986). Processes underlying the construction, maintenance, and enhancement of the self-concept in children. *Psychological perspectives on the self, 3*(13), 7–181.

Harter, S. (1988). Developmental processes in the construction of the self. In T.D. Yawkey & J.E. Johnson (Eds.), *Integrative processes and socialization: Early to middle Childhood* (pp. 45–78). Hillside, NJ: Lawrence Erlbaum Associates.

Hawley, L.L., Padesky, C.A., Hollon, S.D., Mancuso, E., Laposa, J.M., Brozina, K., & Segal, Z.V. (2017). Cognitive-behavioral therapy for depression using mind over mood: CBT skill use and differential symptom alleviation. *Behavior Therapy, 48*(1), 29–44. http://doi.org/10.1016/j.beth.2016.09.003

Hayes, S.C., & Strosahl, K.D. (2004). *A practical guide to acceptance and commitment therapy*. New York, NY: Springer. http://doi.org/10.1007/978-0-387-23369-7

Health Insurance Portability and Accountability Act of 1996, Pub. L. No. 104–191; §264, 110 Stat. 1936 (August 21, 1996).

Healy, J.M., Jr., Stewart, A.J., & Copeland, A.P. (1993). The role of self-blame in children's adjustment to parental separation. *Personality and Social Psychology Bulletin, 19*(3), 279–289. http://doi.org/10.1177/0146167293193004

Heffner, M., Greco, L.A., & Eifert, G.H. (2003). Pretend you are a turtle: Children's responses to metaphorical versus literal relaxation instructions. *Child & Family Behavior Therapy, 25*(1), 19–33. http://doi.org/10.1300/J019v25n01_02

Hetherington, E.M. (2006). The influence of conflict, marital problem solving and parenting on children's adjustment in nondivorced, divorced and remarried families. In A. Clarke-Stewart & J. Dunn (Eds.), *Families count: Effects on child and adolescent development* (pp. 203–237). New York, NY: Cambridge University Press.

Hetherington, E.M., & Kelly, J. (2003). *For better or for worse: Divorce reconsidered*. New York, NY: WW Norton & Company.

Hirshfeld-Becker, D.R., & Biederman, J. (2002). Rationale and principles for early intervention with young children at risk for anxiety disorders. *Clinical Child and Family Psychology Review, 5*(3), 161–172. http://doi.org/10.1023/A:1019687531040

Hobson, J.A., Tarver, L., Beurkens, N., & Hobson, R.P. (2016). The relation between severity of autism and caregiver-child interaction: A study in the context of relationship development intervention. *Journal of Abnormal Child Psychology, 44*(4), 745–755. http://doi.org/10.1007/s10802-015-0067-y

Hoffmann, H.C., Byrd, A.L., & Kightlinger, A.M. (2010). Prison programs and services for incarcerated parents and their underage children: Results from a national survey of correctional facilities. *The Prison Journal, 90*(4), 397–416. http://doi.org/10.1177/0032885510382087

Horvath, A.O., & Symonds, B.D. (1991). Relation between working alliance and outcome in psychotherapy: A meta-analysis. *Journal of Counseling Psychology, 38*(2), 139–149. http://doi.org/10.1037/0022-0167.38.2.139

Jackson, A.L., Lucas, S.L., & Blackburn, A.G. (2009). Externalization and victim-blaming among a sample of incarcerated females. *Journal of Offender Rehabilitation, 48*(3), 228–248. http://doi.org/10.1080/10509670902766612

Jacobs, S., & Sillars, A. (2012). Sibling support during post-divorce adjustment: An idiographic analysis of support forms, functions, and relationship types. *Journal of Family Communication, 12*(2), 167–187. http://doi.org/10.1080/15267431.2011.584056

Jacobson, D.S. (1978). The impact of marital separation/divorce on children: Part III: Parent-child communication and child adjustment, and regression analysis of findings from overall study. *Journal of Divorce, 2*(2), 175–194. http://doi.org/10.1300/J279v02n02_03

Jirout, J., & Klahr, D. (2012). Children's scientific curiosity: In search of an operational definition of an elusive concept. *Developmental Review, 32*(2), 125–160. http://doi.org/10.1016/j.dr.2012.04.002

Judge, A.M., Bailey, R., Behrman-Lippert, J., Bailey, E., Psaila, C., & Dickel, J. (2016). The transitioning families therapeutic reunification model in nonfamilial abductions. *Family Court Review, 54*(2), 232–249. http://doi.org/10.1111/fcre.12215

Keenan, B.M., Newman, L.K., Gray, K.M., & Rinehart, N.J. (2016). Parents of children with ASD experience more psychological distress, parenting stress, and attachment-related anxiety. *Journal of Autism and Developmental Disorders, 46*(9), 2979–2991. http://doi.org/10.1007/s10803-016-2836-z

Kelly, J.B. (2000). Children's adjustment in conflicted marriage and divorce: A decade review of research. *Journal of the American Academy of Child & Adolescent Psychiatry, 39*(8), 963–973. http://doi.org/10.1097/00004583-200008000-00007

Kelly, J.B. (2008). Preparing for the parenting coordination role: Training needs for mental health and legal professionals. *Journal of Child Custody, 5*(1–2), 140–159. http://doi.org/10.1080/15379410802070476

Kelly, J.B., & Emery, R.E. (2003). Children's adjustment following divorce: Risk and resilience perspectives. *Family Relations, 52*(4), 352–362. http://doi.org/10.1111/j.1741-3729.2003.00352.x

Kelly, J.B., & Johnston, J.R. (2001). The alienated child: A reformulation of parental alienation syndrome. *Family Court Review, 39*(3), 249–266. http://doi.org/10.1111/j.174-1617.2001.tb00609.x

Kim, S., Thibodeau, R., & Jorgensen, R.S. (2011). Shame, guilt, and depressive symptoms: A meta-analytic review. *Psychological Bulletin, 137*(1), 68–96. http://doi.org/10.1037/a0021466

Knapp, S.J., & VandeCreek, L.D. (2006). *Practical ethics for psychologists: A positive approach.* Washington, DC: American Psychological Association. http://doi.org/10.1037/11331-000

Ko, C., Faust, J., Painter, K., & Hoefling, K. (2015). *Predicting child adjustment: Impact of length of litigation and parental acrimony.* Paper presented at the 123rd annual convention of the American Psychological Association, Toronto, Canada.

Krause-Parello, C.A., & Kolassa, J. (2016). Pet therapy: Enhancing social and cardiovascular wellness in community dwelling older adults. *Journal of Community Health Nursing, 33*(1), 1–10. http://doi.org/10.1080/07370016.2016.1120587

Lambert, M.J., & Barley, D.E. (2001). Research summary on the therapeutic relationship and psychotherapy outcome. *Psychotherapy: Theory, Research, Practice, Training, 38*(4), 357–361. http://doi.org/10.1037/0033-3204.38.4.357

Lamela, D., Figueiredo, B., Bastos, A., & Feinberg, M. (2016). Typologies of post-divorce coparenting and parental well-being, parenting quality and children's psychological adjustment. *Child Psychiatry & Human Development, 47*(5), 1–13.

Laser, J.A., & Stephens, P.M. (2011). Working with military families through deployment and beyond. *Clinical Social Work Journal, 39*(1), 28–38. http://doi.org/10.1007/s10615-010-0310-5

Latham, R.M., Mark, K.M., & Oliver, B.R. (2016). A harsh parenting team? Maternal reports of coparenting and coercive parenting interact in association with children's disruptive behaviour. *Journal of Child Psychology and Psychiatry, 58*(5), 603–611.

Lavner, J.A., & Bradbury, T.N. (2012). Why do even satisfied newlyweds eventually go on to divorce? *Journal of Family Psychology, 26*(1), 1–10. http://doi.org/10.1037/a0025966

Lebowitz, E.R., Shic, F., Campbell, D., Basile, K., & Silverman, W.K. (2015). Anxiety sensitivity moderates behavioral avoidance in anxious youth. *Behaviour Research and Therapy, 74*, 11–17. http://doi.org/10.1016/j.brat.2015.08.009

Lee, P.T., Dakin, E., & McLure, M. (2016). Narrative synthesis of equine-assisted psychotherapy literature: Current knowledge and future research directions. *Health & Social Care in the Community, 24*(3), 225–246. http://doi.org/10.1111/hsc.12201

Leeman, J., Crandell, J.L., Lee, A., Bai, J., Sandelowski, M., & Knafl, K. (2016). Family functioning and the well-being of children with chronic conditions: A meta-analysis. *Research in Nursing & Health, 39*(4), 229–243. http://doi.org/10.1002/nur.21725

Leichty, G., & Applegate, J. L. (1991). Social-cognitive and situational influences on the use of face-saving persuasive strategies. *Human Communication Research, 17*(3), 451–484. http://doi.org/10.1111/j.1468-2958.1991.tb00240.x

Liu, E., & Roloff, M. E. (2015). Exhausting silence: Emotional costs of withholding complaints. *Negotiation and Conflict Management Research, 8*(1), 25–40. http://doi.org/10.1111/ncmr.12043

Loftus, E. F. (2005). Planting misinformation in the human mind: A 30-year investigation of the malleability of memory. *Learning & Memory, 12*(4), 361–366. http://doi.org/10.1101/lm.94705

Maclean, M. (Ed.). (2007). *Parenting after partnering: Containing conflict after separation.* Oxford, UK: Bloomsbury.

Madanes, C. (1990). *Sex, love, and violence: Strategies for transformation.* New York, NY: Norton.

Main, M., Kaplan, N., & Cassidy, J. (1985). Security in infancy, childhood, and adulthood: A move to the level of representation. *Monographs of the Society for Research in Child Development, 50*(1–2), 66–104. http://doi.org/10.2307/3333827

Maner, J. K., Richey, J. A., Cromer, K., Mallott, M., Lejuez, C. W., Joiner, T. E., & Schmidt, N. B. (2007). Dispositional anxiety and risk-avoidant decision-making. *Personality and Individual Differences, 42*(4), 665–675. http://doi.org/10.1016/j.paid.2006.08.016

Manne, S. L., Bakeman, R., Jacobsen, P. B., Gorfinkle, K., Bernstein, D., & Redd, W. H. (1992). Adult-child interaction during invasive medical procedures. *Health Psychology, 11*(4), 241–249. http://doi.org/10.1037/0278-6133.11.4.241

Margulies, P. (1996). Political lawyering, one person at a time: The challenge of legal work against domestic violence for the impact litigation/client service debate. Michigan. *Journal of Gender & Law, 3*, 493–514.

Martin, D. J., Garske, J. P., & Davis, M. K. (2000). Relation of the therapeutic alliance with outcome and other variables: A meta-analytic review. *Journal of Counseling and Clinical Psychology, 68*(3), 438–450. http://doi.org/10.1037/0022-006X.68.3.438

McCauley, E., Gudmundsen, G., Schloredt, K., Martell, C., Rhew, I., Hubley, S., & Dimidjian, S. (2016). The adolescent behavioral activation program: Adapting behavioral activation as a treatment for depression in adolescence. *Journal of Clinical Child & Adolescent Psychology, 45*(3), 291–304. http://doi.org/10.1080/15374416.2014.979933

McIntosh, J., Smythe, B., & Kelaher, M. (2013). Overnight care patterns following parental separation: Associations with emotional regulation in infants and young children. *Journal of Family Studies, 19*(3), 224–239. http://doi.org/10.5172/jfs.2013.19.3.224

McIntosh, J., Smythe, B., Kelaher, M., Wells, Y., & Long, C. (2011). *Post-separation parenting arrangements: Studies of two risk groups.* Paper presented at the annual meeting of the Association of Family and Conciliation Courts, Orlando, FL.

McWey, L. M., & Mullis, A. K. (2004). Improving the lives of children in foster care: The impact of supervised visitation. *Family Relations, 53*(3), 293–300.

Meierding, N. R. (1993). Does mediation work? A survey of long-term satisfaction and durability rates for privately mediated agreements. *Conflict Resolution Quarterly, 11*(2), 157–170.

Merlot, E., Couret, D., & Otten, W. (2008). Prenatal stress, fetal imprinting and immunity. *Brain, Behavior, and Immunity, 22*(1), 42–51. http://doi.org/10.1016/j.bbi.2007.05.007

Miller, W. R., & Rollnick, S. (1991). *Preparing people to change addictive behavior.* New York, NY: Guilford Press.

Miller, W. R., & Rollnick, S. (2002). *Motivational interviewing: Preparing people for change.* New York, NY: Guilford Press.

Mills, J. C., & Crowley, R. J. (2014). *Therapeutic metaphors for children and the child within.* New York, NY: Routledge.

Minuchin, P. (1985). Families and individual development: Provocations from the field of family therapy. *Child Development, 56*(2), 289–302 http://doi.org/10.2307/1129720

Minuchin, S. (1974). *Families and Family Therapy.* Cambridge, MA: Harvard University Press.

Minuchin, S., Baker, L., Rosman, B. L., Liebman, R., Milman, L., & Todd, T. C. (1975). A conceptual model of psychosomatic illness in children: Family organization and family therapy. *Archives of General Psychiatry, 32*(8), 1031–1038. http://doi.org/10.1001/archpsyc.1975.01760260095008

Mitchell, B. A. (2006). The boomerang age from childhood to adulthood: Emergent trends and issues for aging families. *Canadian Studies in Population, 33*(2), 155–178. http://doi.org/10.25336/P6V32J

Mmari, K., Roche, K., Sudhinaraset, M., & Blum, R. (2009). When a parent goes off to war: Exploring issues faced by adolescents and their families. *Youth and Society, 40*(4), 455–475. http://doi.org/10.1177/0044118X08327873

Modification of Order Based on Military Duty, Tex. Family Code § 156.105 (2009).

Moss, M. (2004). Grief on the web. *Omega: Journal of Death and Dying, 49*(1), 77–81. http://doi.org/10.2190/CQTK-GF27-TN42-3CW3

Murray, L., Creswell, C., & Cooper, P. J. (2009). The development of anxiety disorders in childhood: An integrative review. *Psychological Medicine, 39*(9), 1413–1423. http://doi.org/10.1017/S0033291709005157

Naar-King, S., & Suarez, M. (2011). *Motivational interviewing with adolescents and young adults.* New York, NY: Guilford Press.

Nelson, R. H., Mitrani, V. B., & Szapocznik, J. (2000). Applying a family-ecosystemic model to reunite a family separated due to child abuse: A case study. *Contemporary Family Therapy, 22*(2), 125–146. http://doi.org/10.1023/A:1007722501848

Nielsen, L. (2011). Divorced fathers and their daughters: A review of recent research. *Journal of Divorce & Remarriage, 52*(2), 77–93. http://doi.org/10.1080/10502556.2011.546222

Office of Child Support Enforcement. (2015). *Essentials for attorneys in child support enforcement* (3rd ed.). Washington, DC: US Department of Health & Human Services. Retrieved from https://www.acf.hhs.gov/css/resource/essentials-for-attorneys-in-child-support-enforcement-3rd-edition

Office of the Deputy Assistant Secretary of Defense. (2014). *2014 Demographics: Profile of the military community*. Washington, DC: Author. Retrieved from http://download.militaryonesource.mil/12038/MOS/Reports/2014-Demographics-Report.pdf

Okorodudu, G. N. (2010). Influence of parenting styles on adolescent delinquency in delta central senatorial district. *Edo Journal of Counselling, 3*(1), 58–86. http://doi.org/10.4314/ejc.v3i1.52682

Olson, D. h. (2000). Circumplex model of marital and family systems. *Journal of Family Therapy, 22*(2), 144–167. http://doi.org/10.1111/1467-6427.00144

Park, C. B., & Cho, N. H. (1995). Consequences of son preference in a low-fertility society: Imbalance of the sex ratio at birth in Korea. *Population and Development Review, 21*(1), 59–84. http://doi.org/10.2307/2137413

Park, N. (2011). Military children and families strengths and challenges during peace and war. *American Psychologist, 66*(1), 65–72. http://doi.org/10.1037/a0021249

Parks, L. S., Tindall, H. L., & Yingling, L. C. (2011). Defining parenting coordination with state laws. *Family Court Review, 49*(3), 629–641. http://doi.org/10.1111/j.1744-1617.2011.01398.x

Patterson, G. R. (1982). *Coercive family process.* (Vol. 3). Eugene, OR: Castalia.

Paulus, M. P., & Stein, M. B. (2006). An insular view of anxiety. *Biological Psychiatry, 60*(4), 383–387. http://doi.org/10.1016/j.biopsych.2006.03.042

Pearson, J. (2015). Establishing parenting time in child support cases: New opportunities and challenges. *Family Court Review, 53*(2), 246–257. http://doi.org/10.1111/fcre.12147

Piaget, J. (2000). Piaget's theory of cognitive development. In K. Lee (Ed.), *Childhood cognitive development: The essential readings* (pp. 33–47). Malden, MA: Wiley-Blackwell.

Picoult, J. (2012). *Lone wolf.* New York, NY: Washington Square Press.

Potter, D. (2010). Psychosocial well-being and the relationship between divorce and children's academic achievement. *Journal of Marriage and Family, 72*(4), 933–946. http://doi.org/10.1111/j.1741-3737.2010.00740.x

Rand, D. C., & Rand, R. (2005). The spectrum of parental alienation syndrome: Part III: The Kopetski follow-up study. *American Journal of Forensic Psychology, 23*(1), 15–43.

Reay, K. M. (2015). Family reflections: A promising therapeutic program designed to treat severely alienated children and their family system. *American Journal of Family Therapy, 43*(2), 197–207. http://doi.org/10.1080/01926187.2015.1007769

Reconciliation. (n.d.). In *Merriam-Webster's online dictionary* (11th ed.). Retrieved from https://www.merriam-webster.com/dictionary/reconciliation

Reiter, S. L., & El-Sheikh, M. (1999). Does resolution of interadult conflict ameliorate children's anger and distress across covert, verbal, and physical disputes? *Journal of Emotional Abuse, 1*(3), 1–21. http://doi.org/10.1300/J135v01n03_01

Reunification. (n.d.). In *American Heritage dictionary of the English language* (5th ed.). Retrieved from http://www.thefreedictionary.com/reunification

Reunite. (n.d.). In *Collins English dictionary* (10th ed.). Retrieved from http://www.dictionary.com/browse/reunite

Robinson, N. J., Tharinger, D., Urbina, S., & Witt, P. (1994). Guidelines for child custody evaluations in divorce proceedings. *American Psychologist, 49*(7), 677–680. Retrieved from http://floridaspsychology.gov/forms/apa-guidelines-child-custody-eval-divorce-proceedings.pdf

Ropar, D., & Peebles, D. (2007). Sorting preference in children with autism: the dominance of concrete features. *Journal of Autism and Developmental Disorders, 37*(2), 270–280. http://doi.org/10.1007/s10803-006-0166-2

Rowen, J., & Emery, R. (2014). Examining parental denigration behaviors of co-parents as reported by young adults and their association with parent–child closeness. *Couple and Family Psychology: Research and Practice, 3*(3), 165–177. http://doi.org/10.1037/cfp0000026

Rules of Superintendence for the Courts of Ohio, Adopted by the Supreme Court of Ohio, Sup. R, §90.01 (2014).

Sae, K., & Yoko, K. (2004). A review of parents' acceptance of their child's developmental disabilities. *Japanese Journal of Child and Adolescent Psychiatry, 45*(4), 15–33.

Sam Houston State University. (2015, June 25). Investigating parent-child visitation in prison. *ScienceDaily*. Retrieved from www.sciencedaily.com/releases/2015/06/150625130000.htm

Sanders, M. J. (1995). Symptom coaching: Factitious disorder by proxy with older children. *Clinical Psychology Review, 15*(5), 423–442. http://doi.org/10.1016/0272-7358(95)00024-J

Satiansukpong, N., Pongsaksri, M., Sung-U, S., Vittayakorn, S., Tipprasert, P., Pedugsorn, M., ... Sung-U, S. (2008). Thai elephant-assisted therapy program: The feasibility in assisting an individual with autism. *World Federation of Occupational Therapists Bulletin, 58*(1), 17–26. http://doi.org/10.1179/otb.2008.58.1.004

Scharp, K. M., Thomas, L. J., & Paxman, C. G. (2015). "It was the straw that broke the camel's back": Exploring the distancing processes communicatively constructed in parent-child estrangement backstories. *Journal of Family Communication, 15*(4), 330–348. http://doi.org/10.1080/15267431.2015.1076422

Schrodt, P., Witt, P. L., & Messersmith, A. S. (2008). A meta-analytical review of family communication patterns and their associations with information processing, behavioral, and psychosocial outcomes. *Communication Monographs, 75*(3), 248–269. http://doi.org/10.1080/03637750802256318

Servicemembers Civil Relief Act, 50 U.S.C. §§3901–4043 (2014).

Shapiro, A.F., Gottman, J.M., & Fink, B.C. (2015). Short-term change in couples' conflict following a transition to parenthood intervention. *Couple and Family Psychology: Research and Practice, 4*(4), 239–251. http://doi.org/10.1037/cfp0000051

Shaw, L.A. (2010). Divorce mediation outcome research: A meta-analysis. *Conflict Resolution Quarterly, 27*(4), 447–467. http://doi.org/10.1002/crq.20006

Shumaker, D.M., Miller, C., Ortiz, C., & Deutsch, R. (2011). The forgotten bonds: The assessment and contemplation of sibling attachment in divorce and parental separation. *Family Court Review, 49*(1), 46–58. http://doi.org/10.1111/j.1744-1617.2010.01352.x

Silver, M.A. (1999). Love, hate, and other emotional interference in the lawyer/client relationship. *Clinical Law Review, 6*(1), 259–314.

Silveri, M.M., Sneider, J.T., Crowley, D.J., Covell, M.J., Acharya, D., Rosso, I.M., & Jensen, J.E. (2013). Frontal lobe γ-aminobutyric acid levels during adolescence: Associations with impulsivity and response inhibition. *Biological Psychiatry, 74*(4), 296–304. http://doi.org/10.1016/j.biopsych.2013.01.033

Simon, E., & Verboon, P. (2016). Psychological inflexibility and child anxiety. *Journal of Child and Family Studies, 25*(12), 3565–3573. http://doi.org/10.1007/s10826-016-0522-6

Simons, D.J. (2014). The value of direct replication. *Perspectives on Psychological Science, 9*(1), 76–80. http://doi.org/10.1177/1745691613514755

Slesnick, N., & Zhang, J. (2016). Family systems therapy for substance-using mothers and their 8- to 16-year-old children. *Psychology of Addictive Behaviors, 30*(6), 619–629. http://doi.org/10.1037/adb0000199

Slifer, K.J. (2013). *A clinician's guide to helping children cope and cooperate with medical care: An applied behavioral approach.* Baltimore, MD: John Hopkins University Press.

Smith, B.D. (2003). How parental drug use and drug treatment compliance relate to family reunification. *Child Welfare, 82*(3), 335–365.

Sobell, L.C., & Sobell, M.B. (2013). *Motivational techniques and skills for health and mental health coaching/counseling.* Retrieved from http://www.nova.edu/gsc/forms/mi-techniques-skills.pdf

Stallman, H.M., & Sanders, M.R. (2014). A randomized controlled trial of Family Transitions Triple P: A group-administered parenting program to minimize the adverse effects of parental divorce on children. *Journal of Divorce & Remarriage, 55*(1), 33–48. http://doi.org/10.1080/10502556.2013.862091

Stamps, L.E., Kunen, S., & Lawyer, R. (1996). Judicial attitudes regarding custody and visitation issues. *Journal of Divorce & Remarriage, 25*(1–2), 23–37. http://doi.org/10.1300/J087v25n01_02

Stavrou, E.T. (1999). Succession in family businesses: Exploring the effects of demographic factors on offspring intentions to join and take over the business. *Journal of Small Business Management, 37*(3), 43–61.

Sturge-Apple, M.L., Davies, P., & Cummings, E.M. (2006). Impact of hostility and withdrawal in interparental conflict on parental emotional unavailability and children's adjustment difficulties. *Child Development, 77*(6), 1623–1641. http://doi.org/10.1111/j.1467-8624.2006.00963.x

Sullivan, W.E., Martens, B.K., Morley, A.J., & Long, S.J. (2017). Reducing transition latency and transition-related problem behavior in children by altering the motivating operations for task disengagement. *Psychology in the Schools, 54*(4), 404–420. http://doi.org/10.1002/pits.22008

Temporary Time-Sharing Modification and Child Support Modification Due to Military Service, Fla. Stat. §61.13002 (2016).

Timmer, S.G., Llrquiza, A.I., Herschell, A.D., McGrath, J.M., Zebell, N.M., Porter, A.L., & Vargas, E.C. (2006). Parent-child interaction therapy: Application of an empirically supported treatment to maltreated children in foster care. *Child Welfare, 85*(6), 919–939.

Ultee, C.A., Griffioen, D., & Schellekens, J. (1982). The reduction of anxiety in children: A comparison of the effects of "systematic desensitization in vitro" and "systematic desensitization in vivo". *Behaviour Research and Therapy, 20*(1), 61–67. http://doi.org/10.1016/0005-7967(82)90009-2

US Department of Health and Human Services, National Center on Child Abuse and Neglect (1996). *Third national incidence study of child abuse and neglect (NIS-3).* Washington, DC: US Government Printing Office.

VanBuskirk, K.A., & Wetherell, J.L. (2014). Motivational interviewing with primary care populations: A systematic review and meta-analysis. *Journal of Behavioral Medicine, 37*(4), 768–780. http://doi.org/10.1007/s10865-013-9527-4

Van Starrenburg, M.L., Kuijpers, R.C., Kleinjan, M., Hutschemaekers, G.J., & Engels, R.C. (2017). Effectiveness of a cognitive behavioral therapy-based indicated prevention program for children with elevated anxiety levels: A randomized controlled trial. *Prevention Science, 18*(1), 31–39. http://doi.org/10.1007/s11121-016-0725-5

Vélez, C.E., Wolchik, S.a., Tein, J.Y., & Sandler, I. (2011). Protecting children from the consequences of divorce: A longitudinal study of the effects of parenting on children's coping processes. *Child Development, 82*(1), 244–257. http://doi.org/10.1111/j.1467-8624.2010.01553.x

Viry, G. (2014). Coparenting and children's adjustment to divorce: The role of geographical distance from fathers. *Journal of Divorce and Remarriage, 55*, 503–526.

Wade, C., Llewellyn, G., & Matthews, J. (2015). Parent mental health as a mediator of contextual effects on parents with intellectual disabilities and their children. *Clinical Psychologist, 19*(1), 28–38. http://doi.org/10.1111/cp.12055

Wallerstein, J.S. (1985). Children of divorce: Preliminary report of a ten-year follow-up of older children and adolescents. *Journal of the American Academy of Child Psychiatry, 24*(5), 545–553. http://doi.org/10.1016/S0002-7138(09)60055-8

Wallerstein, J. S., & Kelly, J. B. (1980). Effects of divorce on the visiting father–child relationship. *American Journal of Psychiatry, 137*(12), 1534–1539. http://doi.org/10.1176/ajp.137.12.1534

Wallerstein, J., Lewis, J., & Packer Rosenthal, S. (2013). Mothers and their children after divorce: Report from a 25-year longitudinal study. *Psychoanalytic Psychology, 30*(2), 167–187. http://doi.org/10.1037/a0032511

Walsh, T. B., Dayton, C. J., Erwin, M. S., Muzik, M., Busuito, A., & Rosenblum, K. L. (2014). Fathering after military deployment: Parenting challenges and goals of fathers of young children. *Health & Social Work, 39*(1), 35–44. http://doi.org/10.1093/hsw/hlu005

Warner, C. M., Colognori, D., Brice, C., Herzig, K., Mufson, L., Lynch, C., ... Ryan, J. (2016). Can school counselors deliver cognitive-behavioral treatment for social anxiety effectively? A randomized controlled trial. *Journal of Child Psychology and Psychiatry, 57*(11), 1229–1238. http://doi.org/10.1111/jcpp.12550

Warshak, R. A. (2015a). Parental alienation: Overview, management, intervention, and practice tips. *Journal of the American Academy of Matrimonial Lawyers, 28*, 181–248.

Warshak, R. A. (2015b). Ten parental alienation fallacies that compromise decisions in court and in therapy. *Professional Psychology: Research and Practice, 46*(4), 235–249. http://doi.org/10.1037/pro0000031

Wells, K., & Marcenko, M. O. (2011). Introduction to the special issue: Mothers of children in foster care. *Children and Youth Services Review, 33*(3), 419–423. http://doi.org/10.1016/j.childyouth.2010.06.022

Wenzel, A. (2013). Exposure. In A. Wenzel (Ed.), *Strategic decision making in cognitive behavioral therapy* (pp. 169–186). Washington, DC: American Psychological Association.

Westra, H. A., Constantino, M. J., & Antony, M. M. (2016). Integrating motivational interviewing with cognitive-behavioral therapy for severe generalized anxiety disorder: An allegiance-controlled randomized clinical trial. *Journal of Consulting and Clinical Psychology, 84*(9), 768–782. http://doi.org/10.1037/ccp0000098

Williams, K. D., Shore, W. J., & Grahe, J. E. (1998). The silent treatment: Perceptions of its behaviors and associated feelings. *Group Processes & Intergroup Relations, 1*(2), 117–141. http://doi.org/10.1177/1368430298012002

Wilson, S. R., Chernichky, S. M., Wilkum, K., & Owlett, J. S. (2014). Do family communication patterns buffer children from difficulties associated with a parent's military deployment? Examining deployed and at-home parents' perspectives. *Journal of Family Communication, 14*(1), 32–52. http://doi.org/10.1080/15267431.2013.857325

Wilson, C., & Hughes, C. (2011). Worry, beliefs about worry and problem solving in young children. *Behavioural and Cognitive Psychotherapy, 39*(05), 507–521. http://doi.org/10.1017/S1352465811000269

Wolfram, C. W. (1979). The code of professional responsibility as a measure of attorney liability in civil litigation. *South Carolina Law Review, 30*, 281–320.

Zeman, J., Dallaire, D., & Borowski, S. (2015). Emotion socialization in the context of risk and psychopathology: Maternal emotion socialization in children of incarcerated mothers. *Social Development, 25*(1), 66–81. http://doi.org/10.1111/sode.12117

Appendices

APPENDIX A
Reunification Therapy: Motivational Interviewing Questions

I. Motivational Interviewing Questions for Children

The therapist should use developmentally appropriate language when asking children these questions and use the terms father *or* mother *in place of* time-sharing *and* non-time-sharing parent.

A. Initial and Early Sessions

1. What are some of the good things about having a relationship with your non-time-sharing parent?

2. What are some of the good things about improving the relationship you have with your non-time-sharing parent?

3. If you have to see your non-time-sharing parent, what would you like to see happen differently?
   If you are receiving resistance such as in statements that "she will never change" or "I have already given him a million chances," then ask, "If you waved your magic wand, and we could get your non-time-sharing parent to change, what would you like to see your non-time-sharing parent do differently?"

4. What are the downsides or not good things about *not* having a relationship with your non-time-sharing parent?

5. What do you think other children miss out on if they don't have a relationship with their non-time-sharing parent?
   By distancing the problem by referring to other children, you may enable the child to reflect differently about the problem at hand, thereby contributing to cognitive reorganization in this regard.

6. What do you think you could do differently to get to the end goal of spending time with your non-time-sharing parent?

7. How might your life or things be different if you did not have anxiety about your non-time-sharing parent?
   If the child has notable anxiety, how is the anxiety helpful?

B. During Treatment

8. When you went out with your non-time-sharing parent, what worked for you?

9. What was positive or pleasant about the interaction that you would like to see happen again?

10. What surprised you about the outing?

    The term surprised *is not a term that children typically expect in the context of assessing the quality of their interaction with their non-time-sharing parent and in the context of therapy. It often positively unbalances the child's cognitive orientation to the process and causes them to reflect differently on the interaction.*

11. What was different in your non-time-sharing parent's behavior? Was that surprising?

12. What was different in your behavior? What surprised you about yourself that you liked (or could use in the future to your benefit)?

13. What didn't work as well as you wanted?

14. What are the good things about moving forward and spending additional time with your parent?

15. What are the not so good things about moving forward and spending additional time with your parent?

II. Motivational Interviewing Questions for Non-Time-Sharing Parent

1. What are the benefits of you and your child engaging in reunification therapy?

   This question is useful when the non-time-sharing parent feels victimized by the time-sharing parent and the court. Occasionally these parents are unable to understand the benefits of the process, as their thinking is clouded by feelings of victimization.

   ____

   ____

   ____

   ____

2. What are the benefits of having immediate contact with your child without engaging methodically in the treatment? What are the downsides of rushing the process?

   These questions are useful when working with non-time-sharing parents who are impatient and demand immediate live contact with the child.

   ____

   ____

   ____

   ____

3. How did altering our outside-of-session homework work for you and your child? What were the upsides of making these changes for you and your child? What were the downsides of making these changes, for you and your child?

   Questions 3 and 4 are useful for the non-time-sharing parent who unilaterally decides to change the homework (outside-of-session parent–child contact) assignments.

   ____

   ____

   ____

   ____

4. How did altering our outside-of-session homework work for you and your coparent? What were the upsides for you and your coparent of making these changes? What were the downsides for you and your coparent of making these changes?

   ____

   ____

   ____

   ____

5. What are the benefits of not working cooperatively with the time-sharing parent? What are the drawbacks to staying stuck in your conflictual relationship with them?

III. Motivational Interviewing Questions for Time-Sharing Parent

1. What are the positive benefits about your child having a relationship with the non-time-sharing parent?
   Many time-sharing parents are worried about the parenting ability of the non-time-sharing parent; it is important to delineate for the time-sharing parent that via reunification therapy not only does the therapist address parenting skills with that parent, but they are also a second set of eyes and ears. To this end, the therapist can inform the parent that once reunification therapy has been completed, the therapist can conduct follow-up sessions: every 2 months, 3 months, quarterly, or semi-annually, for example.

2. What are some of the downsides of your child *not* reunifying with their other parent?

3. What are some of the benefits of having another primary caretaker in your child's life?

4. What would it mean or what is the impact if you were the one to enable your child to share time with the non-time-sharing parent?

5. What are the benefits of letting a third party (e.g., a judge) decide whether or not the non-time-sharing parent has a relationship with the child? What are the downsides to letting them decide?

____

____

____

____

6. What are the benefits of not working cooperatively with the non-time-sharing parent? What are the drawbacks to staying stuck in your conflictual relationship with them?

____

____

____

____

APPENDIX B
Reunification Therapy: Behavioral Activation

Photocopy this list and cut out the events that are potential activities for the clients. Make four envelope packets or small bags, one for each category. The non-time-sharing parent and child can discuss other possible activities and add these to each of the four categories. If the child does not or will not express an interest as to the activity, they reach into the envelope that indicates the category of activity for which they are ready, and pull out an activity.

I. Time-Intensive Interaction, With Direct Contact	II. Less Time Intensive, But With Direct Interaction	III. Less Direct Interaction, Circumscribed Interaction, or Interaction That Has Elements of Distraction (Diluted Interaction)	IV. Activities That Can Be Modified by Level of Contact
Bicycle ride	Coffee house	Going to a movie at a theater	Downhill snow skiing
Kayak ride	Going for a yogurt/ice cream	Going to a music concert	Horseback riding
Fishing	Visiting an animal shelter	Bowling	Bookstore
Making your own pottery at a pottery store	Selecting holiday decorations (e.g., pumpkin, Christmas tree)	Cooking or attending an art class	Library
Cooking a meal together	Baking cookies or cupcakes	Miniature golf	Surfing
Park and/or picnic	Small crafting projects	Dog park or dog beach with dog	Ice skating
Hiking	One-store shopping (e.g., electronics)	Attending a play, musical, ballet, or opera	Laser tag

Multistore or mall shopping	Manicure/pedicure	Afternoon at the spa	Arcade
Zoo	High tea at a hotel or restaurant	Museum	Four wheeling
Aquarium	Professional sporting event	Barbecue with special family members and friends	Indoor play arena or trampoline park
Theme park	Building a model or build a stuffed animal at the mall	Pool party with family members and friends	Playing sports together (e.g., basketball, soccer)
Eating a meal at a restaurant	Farmer's market	Game night with fiends or family	Go kart racing
Pool	Fruit or vegetable picking	Cake decorating class	Holiday festival/ or art fair
Beach	Conjoint videogaming	Marshmallow or whip creme fight	Volunteer together
Redecorating child's room at reunifying parent's house	Make a sundae	Remote online videogames with parent and child	Create an obstacle course
Scrap booking	Observatory-stargazing	Collecting shells, leaves, bugs, sea glass	Do a science experiment
Making a garden	Roast marshmallows and tell stories	Scavenger hunt	Fly kites
Going to a movie at a drive-In	Board game	Water balloon or water gun fight	Indoor daytime "camping"

APPENDIX C
Empathy Training for Parents

Teach your kids about love; one day they will teach their own.

US Department of Health and Human Services (1996)

Empathy is a comprehensive understanding or knowledge of another person's feelings. When using a web-based search engine to locate synonyms for the term, the first word listed is *understanding*. People often confuse empathy and sympathy, and while these concepts share similarities they also share differences. *Sympathy* is defined as sorrow for another's pain. The difference in the two lies in the depth and to some extent the quality of feeling, such that empathy is the capacity to truly understand and even to vicariously experience what another individual has experienced, whereas sympathy does not require that degree of feeling or even the knowledge about the feeling, but rather, as socialized human beings we have an understanding about what is expected in the circumstance and we know that the person is experiencing distress but may not know the degree or the complete quality of the distress.

For example, when a coworker's neighbor's son is killed in military combat, we know that the loss of an adult child must be a devastating experience, even though we may not have first-hand knowledge about these feelings, and we can express to that parent our sorrow for their loss despite not feeling it directly. However, to experience empathy for the individual experiencing the loss requires an element of imagination regarding the feeling and placing ourselves in the same position as the neighbor of the coworker. This empathic experience will have a notable emotional effect on us and may include profound sadness including crying and anger.

The experience and communication of empathy requires much greater emotional and cognitive (thinking) effort than the transmission of sympathy to others. Empathy requires you to think about the quality of pain the person is experiencing and to place yourself both emotionally and conceptually in that person's life experience. It requires you to feel pain as closely as possible to how the person does, and since we are naturally developed to protect ourselves from negative feelings, we automatically resist feeling discomfort and pain. So the first step is to be aware of your resistance to the process of attempting to feel what the other person is feeling.

Below are exercises to build empathy skills. These questions are designed to be completed sequentially (in order). After you complete these exercises, review them with your therapist.

1. Describe the time you felt the most sad or depressed in your life as an adult. Write first about the nature of the triggering situation, what you were feeling, and what you were thinking about the situation. Also write how you felt while you were thinking about the situation and immediately afterwards. Finally, write about who knew about your sadness and how they knew about your sadness and other feelings. Did they respond to you as you would have wished, and if not (or if no one knew), write about how you wished someone would have responded to you.

   Situation: ______________________________

   Feelings: ______________________________

   Thoughts: ______________________________

   Feelings in Response to Your Thoughts: ______________________________

   How Did People Respond (or Not Respond)? ______________________________

   How Would You Have Wished They Had Responded? ______________________________

2. Describe the time you felt the most sad or depressed in your life as a child. Write first about the nature of the triggering situation, what you were feeling, and what you were thinking about the situation. Also write how you felt while you were thinking about the situation and immediately afterwards. Finally, write about who knew about your sadness and how they knew about your sadness and other feelings. Did they respond to you as you would have wished, and if not (or if no one knew), write how you wished someone would have responded to you.

   Situation: ____

   Feelings: ____

   Thoughts: ____

   Feelings in Response to Your Thoughts: ______________________________

   How Did People Respond (or Not Respond)? ____________________________

   How Would You Have Wished They Had Responded? _______________________

3. Describe one time when you felt the most fearful and anxious in your life as an adult. Write first about the nature of the triggering situation, what you were feeling, and what you were thinking about the situation. Also write how you felt while you were thinking about the situation and immediately afterwards. Finally, write about who knew about your fear and anxiety and how they knew about your anxiety. Did they respond to you as you would have wished, and if not (or if no one knew), write about how you wished someone would have responded to you.

   Situation: __________

   Feelings: __________

   Thoughts: __________

   Feelings in Response to Your Thoughts: __________

   How Did People Respond (or Not Respond)? __________

   How Would You Have Wished They Had Responded? __________

4. Describe one time you felt the most fearful and anxious in your life first as a child. Write first about the nature of the triggering situation, what you were feeling, and what you were thinking about the situation. Also write how you felt while you were thinking about the situation and immediately afterwards. Finally, write about who knew about your fear and anxiety and how they knew about your anxiety. Did they respond to you as you would have wished, and if not (or if no one knew), write about how you wished someone would have responded to you.

Situation: ______________________________

Feelings: ______________________________

Thoughts: ______________________________

Feelings in Response to Your Thoughts: ______________________________

How Did People Respond (or Not Respond)? ______________________________

How Would You Have Wished They Had Responded? ______________________________

5a. Write about the last five times you became extremely angry, as an adult, to the point where your anger became problematic, legally and/or interpersonally such that it hurt those you love or loved or caused people to distance themselves from you.

First Situation: ______________________________

____

____

____

Feelings: ______________________________

____

____

____

Thoughts: ______________________________

____

____

____

Feelings in Response to Your Thoughts: ______________________________

____

____

____

____

Behavioral and Environmental Impact Your Anger Had on You for This Event (e.g., Repercussions): __________

____

____

____

____

Impact Your Anger Had on Others for This Event: ______________________________

____

____

____

____

Your Feelings in Response to How Others Responded to Your Anger: ______________________________

____

____

____

____

Second Situation: ____________________

____

____

____

Feelings: ____________________

____

____

____

Thoughts: ____________________

____

____

____

Feelings in Response to Your Thoughts: ____________________

____

____

____

____

Behavioral and Environmental Impact Your Anger Had on You for This Event (e.g., Repercussions): ____________________

____

____

____

____

Impact Your Anger Had on Others for This Event: ____________________

____

____

____

____

Your Feelings in Response to How Others Responded to Your Anger: ____________________

____

____

____

____

Third Situation: ____

____

____

____

Feelings: ____

____

____

____

Thoughts: ____

____

____

____

Feelings in Response to Your Thoughts: ______________________________

____

____

____

____

Behavioral and Environmental Impact Your Anger Had on You for This Event (e.g., Repercussions): __________

____

____

____

____

Impact Your Anger Had on Others for This Event: ______________________

____

____

____

____

Your Feelings in Response to How Others Responded to Your Anger: ______________

____

____

____

____

Fourth Situation: ______________________________

____

____

____

Feelings: ______________________________

____

____

____

Thoughts: ______________________________

____

____

____

Feelings in Response to Your Thoughts: ______________________________

____

____

____

____

Behavioral and Environmental Impact Your Anger Had on You for This Event (e.g., Repercussions): __________

____

____

____

____

Impact Your Anger Had on Others for This Event: ______________________________

____

____

____

____

Your Feelings in Response to How Others Responded to Your Anger: ______________________________

____

____

____

____

Fifth Situation: ____

____

____

____

Feelings: ____

____

____

____

Thoughts: ____

____

____

____

Feelings in Response to Your Thoughts: ____

____

____

____

____

Behavioral and Environmental Impact Your Anger Had on You for This Event (e.g., Repercussions): __________

____

____

____

____

Impact Your Anger Had on Others for This Event: ____

____

____

____

____

Your Feelings in Response to How Others Responded to Your Anger: ____

____

____

____

____

5b. For each of the times you became angry in number 5a above, write the pain and sadness you were feeling; even if you do not believe you were feeling pain and sadness, please guess what you might have been feeling. Anger masks pain because it is energizing and serves the purpose of protection against vulnerable feelings. Human beings' pain renders them vulnerable as it can immobilize; consequently, it places the organism at risk. Therefore there is a motivation to counteract feelings of pain and vulnerability through mobilizing of resources (fight and/or flight). List the *Feelings in the Spaces Below, Other Than Anger, That Made You Feel Vulnerable*:

Situation 1: ______________________________

____

____

____

____

____

Situation 2: ______________________________

____

____

____

____

____

Situation 3: ______________________________

____

____

____

____

____

Situation 4: ______________________________

____

____

____

____

____

Situation 5: ______________________________

____

____

____

____

____

6a. Write about the last five times you became extremely angry, as a child, to the point where your anger became problematic, legally and/or interpersonally such that it hurt those you loved or caused people to distance themselves from you.

First Situation: ______________________

Feelings: ______________________

Thoughts: ______________________

Feelings in Response to Your Thoughts: ______________________

Behavioral and Environmental Impact Your Anger Had on You for This Event (e.g., Repercussions): ______________________

Impact Your Anger Had on Others for This Event: ______________________

Your Feelings in Response to How Others Responded to Your Anger: ______________________

Second Situation: ____

____

____

____

Feelings: ____

____

____

____

Thoughts: ____

____

____

____

Feelings in Response to Your Thoughts: ____

____

____

____

____

Behavioral and Environmental Impact Your Anger Had on You for This Event (e.g., Repercussions): __________

____

____

____

____

Impact Your Anger Had on Others for This Event: ____

____

____

____

____

Your Feelings in Response to How Others Responded to Your Anger: ____

____

____

____

____

Third Situation: ____

____

____

____

Feelings: ____

____

____

____

Thoughts: ____

____

____

____

Feelings in Response to Your Thoughts: ____

____

____

____

____

Behavioral and Environmental Impact Your Anger Had on You for This Event (e.g., Repercussions): __________

____

____

____

____

Impact Your Anger Had on Others for This Event: ____

____

____

____

____

Your Feelings in Response to How Others Responded to Your Anger: ______________________________

____

____

____

____

Fourth Situation: ______________________________

____

____

____

Feelings: ______________________________

____

____

____

Thoughts: ______________________________

____

____

____

Feelings in Response to Your Thoughts: ______________________________

____

____

____

____

Behavioral and Environmental Impact Your Anger Had on You for This Event (e.g., Repercussions): __________

____

____

____

____

Impact Your Anger Had on Others for This Event: ______________________________

____

____

____

____

Your Feelings in Response to How Others Responded to Your Anger: ______________________________

____

____

____

____

Fifth Situation: ____

____

____

____

Feelings: ____

____

____

____

Thoughts: ____

____

____

____

Feelings in Response to Your Thoughts: ____

____

____

____

____

Behavioral and Environmental Impact Your Anger Had on You for This Event (e.g., Repercussions): __________

____

____

____

____

Impact Your Anger Had on Others for This Event: ____

____

____

____

____

Your Feelings in Response to How Others Responded to Your Anger: ______________________________

____

____

____

____

6b. For each of the times you became angry in number 6a above, write about the pain and sadness you were feeling; even if you do not believe you were feeling pain and sadness, please guess what you might have been feeling. Anger masks pain because it is energizing and serves the purpose of protection against vulnerable feelings. Human beings' pain renders them vulnerable as it can immobilize; consequently, it places the organism at risk. Therefore there is a motivation to counteract feelings of pain and vulnerability through mobilizing of resources (fight and/or flight). List the *Feelings in the Spaces Below, Other Than Anger, That Made you Feel Vulnerable*:

Situation 1: ______________________________

Situation 2: ______________________________

Situation 3: ______________________________

Situation 4: ______________________________

Situation 5: ______________________________

7. Describe a time you felt *the most frightened* for the safety of your child, such that their life was in danger or could have been in danger (e.g., high fever as a small child). First write about your feelings, then write your thoughts and your feelings in response to your thoughts. Subsequently, write what you imagine your child was feeling and thinking.

   Situation: ______________________________

   Your Feelings: ______________________________

   Your Thoughts: ______________________________

   Your Feelings in Response to Your Thoughts: ______________________________

   Your Child's Feelings: ______________________________

   Your Child's Thoughts: ______________________________

8. Describe five times you witnessed your child in significant emotional distress, either in fear or with notable sadness. First write about your feelings and then your thoughts. Subsequently, write first all of the feelings you imagined your child was having during these events, and then write what you believe they were thinking. Also write the reasons *your child believed* they were afraid or sad.

First Situation: ______________________________

____

____

____

Your Feelings: ______________________________

____

____

____

Your Thoughts: ______________________________

____

____

____

Your Feelings in Response to Your Thoughts: ______________________________

____

____

____

Your Child's Feelings: ______________________________

____

____

____

____

Your Child's Thoughts: ______________________________

____

____

____

____

What You Believe to Be the Reasons Your Child Was Feeling This Way: ______________________________

____

____

____

____

Second Situation: ______________________________

____

____

____

____

Your Feelings: ______________________________

____

____

____

Your Thoughts: ______________________________

____

____

____

____

Your Feelings in Response to Your Thoughts: ______________________________

____

____

____

____

Your Child's Feelings: ______________________________

____

____

____

____

Your Child's Thoughts: ______________________________

____

____

____

____

What You Believe to Be the Reasons Your Child Was Feeling This Way: ______________________________

____

____

____

____

Third Situation: ____

____

____

____

____

Your Feelings: ____

____

____

____

Your Thoughts: ____

____

____

____

____

Your Feelings in Response to Your Thoughts: ______________________________

____

____

____

____

Your Child's Feelings: ____

____

____

____

____

Your Child's Thoughts: ____

____

____

____

____

What You Believe to Be the Reasons Your Child Was Feeling This Way: ______________

____

____

____

____

Fourth Situation: ____

____

____

____

____

Your Feelings: ____

____

____

____

Your Thoughts: ____

____

____

____

____

Your Feelings in Response to Your Thoughts: ______________________________

____

____

____

____

Your Child's Feelings: ____

____

____

____

____

Your Child's Thoughts: ____

____

____

____

____

What You Believe to Be the Reasons Your Child Was Feeling This Way: ____________________

____

____

____

____

Fifth Situation: ____________________

____

____

____

____

Your Feelings: ____________________

____

____

____

Your Thoughts: ____________________

____

____

____

____

Your Feelings in Response to Your Thoughts: ____________________

____

____

____

____

Your Child's Feelings: ____________________

____

____

____

____

Your Child's Thoughts: ____________________

____

____

____

____

What You Believe to Be the Reasons Your Child Was Feeling This Way: ____________________

____

____

____

____

9. For divorced or separated parents: First describe your feelings and those you believe your child and partner were experiencing at the time of deciding to leave the relationship with the other parent or learning your partner wished to vacate the relationship (Situation A). Describe your feelings and those you believe your child and partner were experiencing at the time of the actual physical separation (Situation B). Describe your child's feelings on three different occasions when they witnessed you and your former partner engaged in conflict (Situations C1 to C3). First, write down your feelings, and then your thoughts and your feelings in response to the thoughts about these. Subsequently, write down all of the feelings you imagined your child and the other parent were feeling during these events. Also write about the reasons *you believe your child and the other parent were feeling this way*. Finally write down your feelings and then your thoughts about being separated from your child. Write down all of the feelings you imagine your child and the other parent are feeling due to the separation and the ongoing conflict (if applicable) between you and the other parent.

Situation A: Deciding to Leave the Relationship or Being Informed the Other Parent Desired to Leave the Relationship

Your Feelings: ______________________________

____

____

____

Your Thoughts: ______________________________

____

____

____

Your Feelings in Response to Your Thoughts: ______________________________

____

____

____

Your Child's Feelings: ______________________________

____

____

____

Your Child's Thoughts: ______________________________

____

____

____

What You Believe to Be the Reasons Your Child Was Feeling This Way: ______________________________

____

____

____

The Other Parent's Feelings: ______________________________

____

____

____

The Other Parent's Thoughts: ______________________________

____

____

____

The Reasons You Believe The Other Parent Was Feeling This Way: ______________________________

____

____

____

Situation B: The Actual Physical Separation

Your Feelings: ______________________________

____

____

____

Your Thoughts: ______________________________

____

____

____

Your Feelings in Response to Your Thoughts: ______________________________

____

____

____

Your Child's Feelings: ______________________________

____

____

____

Your Child's Thoughts: ______________________________

____

____

____

What You Believe to Be the Reasons Your Child Was Feeling This Way: ______________________

____

____

____

The Other Parent's Feelings: ______________________

____

____

____

The Other Parent's Thoughts: ______________________

____

____

____

The Reasons You Believe The Other Parent Was Feeling This Way: ______________________

____

____

____

Situation C1: Open (Observed by Child) Conflict With Other Parent

Your Feelings: ______________________

____

____

____

Your Thoughts: ______________________

____

____

____

Your Feelings in Response to Your Thoughts: ______________________

____

____

____

Your Child's Feelings: ______________________

____

____

____

Your Child's Thoughts: ______________________________

____

____

____

What You Believe to Be the Reasons Your Child Was Feeling This Way: ______________________________

____

____

____

The Other Parent's Feelings: ______________________________

____

____

____

The Other Parent's Thoughts: ______________________________

____

____

____

The Reasons You Believe The Other Parent Was Feeling This Way: ______________________________

____

____

____

Situation C2: Open (Observed by Child) Conflict With Other Parent

Your Feelings: ______________________________

____

____

____

Your Thoughts: ______________________________

____

____

____

Your Feelings in Response to Your Thoughts: ______________________________

____

____

____

Your Child's Feelings: ______________________________

____

____

____

Your Child's Thoughts: ______________________________

____

____

____

What You Believe to Be the Reasons Your Child Was Feeling This Way: ______________________________

____

____

____

The Other Parent's Feelings: ______________________________

____

____

____

The Other Parent's Thoughts: ______________________________

____

____

____

The Reasons You Believe The Other Parent Was Feeling This Way: ______________________________

____

____

____

Situation C3: Open (Observed by Child) Conflict With Other Parent

Your Feelings: ______________________________

____

____

____

Your Thoughts: ______________________________

____

____

____

Your Feelings in Response to Your Thoughts: ______________________________

Your Child's Feelings: ______________________________

Your Child's Thoughts: ______________________________

What You Believe to Be the Reasons Your Child Was Feeling This Way: ______________________________

The Other Parent's Feelings: ______________________________

The Other Parent's Thoughts: ______________________________

The Reasons You Believe The Other Parent Was Feeling This Way: ______________________________

Situation D: Being Separated From Your Child and Continuing Conflict With the Other Parent

Your Feelings: ______________________________

Your Thoughts: ____

____

____

____

Your Feelings in Response to Your Thoughts: ____

____

____

____

Your Child's Feelings: ____

____

____

____

Your Child's Thoughts: ____

____

____

____

What You Believe to Be the Reasons Your Child Was Feeling This Way: ____

____

____

____

The Other Parent's Feelings: ____

____

____

____

The Other Parent's Thoughts: ____

____

____

____

The Reasons You Believe The Other Parent Was Feeling This Way: ____

____

____

____

10. Based on completion of your empathy training, please write down eight ways you can convey empathy to your child and your child's other parent; give examples of each.

Convey to Your Child:

1. ____________________

2. ____________________

3. ____________________

4. ____________________

5. ____________________

6. ____________________

7. ____________________

8. ____________________

Convey to the Other Parent:

1. ______________________________

2. ______________________________

3. ______________________________

4. ______________________________

5. ______________________________

6. ______________________________

7. ______________________________

8. ______________________________

11. Please complete this question last in the module. In reflecting back on the empathy training exercises you have recently completed, please (A) write down why you were asked to answer questions about your feelings, thoughts, behaviors, and others' responses to your behaviors before answering questions related to those of your child. (B) Also write about how you think your feelings, thoughts, and behavior are *related* to your child's feelings, thoughts, and behaviors, and to the other parent's feelings, thoughts, and behaviors, and (C) how they are *unrelated* to your child's feelings, thoughts, and behaviors, and the other parent's feelings, thoughts, and behaviors.

A. ____________________

B. ____________________

C. ____________________